# SRI KANDHA PURÂNAM

### (English Version)

**Dr. AKILA SIVARAMAN**

# GIRI

# GIRI TRADING AGENCY PRIVATE LIMITED

**SRI KANDHA PURANAM**
(ENGLISH)
ISBN : 978-81-397-6

1st Edition : March 2006 | 12th Reprint : June-2019
Pages 448 | Demi | N.S. Maplitho | 500 Copies

Published by : GIRI TRADING AGENCY PRIVATE LIMITED
© Publisher | All rights reserved.
*Regd. Office* : Modi Niwas, Opp.Post Office, Matunga, Mumbai - 19. ✆ (022) 2412 1344
*Admn. Office*: No.372/1, Mangadu Pattur Koot Road, Mangadu, Chennai - 600 122.
✆ +91 44 66 93 93 93 (Multiple Lines), +91 44 2679 3190, 3100
www.giri.in  ✉ sales@giri.in
SHOWROOMS : MUMBAI · CHENNAI · KANCHIPURAM · COIMBATORE · MADURAI
TRICHY · PUDUCHERRY · SECUNDERABAD · BENGALURU · NEW DELHI

**III**

# FROM THE PUBLISHER'S DESK

*Sri Kandha Puranam is the divine story of Lord Kandha, popularly known as Muruga in Tamil Nadu. Karthikeya, Kumara, Saravana, Velava, Shanmukha, Arumugha are among the other names by which devotees all over the world pray to Him. There are sevaral incidents which are associated with these names and these are told in a narrative form in this work which deserves wide reading by Indians and International readers also. This humble attempt made to serve His noble cause, as we have been in this task of publishing all religious texts, to popularise them world-wide.*

*Dr. (Mrs.) Akila Sivaraman, a retired office Indian Broad casting Service, has taken great pains to communicate Lord Murugas greatness in this book in an effective style with her rich experience in the mass media.*

*It is our fervent hope that this literary work devoted to Lord Muruga would be useful for all our avid readers, wherever they live and whatever their faith.*

*We humbly submit this work at the feet of Lord Muruga at Kandhakottam at Kanchipuram. Where He, Lord Muruga initiated this work through Kachiapha Shivachariyar.*

*"May Lord Muruga shower his blessing on all of us."*

,

# IV

## FOREWORD

Maugre the Mouna Matam's publication of the English translation of the Kandha Puranam by the late-lamented S.Swaminatha Iyer, the need for a fresh and more comprehensive version was persistently felt by scholars. No doubt Iyer's translation sharpened our taste for the Puranam and like Oliver Twist we demanded more of the fare. This demand is now met with by Dr.Akila Sivaraman to a great extent. Indeed her work brings to the fore the salient features of Hinduism as inculcated by our Puranas.

Hinduism, I daresay, has declared ex cathedra, long, long ago that God is one only and all lives constitute but one family (Ondre Kulamum Oruvane Devanum). Yet God is worshipped in His threefold nature, they being paternal, maternal and filial. In this context it should be remembered that God is the transcendental Ens that is neither male nor female and is neither of either sex. It is the Self-Born and also the Self-Existent. Yet the deity which is sex-transcending is also androgynic. No wonder Hinduism which is the Sanatana Dharma (the Aeviternal Way of Life) is more admired than understood or followed in its nascent splendour. It is given to a few only to pursue Hinduism.

There are two distinct versions of the Kandha Purânam. The Sanskrit version, hailed as the original, is known as the Skaanda Maha Puranam. It is yet to be translated in full. The Tamil Kandha Purânam is but a part of the Sanskrit original which is made up of Sanatkumara, Suta, Brahma, Vishnu, Sankara and Sura Samhitas. These respectively contain 55,000, 6,000, 3,000, 5,000, 30,000 and 1,000 slokas. Sankara Samhita is composed of twelve Kandas. The first Kanda is Siva Rahasya Kanda comprising 13,000 granthas. It is made up of Sambhava, Asura, Mahendra, Yuddha, Deva, Daksha and Upadesa Kaandas. Of these the first six were translated into Tamil by Kacchiyappa Sivacharya. It is these six that consitute the Tamil Kandha Purânam. As commmanded by Kacchiyappa himself, his chela Koneriyappa (also known as Guha Neriyappa) translated into Tamil the Upadesa Kaandam. This work is composed of 4,348 verses.

Skanda, hailed as Muruga in the Tamil Nadu, made His avatar long before Sri Rama. Sarga 37 of Sri Valmiki's Ramayana speaks with rapture on the multifoliate glory of Skanda. It is said that history repeats itself. The exploits occurring in the Ramayana are truly the replicas of those of the Skannda Puranam. However it should be observed here that before Surapadhama, Ravana is but a Lilliputian.

Muruga who is the Vedic Subrahmanya is the divine rebel par excellence. His wedding with Valli pioneered intercaste connubium. The esoteric significance of this matrimony is never to be lost sight of. Valli is truly the soul that is referred to in the eighth sutra of the Siva Gnaana Bhodam. The Guru, like the Hound of Heaven, chases the soul that is fleeing from him, stakes his claim and eventually possesses it only to confer on it sempiternal bliss. Valli the lass belonging to the cynegetic clan deemed untouchable, becomes the Consort of Muruga and what is more, She thereafter rules Him. Muruga gladly implements all her behests (Pani Yaa Yena Valli Padam Paniyum).

Kacchiyappa's Kanda Puranam is in 10,345 verses. A concise version in English was indited by S.Swaminatha Iyer and it was published about fifteen years ago. It was my good fortune to contribute a Foreword to this work also.

The Periya Purânam, the Tiruvilaiyaadal Purânam and the Kandha Purânam are hailed as the three eyes of the Lord Siva. The three Purânas which are in vogue in Sri Lanka are the Periya, the Vathavur Adikal and the Kanda Puranas. Before translating the Saiva Sastras, the American missionary Rev. Hoisington studied the Kandha Puranam in depth and prescribed portions of it as part of the curriculum in his school. It is Sri Lanka which totally embraced the Kanda Purana culture. "Kandha Purâna Kalaachaaram" by Ganapathy-p-Pillai of Sri Lanka is even today cultivated with care by the Sri Lankans. His another work known as "Kanda Purana Bhothanai" is equally popular. S. Shivapadasundaram of Sri Lanka is the author of "Kanda Puranam Vilakkam". Kasivaasi Senthi Naatha Iyer - a chela of Sri-la-Sri Arumukha Naavalar -, indited the "Kanda Purana Navanitam" - a work small in size but great in content. The Tiruvaavaduthurai Aadheenam supplied a felt want by republishing this work in 1969 under the name and style of "Kanda Purana Navanitiyam".

As Sri-la-Sri Arumukha Naavalar could not complete his concise prose version of the Kanda Puranam, his disciple took upon himself the task of completing it and brought it to a close. Pattuswami Othuvaar's prose version was published by Kasi Matam in 1953.

The earliest prose version of the Kandha Purânam including the Upadesa Kaandam by Mutthuswami Mudaliyaar appeared in two volumes during the last decade of the nineteenth century.

The propagators of the Kandha Purânam in Tamil Nadu were Guha Sri Krupaananda Vaariyaar - the author of the prose version of the Kanda Puranam namely the Kandar Tiruvilaiyaadal and the Kanda Puranak kaviyamudam, and Vaakisa Kalaanidhi K.V. Jagannathan - the author of the Kandavell Kathai Amudam.

Devotees of Muruga insist that one should read the whole of the Kanda Puranam at least once a gear, and once a month a work called "Kanda Puranacchurukkam" and should recite every day "Kandar Kali Vennpaa".

The Kandha Purânam is a major puranam. It is encyclopaedic. It provides the reader with the key to open all the other Puranas which in the dim, distant past, was propagated by Suta Pauraanika. Kandhan hailed as Murugan - the ever-young and handsome God -, is the divine Guru par excellence. His Puranam should be known the world over. So, to begin with, at least a concise version of His puranam is a pressing desideratum.

Fortunately for us, this work was undertaken by Dr. Akila Sivaraman - a competent scholar and an earnest devotee of Murugan. Small wonder that she is endowed with the vision required for fulfilling her mission.

A perusal of her work reveals that it is a labour of love, yes - immense love for the filial Godhead that not only shows the WAY, but guides us through it to reach the goal. Her opus is in simple and highly readable English. A few Indianisms found here and there in her work, do not mar its beauty. Strangely these bring the reader closer to the Indian way of thinking. Her work is at once readable and dependable. It has a beckoning intimacy, in particular, with the Tamil tradition of Bhakti which is truly representative of the pan-Indian Bhakti movement. The talented autor is able to bring home the message to the careful reader both imperceptibly and palpably, as the occasion demands. She has by the grace of Grace, earned our thanks.

**Sekkizhaar Adi-ppodi**
**Dr. T.N. Ramachandran, D.Lit (Jaffna)**

# x

# TABLE OF CONTENTS

# XI

,

# XIII

# XIV

## XV

# SRI KANDHA PURÂNAM

## 1. A Poser to ponder

The august assembly was awaiting the auspicious event. It was a great gathering of scholars, savants and seers. There was immense enthusiasm among the audience to listen to the inaugural address for the new classic work to be introduced on that day.

Kachiappa Sivachariar, a great devotee of Lord Muruga, performed the traditional puja in His Shrine at Kumarakkottam. His literary work, Sri Kandha Purânam, written on palm leaves and wrapped in pure silk, had been placed at His feet. Kachiappar took it in his hands and looked at the smiling face of the Lord.

"Muruga! My Lord! Please help me with your grace for a smooth inaugural function today". With this prayer, he respectfully took his work and started moving towards the hall.

The audience welcomed him with great applause and his heart was filled with joy at the reception. This was the day of his dreams that he had long awaited for. He proceeded to the centre-stage and addressed the audience.

"My dear friends! I have written this work with my limited knowledge and capacity. Kindly allow me to present it to you as my humble submission", he said.

"Please begin, Let us hear you." Several voices from the audience greeted him.

He sat on the stage and raised his work to his eyes in reverence. He opened his eyes after meditating on Lord

Muruga for a short while, offered a few flowers on the literary work on palm leaves and then started his presentation in a bold voice.

He read out the invocatory passage addressing Lord Ganesa which started like this: "Thigada chakkara chemuga maindulân: Paraphrasing the first line, he said, "Lord Siva with His ten glorious hands and five divine faces…"

**A scholar stood up from the audience and interrupted the presentation.**

"Yes, Sir, Do you want me to read the passage again?" asked the presenter.

"I have a doubt here. Please clarify it and then proceed", the intruder said.

"May I know your doubt, Sir?"

"There is no grammatical sanction for the formation of the first word - Tigada Chakkaram - in the very first line. Tolkappiam, the ancient grammatical text is silent on this point".

"He is right" joined a few more voices in the crowd. "Where is the authority for such a formation of the phrase?"

"I am afraid, I am not aware of it. The first line was given to me by Lord Muruga Himself and hence I have just continued and completed the stanza suitably"

There was a mild flutter in the audience. "Lord Muruga might have helped you with the first line. But, how do we approve it as correct? Let your Lord testify before us that He was the author of this line. Or you may show us the relevant authority from any grammatical text. Otherwise, we cannot accept its authenticity".

A section of the audience agreed with this group and demanded a proper explanation. Kachiappar had started the presentation with the invocation to Lord Ganesa with great joy. Should there be an objection to the very first word itself? Such a hassle right at the start was unexpected.

He stood flabbergasted, as he least anticipated such a turn of events.

Tears rolled down his cheeks. How is he going to prove that God himself had taken the initiative for this work? He could not decide on how to overcome the hurdle. He has to ponder and arrive at a solution to the problem. He has to face the challenge and prove the veracity of his statements. So, he got up with folded hands and announced that the meeting was postponed to the next day when he would produce the proof required by the audience.

The assurance given was well taken and the meeting ended abruptly. Kachiappar stared at the dispersing crowd with tears in his eyes. He gathered himself slowly after the last man left the hall. He took his work with the silk wrapper and moved towards Kumarakkottam. One could see the big difference between the confident way he walked into the hall and the  way he walked out of it now, totally embarrassed.

## 2. Lord Muruga comes to clarify

Kâlathiappa Sivachariar belonged to the ancient Saiva brahmin family. He was a great scholar of all religious texts. As an ardent devotee of Lord Muruga, enshrined in Kumarakkottam at Kanchipuram, one of the seven centres assuring salvation to souls, he worshipped Him daily with great devotion and traditional rituals.

Though endowed with all blessings in life, Kâlathiappar had one grievance. Even after a long married life, he was yet to get a child to carry on the family traditions. He had a firm belief in God's grace and prayed daily to Lord Muruga for the fulfilment of his desire.

Kâlathiappar's immense faith and devotion fructified, God granted his prayers and his wife gave birth to a male child. Kâlathiappar's happiness knew no bounds as he rejoiced in His abundant grace and named the new born as Kachiappan.

The young Kachiappan was quite brilliant right from his childhood and grew up with all good qualities, as an intelligent, affectionate and obedient person. He was well versed in both Tamil and Sanskrit and read quite a number of books in both the languages.

Kâlathiappar was highly pleased with his son's accomplishments. He wanted his son to take up the services to Lord Muruga at Kumarakkottam temple. Accordingly, Kachiappar took upon himself the routine procedure of worship at Kumarakkottam, alongside his other duties.

Initiated by the ancient traditional order, Kachiappar mastered the great saivite works viz. Thevaram and Thiruvachagam and understood their significant similarities to Vedas and Upanishads.

As he grew up intellectually and spiritually, he worshipped Lord Muruga with increasing devotion day after day. One day, Lord appeared in his dreams and directed him to write about his celestial glory, as described in the first chapter of Sankara Samhita of Skanda purâna. The Lord initiated him into the job by giving him the first line of the invocation - **Tigada chakkara chemmuga maindulân** which meant "Lord with the ten hands and five faces".

When Kachiappar woke up from his dreams, he was thrilled and his heart was full of joy. He was greatly moved and extremely delighted by His grace and kindness showered on him.

"Oh! Muruga! You have chosen me for such an arduous task of singing your praise. Do I deserve this honour? You have to stand by me throughout, to enable me to complete this assignment creditably", he said.

After his usual prayers, Kachiappar started his work. The invocation was followed by poetic verses of exceeding merit. Whenever he was in doubt about his compositions, he would pause and rethink till such time he was fully satisfied with them.

Though he was happy with his work, he wanted an approval for the same. Who could be the right person for it? None else than the Lord himself was capable of it, he thought. As soon as every hundred stanzas were ready, he made it a point to submit them at His feet at the end of the day. Next day morning, he observed that Lord Himself had done some corrections in the manuscript.

The way in which Lord Muruga initiated Kachiappar into the work and approved his verses, after carrying out corrections wherever required, was unique and hence, Kachiappar rejoiced in His grace everyday.

With 10,345 verses, the monumental work of Sri Kandha Purânam was completed. Kachiappar wanted it to be presented to scholars, for which he decided to call an assembly of all worthy stalwarts. He chose an auspicious time for the presentation and sent out invitations. Having known Kachiappar's scholarship, everyone readily accepted the invitation. Kumarakkottam was decorated tastefully and there was a huge crowd awaiting the event. Kachiappar was eagerly looking forward to the great occasion when the task assigned by the Lord would be completed.

But unexpectedly, an objection has been raised in the assembly. If the work is to be accepted, the relevant grammatical point has to be cited in support of the usage made. Otherwise, Lord Muruga himself should appear in person before the devotees and proclaim that He was the author of the line in dispute. To tide over the crisis, the meeting was postponed for a day. Can a miracle take place, to resolve the issue?

Kachiappar was terribly disturbed. The whole day, he did not eat. He completed the pujas and stayed in the temple itself.

"God loved me and hence chose me for this great task. When a problem has cropped up, will He not solve it Himself?" he thought.

"Oh Muruga! How shall I face the people tomorrow? When you have approved my work, can that face a rejection? I have promised to meet the audience with the explanation. Let me not live tomorrow if I am to fail and please accept me at your feet".

Soon he fell asleep and Lord appeared in his dream, just as He had done earlier when He ordered him to start the work.

"Don't grieve, my friend! There is a grammatical work called Veera Chozhiyam, which is in vogue in Chola Country. 18th verse of this work gives the sanction for the fusion of the two words as given by me in the first line. A poet from Chola Kingdom will be present in the assembly tomorrow to solve the puzzle". Lord said and disappeared.

Kachiappar woke up from his slumber and thanked Lord profusely. He felt relieved and was very happy.

The next day, Kachiappar did his routine pujas with great joy and at the appointed time went to the assembly. As God Himself was to settle the dispute, a hectic crowd of devotees had gathered.

There was the same reception to Kachiappar as in the previous day. He took his seat after greeting the crowd. A slight disturbance was there at the entrance. Some one wanted to meet Kachiappar and he was duly directed to the stage. The newcomer introduced himself as a poet from Chola Kingdom.

The scholar who raised the doubt the previous day came forward to get his doubt cleared.

"My dear friend! This is "Veerachozhiyam" a grammar book which is followed in Chola Country. You can find an answer to your query in the 18th verse of the chapter on 'fusion'."

The scholar read out the verse aloud and that was the authority for the fusion of the words. (Tigazh + dasakkaram merged as Tigada chakkaram).

The poet from Chola kingdom wanted the person, who raised the doubt to read the verse once again, so that everyone could hear clearly.

"Dear friends, are you all satisfied now?" he asked.

"Yes, by all means. Kachiappar may continue" answered the voices from the crowd.

God's help at the right time was a blessing for Kachiappar. He bowed before the audience with folded hands.

There was a sudden glow on the spot. People got perplexed. The poet from Chola kingdom was no longer there! God who came in disguise had finished His work and hence had disappeared.

The audience were curious. They started searching for the new entrant. Kachiappar knew that the miracle had taken place. He explained to the audience and declared that Lord Muruga Himself came as a poet and clarified their doubt.

The crowd was stunned. They did not realise His presence among them! Kachiappar's great devotion and strength of his prayers came to light. Everyone bowed at his feet and sought pardon for the mistake of finding fault in his work.

The poet who raised the question felt greatly ashamed and fell at Kachiappar's feet.

"I did not know your worth. I was so silly to have put a stumbling block for the great divine task and to have hurt you so badly. Unless you forgive me, I cannot come out of my guilty feeling. Please forgive me for my stupidity."

Kachiappar embraced him and said, "My friend! Do not feel guilty. Only because of your objection, the Lord appeared before us to bless us all."

When God Himself has testified in person, how could there be a further hurdle? All the scholars in the audience asked Kachiappar to proceed with the presentation. Kachiappar continued his discourse explaining each and every verse of his work.

# 3. The wheel sent to  Earth by Lord Brahma

Among the many holy places on Earth, Lord Siva prefers Kanchipuram situated on the banks of the river Kampa. Once

when Lord Brahma and his consort Saraswati came to Kanchipuram to worship Lord Siva, some sages called on Him. They prayed to him for guidance as to what would be the ideal place on Earth where they can quietly worship Lord Siva, after renouncing all worldly desires and embracing the ascetic dharma.

**Lord Brahma took a piece of "darbha" grass, made it like a wheel and sent it rolling down on the ground. He asked the sages to follow the wheel and stop at the place where it rests.**

The sages accordingly followed the wheel, which went on and on till it reached the foot of the Himalayas. It was a thick forest, full of trees, quite suitable for meditation. Rivulets and streams made the place quite pleasant. The sages called the place "***Naimisâranyam***" as Nemi in Sanskrit meant a wheel. A few hermitages were put up there for the sages to stay and meditate.

After sometime the sages planned to conduct a **Yâga**, a religious ritual of worship. To witness the Yâga, many illustrious saints visited Naimisâranyam and sage Sootha was one of the prominent visitors. All the sages were delighted to see him and they enjoyed his presence. They requested him to narrate the story of Lord Muruga who fought Soora padhman to release the Devas from their imprisonment.

Sage Sootha was immensely happy to narrate the story and gave a brief sketch of the same. The sages further requested him for a detailed account of Lord Muruga's glorious birth and various meritorious acts to help his devotees. Sage Sootha conceded and began his narration.

## 4. The Divine child on the Lotus

Indra, Devas, Sages, Siddhas and all the rest have a great reverence for the ancient mountain of Himalayas where Nandideva is guarding the great Mount Kailas, the divine abode of Lord Siva. There lies a beautiful temple wherein a hall decorated with precious gems is the central attraction and Lord Siva with his consort Parvathi sits there, on a golden throne to give audience to the great sages and devotees assembled all around to sing His praise delightfully.

On one such occasion, Parvathi Devi expressed her desire, which was agitating her mind for some time. "My father Daksha has not cared to worship you, for all your mighty accomplishments held in high esteem by one and all. I am ashamed to call myself his daughter. In fact I want to be born again to be worthy of my status as your wife. Kindly guide me to achieve my goal and get peace of mind."

Lord Siva smiled at her request. "My beloved Devi, as your desire will also help to protect and bless your devotees, I shall grant your prayer. The king of Himalayas is meditating on me on the banks of Lake Padma. He wants you as his daughter and desires to give you in marriage to me. I am pleased to grant his wish. You may take birth as his daughter and start meditating on me as soon as you are five years old. I shall meet you at the right time and marry you." Devi was immensely happy about this boon and took leave of the Lord and left Mount Kailas.

The beautiful Lake Padma, at the foot of Himalayas, is full of lotus flowers. The king of Himalayas Himavan was meditating on Lord Siva on the banks of this lake, duly observing the traditional practices of worship.

One day, he took his bath as usual in the lake and suddenly he sighted a beautiful girl child on a lotus flower in the centre. The child smiled at him as if she invited him to take her in his hands. The king did just the same and his joy knew no bounds. He hugged and kissed her with great love and affection.

God has answered his prayers. He now has Devi herself as his daughter. Exuberant with joy, he reached his palace, where his wife Mena joined him with great happiness.

"My honey, God has granted our prayer. Our long felt desire has been fulfilled. This baby is a blessing for our dynasty. Here is your sweet little daughter", said the king of Himalayas and gave the child to his wife. She was so overwhelmed with joy that her breasts were filled with milk. She took the child inside and fed her.

There were celebrations everywhere. Everyone rejoiced at King of Himalayas' fortune. Gifts poured from one and all. Sages and Devas visited the palace to have a glimpse of the divine child who was none other than the Mother of the Universe.

## 5. The maiden at the hermitage

Parvatam in Sanskrit means 'mountain' and Parvataraja was the king of Himalayas. He named his daughter Pârvathi. She grew in the palace to the happiness of everyone around and especially King Parvataraja and Queen Mena. Her childish pranks delighted one and all.

Pârvati was five years old now. One day the cute little girl went to see her father, who was over joyed on seeing her. "My dear father" said Pârvathi.

"Yes, dear, what do you want? Tell me, my child," said the king.

"I am desirous to meet the Lord of the Universe whom you pray to, everyday. I have to meditate on him to win him as my husband. Please allow me to start my prayers".

Parvataraja was stunned.

"Is this possible for a five year old child? Is this not too early to think on these lines?" He did not dwell on such thoughts for long. She was a divine gift for him and from her third year itself she had learnt quite a lot from her parents.

"Did you hear what I said, father?" asked Pârvathi.

"Pârvathi, you are too young, my child, for undertaking such pains. At the right time, I shall do the needful to fulfil your desire."

Pârvathi smiled. "Didn't you like what I said?" she questioned her father. "I don't find anything wrong in meditating on Lord Siva" said Pârvathi.

"I didn't say that, Pârvathi. In fact, I am also eager to give you in marriage to Lord Siva only" said the king.

"Then, why do you hesitate now?" she asked.

"Pârvathi, this is the time for you to play and be happy. It is rather early for a hard life of meditation. When you attain the correct age for marriage, I shall make all arrangements. You better go and play now" said Himavan, the king of Himalayas.

Pârvathi got down from his lap, but did not go to play. She was very unhappy and Himavan understood her disappointment. When he looked at her, he saw tears in her eyes.

"Pârvathi, please listen to what I say. I am very pleased with your desire for meditation for which one has to go to the forest and live there. You cannot think of having even the minimum facilities there. Wild beasts will be there all around. They may pose a danger to you at anytime. That is why I want you to postpone this thought. By the time you grow a little older, you will become fit enough to face such challenges". He pleaded with her.

"I am fully aware of all that you have said, father. You have already told me enough about the life of seers and saints in the jungle. I have thought about everything, before I decided. Whatever be the problem, it is up to Him to take care of me. Why should we then worry?", Pârvathi replied.

What will the king do now? He knew that she was quite firm in her stand. He felt proud of her and at the same time he was quite concerned about her safety in the forest. He evolved a plan and gave his consent. Pârvathi was happy and thanked her father.

"We will have to see if your mother agrees." said Himavan.

"Mother will agree to whatever you say," said Pârvathi.

Queen Mena had already overheard the conversation between the father and the daughter. When Pârvathi ran towards her, announcing her decision and father's consent, Mena hugged her. But she was sad and speechless.

"Are you unhappy, mother?" asked Pârvathi.

"No child. I am happy at your decision," said the queen.

"It is, by God's grace, that I want to meditate on him and I am sure, He, who made me think on these lines, will take care of me adequately."

Mena could not speak. She stood there with tears in her eyes. Himavan made necessary arrangements for Pârvathi's stay at the foot of the Himalayas. On the banks of Lake Padma, he made a hermitage, equipped with all facilities. There were no luxuries or ornamentation there. For Pârvathi's company and help, a few girls were to stay with her so that minimum comforts and safety arrangements were ensured.

On an auspicious day, Pârvathi took leave of her parents and started on her journey to the forest. Himavan accompanied her to the forest and supervised the arrangements before he returned to his kingdom.

Pârvathi took bath in the Lotus Lake and gave up the royal grandeur in dress and ornaments. Attired as an ascetic she began to meditate on Lord Siva with all her heart in full concentration.

## 6. The kind soul under the tree

An asura was born to the sage Kâshyapa and his wife Mâyâ. He was named Soorapadhman. As he was a mighty warrior, he became the king of all kings in the three worlds. His atrocities on his fellow kings were so cruel that even the Devas were reeling under his autocratic rule. None was able to fight against him and hence everyone lived in eternal fear and distress.

Lord Brahma's four sons were Sanaka, Sanandana, Sanâtana and Sanathkumâra. All these four went to Mount Kailas to get mantropadesa from Lord Siva. Nandideva, the celestial guard of Lord Siva, welcomed them and presented them to his Lord. The four scholars chanted the Vedic verses in praise of Lord Siva. They prostrated before Him and prayed thus, "Oh! Lord! We are unable to discern the essence of Vedas, as it is like a search in a big ocean. You may kindly guide us aright to get the real crux of all Vedas to attain liberation".

Pleased with their prayers, Lord Siva agreed to enlighten them on the right path to attain the true knowledge. He then called his guard Nandideva and asked him not to allow any visitors except Manmatha (the guardian of love, Cupid). While he was teaching Brahma's sons, Nandideva stood guard accordingly at the eastern gate of Kailas.

Lord Siva took the four aspiring scholars under the cool shade of Kallâla tree and taught them the three roads to knowledge - Chariyai, Kriya and Yoga (Learning, Action and Meditation). They further requested the Lord to show them the route to the disciplined way of life to attain eternal wisdom.

"My dear sons of Brahma! It cannot be taught by mere words. One has to practice hard to learn it" said Lord Siva and sat with the Chinmudra sign to exercise control over the mind and the body.

Taking the clue from the Lord, the four scholars sat with the Chinmudra sign and went deep into meditation. Though God closed his eyes just for a moment to show his scholarly students the Chinmudra sign and the method to control oneself, it was like a long period for all living beings all over the universe. Earlier, when once Devi covered His eyes in playfulness, the whole world plunged into darkness, causing panic all around. The same scene repeated now also.

**When Lord Siva sat in meditation all his creations also followed suit and desired to stay in Yoga only.** None had any worldly desires. As desire is the root cause of all evils, the world became bereft of all sins. All men sought the path of devotion and dedication to heavenly virtues. The birth rate started falling and even the evil-minded turned away from ignoble deeds.

However, at this time, The asura king Soorapadhman became more powerful. His atrocities grew by leaps and bounds. He tortured everyone, especially the Devas, at their mere appearance before him. His son Bhanugopan was sent to fetch king Indra to his court. When Bhanugopan went in search, Indra and his wife Indrani had gone elsewhere. Annoyed at this, Bhanugopan waged a war and defeated everyone at Amaravati, the capital city of Devas, and took Indra's son Jayantan as hostage.

When the news of Jayanta being taken away as hostage to the Asura's court reached Indra, he was shocked. Unable to counter the asura, he ran for help to Lord Siva. He sat meditating on Him in a suitable place at the foot of Himalayas. Lord Siva appeared before Indra and asked him innocently as to what he wanted of Him.

,

Indra prostrated at His feet and prayed with tears in his eyes.

"Oh My Lord! You are omnipresent. You are fully aware of what has happened. Soorapadhman has gone beyond his limits in torturing Devas. They are reeling in great pain like helpless worms. None has the strength to stand up against him. One of his sons, Bhanugopan, has destroyed my capital Amaravati and also taken away my son Jayantan as captive. We have no other succour other than you. Despite your good will for us, we are suffering a hell. Oh! My Lord, Is there no end to our hardships?"

"Do not grieve Indra! You are paying for your sin of having partaken in the yâga performed by Daksha to insult me. I am to get a son who will put an end to your sufferings. He will kill the asura and protect all of you" said Lord Siva and vanished after blessing him.

Indra heaved a sigh of relief and went to see Bruhaspati, the great teacher of Devas, at the city of Manovati and left his wife Indrani at his palace before he went to see Brahma. Even though God has given him word to help him out of his sufferings, one could not foresee the time by which things would materialize. It may take ages. Who can put up with tortures without the end being in sight?

## 7. Manmatha gets the command

Brahma welcomed Indra with pleasure. Indra narrated about his meditation on Lord Siva and added that He appeared before him and promised to do the needful for his well being. Indra further wanted to know how long he was to wait to get His grace.

"When the children fall sick, the parents take care of them. Likewise the father of the Universe has already agreed to come to your rescue. I am sure that there will be a good turn of events in the near future. But still, let us continue our efforts. It is better to go to Vaikuntam and meet Lord Vishnu there," said Brahma.

When Indra apprised Lord Vishnu about what had happened, He also confirmed that good events were definitely drawing near. "We had foolishly participated in the Yâga conducted by Daksha, which was performed to insult Lord Siva. As a result we had to undergo a lot of sufferings till now. Lord Siva has since decided to help us with His grace and I have no doubt that good times are ahead of us." said Lord Vishnu.

At this juncture, Brahma made an appeal to Him. "I thought that my sons would help me in my task of creations. But they chose to become ascetics and went to Lord Siva, seeking supreme knowledge from Him. Lord Siva has been showing them the path of Gnanayoga under the Kallâla tree. Following in His footsteps, all creatures have taken to a life of seeking wisdom and meditation, with the result, my work of creation has come to a stand still. Devi Pârvathi has gone to Himalayas to meditate on Lord Siva. If the divine couple choose to live away from each other, when will a son be born to them? You have to show us a way out for this problem."

Indra added, "O my Lord! Soorapadhman has since become the mightiest of all and there is no match for him. My kingdom is under his sway now and he is holding my son captive. Though everyone promises an early end to my suffering, it looks so distant and dismal for me."

"Indra, you feel helpless as you have been suffering for long. Lord Siva's promise will not go in vain. Devi is meditating and desires to get united to Lord Siva in wedlock very soon. If only Lord Siva is disturbed from his Yoga, he will get married to Devi, to beget a son for our salvation from evils " said Lord Vishnu.

"O Lord! Is it possible to bring back Lord Siva from his deep meditative status?" questioned Indra.

"Manmatha has to be summoned for this task. He alone is capable of doing it successfully," said Lord Vishnu.

Brahma and Indra returned to the former's abode, which is known as " Satyaloka". Brahma thought of Manmatha and he appeared before him at once. He wanted to know why Brahma, the embodiment of Vedas, summoned him.

"Manmatha, a very important assignment awaits you. Soorapadhman is causing hectic havoc to all of us. When Indra prayed to Lord Siva, he has stated that a son would be born to him to annihilate the asura king. But he is presently engaged in deep meditation, in order to teach my four sons. Devi has taken birth as the daughter of king Himavan and is doing great penance to win Lord Siva as her husband. As soon as both get united in wedlock, a son would be born to them who will be our saviour. You may therefore, set out on a journey with your five arrows to disturb Lord Siva from his yoga" said Brahma.

Manmatha shuddered at this very suggestion. "O Brahma! Have I sinned so much that you want me to take up this hazardous job against the Mighty Lord Siva? Did you really summon me for this?"

"Manmatha! I have said the right course of action, only to save the Devas. Is this wrong?" Brahma asked.

"O Lord! You have asked me to do nothing but my own job. I have made my own father Vishnu to get attracted by Lakshmi. You had married Saraswati only because of my arrows of love. You were also crazy for the dancer Urvasi due to my influence. Indra, Devas and even sages could not resist their temptation when I had kindled a desire in them. That is why, perhaps, you are planning to send me for disturbing the Lord. But are you not aware of Lord Siva's supremacy? Can I approach him at all? Even if I do, will I come back alive? His very presence is enough to silence me. Perhaps you do not want me to survive at all. That is why, you inflict such a cruel punishment on me" pleaded Manmatha.

"Manmatha! You do not seem to understand our predicament. Noble people will sacrifice even their lives to help others. Once upon a time, Devas wanted to get the nectar from the ocean of milk, by churning it with the help of Vasuki, the thousand headed snake, as rope. Vasuki could not stand the strain and spat venom through her thousand mouths. Lord Siva saved the entire universe by consuming it himself and getting a dark permanent patch on his throat.

After fighting with your father Vishnu, Indra once went to sage Dadeechi who made a deadly weapon from his back bone. Though he killed himself thus, the weapon was useful in annihilating Vriddasuran. Those who have sacrificed themselves live eternally with a great name and fame. Soorapadhman is torturing the Devas and for their sake, you must do this" said Brahma.

Manmatha would not still agree, "Lord! Please do not compel me for this task. I shall willingly undertake any other command from you," cried Manmatha.

Despite Brahma's persuasions Manmatha was reluctant to accept the errand. Indra was extremely sad and was afraid that God's promise would never fructify. Brahma consoled him and continued his efforts.

"Manmatha, you do not seem to pay heed to my request. Will you do as I say or not? Be clear. If you do not obey me right away, remember that I will have to curse you. What is your final answer?" asked Brahma angrily.

Manmatha hesitated for a while. "To go" on such a mission to Lord Siva is indeed a point of no return. "Not to go" will also invite Brahma's worst anger and curse. "Instead of losing my life due to a curse, it is better to incur the wrath of Lord Siva and die if necessary. Let others at least benefit by my sacrifice", he thought.

"Well. It is more than certain that I am not going to live long. Let me die, incurring the divine anger of Lord Siva. Please do not get annoyed with me anymore. I am going to Mount Kailas right away", he said.

Indra was happy and hugged Manmatha. "Manmatha, do not fear, you are doing so much good to me. I have no words to praise or thank you. You will be instrumental for the birth of a son for Lord Siva and that will put an end to our agony. Somehow, please disturb Lord Siva to the extent that he comes out of his Yoga and goes in search of a reunion with Devi." he said.

When Lord Siva's yoga is disturbed, Manmatha will not escape His anger too. Fully being aware of this, Manmatha left for Kailas, taking leave of Indra and Brahma.

Brahma wished him well for success and said that he would follow him.

On returning home, Manmatha related to his wife Rathi all that happened in Satyaloka. She was shivering in fear of the consequences and hence wanted to go with him. Manmatha could not persuade her to stay back. He started on his mission with her, in his chariot of southern wind.

## 8. The spark that burnt down Manmatha

When Manmatha reached the eastern gates of Mount Kailas, he saw Nandideva standing guard there. He got down from his chariot and greeted him.

"Manmatha, what is your mission in coming here? If you have come to meet the Lord, this is not the time for that." said Nandideva.

"Nandideva, I am aware of the situation obtaining here. Lord has undertaken to teach Yoga Nishta to the sons of Brahma. This has resulted in prolonging the sufferings of Devas. If I am able to disturb the Lord from his yoga, He will marry Devi Pârvathi and a son will be born to them. Their son alone can put an end to Devas' miseries. So I have been sent by Devas to achieve this end. Kindly allow me to enter", asked Manmatha.

For a moment, Nandideva got wild with anger when he learnt that Manmatha had come there to disturb his Lord. Next moment, he remembered his master's order to allow Manmatha alone inside. So he smiled and said, "Manmatha, Lord has ordered that nobody should be permitted to enter. I suggest that you enter through the Western gate."

When Manmatha left, Nandideva felt sorry for him. "Once Manmatha breaks Lord's Yoganishta, he will not be spared. Devas have decided to sacrifice Manmatha for their happiness." he thought.

As soon as Manmatha entered through the Western gate and sighted the Lord in his yoga posture, he swooned thinking of the consequences if he acted as directed by Brahma. Rathi had to wake him up and still he was very nervous. At the same time, he heard a voice from outside the celestial abode. Indra had followed Manmatha to check if he had carried out the directives. He had persuaded

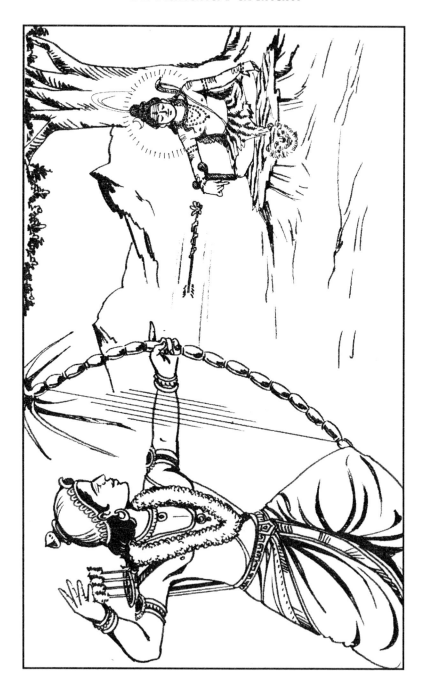

# Sri Kandha Purânam 29

Brahma and Devas also to follow him. All of them were praying to the Lord from outside the eastern gate.

**Gathering courage once again, Manmatha went near Lord Siva. Shivering with fear, he took his sugarcane bow and arrows of flowers and aimed at the Lord.**

His arrows of flowers straight hit the Lord and He woke up from His yoga. His anger knew no bounds. His third eye in the forehead emitted a spark that instantaneously burnt down Manmatha. Mount Kailas was surrounded by smoke.

Devas were shocked to see the smoke all around. They asked Nandideva as to what has happened. Nandideva could rightly guess the cause for the smoke. With tears in his eyes, he said "Knowing fully well what was to follow, Manmatha made bold to shoot his arrows of love at Lord Siva. Alas! Lord Siva, in his anger, has burnt him down and hence the smoke."

There was a mixed reaction for this among the Devas. On one side, they rejoiced that Lord Siva has come out of his yoga now. On the other, they felt sorry for the demise of Manmatha. They expected the Lord to go in search of Devi to marry her.

Rathi saw a lightening like spark from Lord's forehead and next moment Manmatha had been reduced to ashes, right before her eyes. She cried aloud for her husband. She was in tears. Devas have sacrificed her husband to achieve what they wanted. Is this a good outcome? Where are they now? She had lost her husband just as it happened before her in a jiffy.

"You had ruled all the worlds with your sugarcane bow and arrows of flowers. You had vowed before the sacred fire that you would never leave me alone. In order to help the Devas, you have deserted me! How will I face the other women? They may dislike even looking at me. When you were in distress, none has turned up to save you." She went on lamenting the irreparable loss that she suffered.

Lord Siva went into Yoganishta again, as he still wanted to test the patience of Devas. Devas were disappointed at this turn of events and they were further worried that the sacrifice of the life of Manmatha has also gone in vain. All of them started praying unanimously.

"We have surrendered to you totally Lord! Can you still be silent? Are you not the repository of kindness? As long as you are away from Devi, the greater are our woes. Please take pity on us and come to our rescue".

Lord Siva summoned Nandideva and asked him to usher in the waiting Devas.

Nandideva allowed them in and they chanted in chorus, from Vedas, singing His praise profusely. With an air of innocence, Lord asked them for the reason of their visit. Indra and others again pleaded before him. "You are omniscient, my Lord! Devi is meditating at the foot of Himalayas, waiting to marry you. It is high time you concede to her desire and get a son to save us from our sad plight".

"Your wish will be fulfilled soon. Do not fear anymore", Lord said.

Devas once again fell at His feet and took leave of Him. Rathi appeared there in tears and started presenting her pathetic plea.

"Lord almighty! None has come to grieve, once they approach you. Devas have been blessed by you to get what they want. My husband was their messenger and he has been unduly punished. Is this justified? Does this speak well of your abundant grace for the devotees?"

"Calm down, Rathi. None can win over destiny. Your husband is no exception to this rule. Don't grieve too much. I shall go very soon to marry Devi and then your husband also will come back to life," Lord Said.

Rathidevi felt consoled and left in peace. Lord Siva called the sons of Brahma and asked them to continue yoga lessons as they were taught, so that they can attain salvation at the end. Accordingly, the four enlightened sons of Brahma took His blessings and left.

## 9. A man in disguise at the forest

Parvatarajan's daughter Pârvathi was in deep meditation in a forest at the foot of the Himalayas. Lord Siva decided to grant her prayers and hence reached the place where she was meditating. But before accepting her hand in marriage, he wanted to test her strength of mind. He took the guise of an old man wearing a torn dress and Rudrakshas around his neck. He had a 'tilak' in place of His third eye in the forehead. His trident became a staff in His hand.

One of Pârvathi's friends saw this old man walking slowly near the garden. Taking him for a sage she went near him to pay her respects. "O dear old man, the old and weak like you are not to be wandering alone in the forest. Who are you and how are you here? Are you in search of someone?" she asked.

"O dear girl! I heard that the princess Pârvathi is here in the forest meditating hard in a hermitage. She is·certainly great. How do I find her?", He asked.

"O revered old man, it is so good of you to have come to bless her. I shall take you to her place."

Pârvathi also got ready to receive the respectable old man as her guest, having already received the message from her other friends.

"Blessed are you, my child" said the old man as he entered and Pârvathi welcomed him honourably. One of her friends, Vijayai, gave him a seat and another friend brought him fruits to eat.

Lord looked at Pârvathi and commented as follows:

"My dear girl! I am so unhappy to see you here. I have heard a lot about your beauty. Will you be able to undergo the rigorous rules of meditation with your tender figure? You have grown thin by living here like this. What is the big idea? What exactly are you praying for?"

Pârvathi felt rather uncomfortable to answer this question herself. She looked at her friend Vijayai, who readily understood her signal. She replied to the old man "Oh the great one! Pârvathi is desirous of marrying Lord Siva, God almighty of the Universe. She is, therefore, meditating on Him only."

The old man laughed aloud on hearing this. "Why are your laughing, Sir?" asked Vijayai. "My dear girl! There is no doubt that Pârvathi has a lofty desire. But can she ever succeed?" Pârvathi interrupted in haste and asked "Why? Why not?".

"Pârvathi! Please listen. Lord Siva is the source of all Vedas. Do you think He will agree to your proposal? Is it so simple a task? Even Brahma and Vishnu could not even see His head or foot and had to refrain from their attempts. Your efforts will certainly go in vain. Why are you struggling for the unattainable in this young age? Take my advice and go back to your palace and live happily."

When the visitor discouraged her like this, Pârvathi did not relish it. "Dear old man! You have not understood me correctly. I am fully aware as to what I want and what suffering I am to undergo to get it. By any chance, if He does not heed to my prayers and come to marry me, I shall still not give up my penance. I am quite firm in my stand. I shall intensify my prayers and would rather sacrifice my life itself. Please do not talk like a mad person." she said.

Lord smiled and said again:

"Pârvathi ! I congratulate you for your high thinking. All the same, it is not an apt desire for a young maiden like you. When we choose a bridegroom for an eligible girl, we usually look for handsome features, virtues, wealth and the like. Just think of your choice. He is so ugly with three eyes. He walks along like a mad man with open locks of hair. Can he not get even a silk dress to wear? Tiger's skin is adorning Him. Venomous snakes are His bangles. He wears only a garland of skulls and bones. At least can he not wear good flowers in place of ornaments? While the forest is full of beautiful, nice smelling flowers, he chooses to wear the odd ones like Vellerukku, **Angur, Konrai, Nochi and Amathai**".

While he went on and on in these lines, Pârvathi could not stand his blabbering any longer. She closed her ears and chose not to listen.

"Listen, Pârvathi, He lives in the burial ground. He smears ash all over His body and dances with demons day in and day out. If you marry him, you have also to join this dance only. He has no parents. Will any girl fall in love with such a lunatic?"

Pârvathi got wild with anger and looked at Him with disgust. "Stop it! No more nonsense please!" she shouted "I had misjudged you, from your appearance. I mistook you for an ardent devotee of Lord Siva who is my master. You have now shown your true colours. At such a ripe old age, have you learnt only this little about God almighty? Your words do not match your outward appearance. Vedas speak volumes about the Lord of Mount Kailas. Have you never read them? All Devas, led by Brahma himself, always worship at His feet, seeking His grace. Your appearance is so deceptive that I had unnecessarily entertained you here, only to hear such uncharitable comments about my Lord. You have stooped lower than even the lowest creature; it is a sin to talk to you any longer. Please leave me" she said.

Lord roared in laughter. "My dear girl! You are boasting that you now know my true colours. You have hardly understood what I mean. I have come searching for you because I love you very much. Just compare myself with your Lord. I am much better than him in personality and appearance. You better stop your silly meditation. Let us go and meet your father. If you marry me, I shall see to it that you are happy."

When the Lord in his disguise as an old man said like this, Pârvathi was startled out of her wits. Once upon a time, in her previous life, her father Daksha had uttered such uncharitable comments about her husband for which she decided to renounce that birth itself. Now, when she was reborn as the daughter of Himavan, was she destined to undergo the same torture?

When she had already decided upon marrying Lord Siva, should another person express a desire for her? "This wretched person does not even leave me after I have asked him to quit."

"She called her friends and said "Let us all leave this place. This bad man has evil designs in coming here and is talking nonsense. It is better we avoid such fools". As she started moving towards the entrance, God was pleased with her steadfast devotion for Him and hence hastened to say "Pârvathi, please do not go from here. I shall leave. Just take a look at me."

His kind words made Pârvathi turn back. What a surprise! The arguing old man was no longer there. Lord Siva, with his team of Nandideva and the rest was there on his Rishabha vahana. She was thrilled at His great darshan. When she considered it a sin to hear unpleasant words about Lord Siva, she had unknowingly insulted the Lord himself by her crude conduct. She fell at His feet and asked for pardon.

"O my Lord! You were so kind to me that you condescended to come and accept me. I did not realize the truth and spoke utter nonsense to you. I am extremely distressed. Even great wise men have failed to understand your mysterious ways. Where am I, a silly fool? Please forgive me for all that I spoke ill of you," she prayed with sincere remorse.

"**Pârvathi! Don't you worry. I came in disguise to test your strength and will power. I have accepted you for all your words of praise only. You may return to your palace now. I shall come there tomorrow to marry you**" **Lord said and disappeared.** Pârvathi's joy knew no bounds and she continued to stay in the hermitage itself until the king heard the whole episode from her friends. Escorted by his queen Mena, the king came there with immense pleasure and returned with his daughter to his palace.

## 10. The sages arrive to fix the marriage

On returning to Mount Kailas, Lord Siva thought of
Saptarishis, the seven veteran sages. They got the message
of the Lord through their mystic powers and reached
Mount Kailas immediately. Taking permission from
Nandideva, they gained entry to the sanctum sanctorum
where they saw Lord Siva.

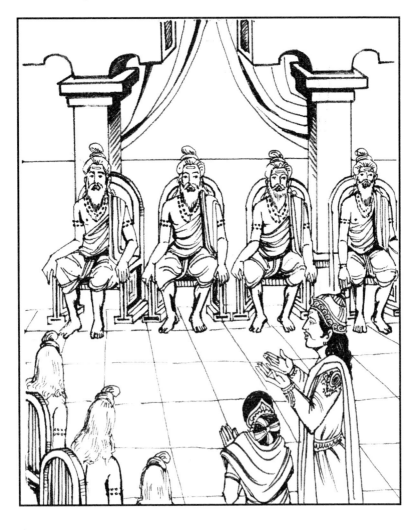

"O Lord! When all the Devas, right from Brahma are awaiting your orders, you have so graciously thought of us for some reason. We feel greatly honoured and we shall carry out your orders right away. So blessed as we are, we shall never be caught again in the cycle of birth and death", they said.

"My dear sages! Parvatarajan's daughter Pârvathi has desired to marry me for which she had been in absolute meditation all along. As I am also eager to accept her, kindly meet Parvatarajan on my behalf and try to find out his opinion in the matter," said the Lord.

The sages accordingly took leave of the Lord and on getting the message of their arrival through his guards, Parvatarajan and his wife received them heartily. After the ceremonial welcome accorded to them as per customs in practice, the king asked them about the purpose of their visit.

**"Parvataraja! Our visit augurs well for your greater fame and name. Lord Siva is desirous of marrying your daughter Pârvathi. We have come here on his behalf to know your views", the sages said.**

Parvatarajan was immensely happy at the proposal. He was blessed with a very rare privilege which none else can even imagine. He bowed before the sages and said "I am extremely delighted to hear your words. I shall readily give my daughter in marriage to Lord Siva and I will also be his slave hence forth." His wife queen Mena was equally elated with joy.

Addressing the sages with due respect, she said "O Great men! Lord Siva who is responsible for all our existence is most welcome to marry our daughter and it is a great honour for us. But, a small doubt lurks in my mind. King

Daksha had earlier given his daughter Dâkshâyani in marriage to Lord Siva. Once when the Lord became angry with him, he ignored the relationship of father in law and punished him severely. He went to the extent of chopping his head off and replacing it with that of a goat. I am afraid to think of a son-in-law who would go so blind in his anger and I shudder to imagine the treatment to be meted out to us. How can my young daughter carry on with him?"

The sages understood queen Mena's hesitation. They consoled her and said, "Fear not, O Queen! King Daksha's case was different. He insulted his own son-in-law, refusing to give him due respect in the yâga performed by him. That triggered Lord's anger and there again he saved him from becoming guilty of the great sin committed against God almighty. He merely punished him gracefully. In your case, Lord is pleased to seek your daughter's hand in marriage and this again means He showers his grace on you. You may rest assured that He is always supreme in His kindness."

Himavan agreed with the sages and queen Mena begged their pardon for her baseless fears. Soon after, the seven sages took leave of them and informed Lord Siva of their approval for the marriage.

# 11. Lord Siva as the bridegroom

No sooner than the sages left for Kailas, King Himavan started his preparation for the wedding scheduled next day. He thought of the divine architect Viswakarma, who readily responded to his call. "O Viswakarma! My daughter Pârvathi is to marry Lord Siva, the God Almighty of Mount Kailas. All Devas numbering thirty-three crores and the rest of the celestial world will certainly grace the auspicious occasion. Our city is to be decorated to look like Indra's capital Amaravati", the King said.

Viswakarma accepted the assignment with pleasure. The city wore a festive look immediately. Great palaces and halls were built on mountain peaks. Broad roads with cool tree shades on either side were truly inviting one and all. Theatres, Yâgasâlâs, wide chariot shelters and the like were erected at suitable places. Plantain trees and aricanut trees were providing the festive arches on the pathways with festoons of mango leaves, bright colourful beads and decorations all along. Separate housing was arranged to accommodate Sages, Siddhas, Yakshas, Gandharvas, Apsara ladies, Kinnaras (musicians) and tastefully equipped for their comfortable stay. On all four sides of the city, compound walls were built with beautiful entrances and welcome arches.

The marriage hall was studded with precious stones and gems of all kinds. Pillars had beautiful images carved on them. Garlands of pearl, ruby, coral, diamond and other gems added grandeur to the place. When they were being tossed about by the gentle wind, different hues were dazzling in the light. There was happiness everywhere and the arrangements were highly appreciated by the King and the Queen.

Invitations for the marriage of Lord Siva and Parvati were sent to all Devas and Gods by King Himavan, with the request to bless the couple and honour him on the occasion. The divine wedding was the talk of the town everywhere in all the worlds.

The next day was an auspicious day in the month of 'phalguna', with the presence of the star 'Uttaraphalguni'. King Himavan got ready early in the morning and reached Mount Kailas with his Queen and relatives. He worshipped the Lord and requested him to come to his palace to accept his daughter in marriage for which He had so kindly consented. He formally invited all His kith and kin, who were none other than all the Gods and Devas.

Lord agreed to reach his palace with his team from Mount Kailas and all sages accompanied him. Himavan was in readiness to receive Him. All the invitees had also gathered at the abode of Himavan. Durga, Kali, the seven rivers, Lakshmi, Saraswati, Indrani, wives of the sages and wives of the Devas, all had congregated there. All the mountains including Meru, the seven oceans, nagas and the eight mighty elephants guarding the eight cardinal directions had already assembled.

After Parvatarajan left, Lord Siva asked Nandideva to get all the Devas, Indras, Brahma, Vishnu and other devotees to Mount Kailas so that He could go with all of them.

Kâlâgni Rudra with his group of ten crore people, armed with their 'trisool' came there. **Panchavaktra** and Rishabhaketu were in this group. Brahmânda Rudra came with his group of 72 crore demons. Adakesa Rudra, Veerabhadra, Mahâsâsthâ and Ékâdasa Rudra came with their crores of subjects. The eight Murtis were present. Gundodaran, Ghantakaranan, Pinaki, Bhanukampan,

Sankhukaranan, Kalakantan, Dandi, Neelan, Karan, Viswamali, Eesânan and others reached Mount Kailas with their army of demons. Indra with Devas, Chandran (Moon) with his stars, the rest of the planets, Vidyadharas and the sages were there to attend the function. All the Sastras beginning from Vedas and all the mantras were available there in their celestial form to accompany the Lord. Brahma came on his swan mount and Vishnu came on his garuda vâhana.

Nandideva announced to Lord Siva about the readiness of all those assembled to escort him. Lord Siva summoned them to his abode, and all of them sang his praise in His august presence.

"O God! You are excessively kind to us, you taught us Yoga mârga, by teaching the four sons of Brahma. We were enlightened about the path to salvation. Now, you are becoming a bridegroom to give us immense pleasure. We are looking forward to the auspicious event when we can see you shining in all glory."

Lord Siva then looked at Brahma, who gave Him the wedding dress. As soon as He touched and accepted them, His entire form changed. The snakes and bones adorning Him till then, vanished. Lord Siva was now fully decked with golden ornaments. Everyone stood there wondering at the gorgeous sight.

**The auspicious time was approaching fast. Nandideva commanded the visitors to order. Lord Siva came out and got on his Rishabha Mount, with the help of Gundodara. All around, "Hara Hara" chanting was heard.** Many types of musical instruments like Berigai, Kokkarai, Salligai, Karaligai, Peeli, Charikai, Udukkai, Mathalam, Kudamuzha, Thabaari, Kakala, Oodukombu were played aloud. Nandideva was leading

the procession with a golden wand in his hand. Demons
were following, chanting His name. Many visitors carried
flags and festoons to add beauty to the occasion. Brahma
and Vishnu came on either side of Lord Siva as his
bodyguards. Sun and the Moon carried the palanquin.

Varuna was making the place cool, spraying water all along. Indra was carrying the umbrella. The big procession was heading towards Himavan's palace, raising lot of dust up to the sky. Musical notes and chanting were sounding as sweet as honey. Tumburu and Narada were playing Vedas on 'yazh'. Sages were singing the praise of the Lord in vedamantras, as they were following, making Him rejoice on the happy occasion.

## 12. Sage Agasthya's greatness

As soon as Parvatarajan got the message that Lord Siva and his party of all-important celestial persons were approaching, he received them all with his relatives at the entrance of the city. He formally requested Lord Siva to come to his palace and the marriage party entered the city.

When the bridegroom was taken in procession along the wide roads with all pomp and grandeur, the people enjoyed the fanfare of the great event. Lord Siva's beautiful darshan gave them the pleasure of all ages. All the women welcomed the Lord in the traditional style. The children greeted Him with the Mantra "Hara Hara". All the Vedas were present with all auspicious gifts.

**At the main entrance to the palace, Queen Mena welcomed them by offering cow's milk as per tradition.** Brahma and Vishnu helped the Lord to get down from his Rishabha Vahana. King Himavan and Queen Mena washed the Lord's feet and worshipped Him with great happiness. Nandideva gave the Lord His footwear and Lord entered the palace. Veda Mantras and auspicious instrumental music filled the whole atmosphere. Demons were enjoying themselves. Vidyadharas sang melodiously. Devas were chanting prayers in praise of God. Brahma and Vishnu escorted Lord Siva to the main Hall to be seated on the throne studded with gems. All the Devas, Indra and other dignitaries were seated all around in their respective positions.

As every soul was present in the Himalayan Kingdom to witness the rare event, the place was heavily loaded with excessive weight, with the result it was being pulled down below the surface of the Earth and the Southern side was high. People living on Earth felt the impact and were

afraid that some havoc awaits them. Even the sages and seers began to worry about the outcome and the entire scene changed into a state of confusion. Lord Siva acted at once and sent for sage Agastya. **Nandideva ushered him in immediately when the sage waited for His orders. Lord Siva directed him to go to Podhigai Mountain in the South, so that the weight of both**

**North and South could be balanced. "That alone will ensure peace of mind for all the souls," He said.**

Agastya was sad that he was being denied the pleasure of witnessing the lifetime event of Lord's marriage with Pârvathi. Lord consoled him and said that he was the greatest of all assembled there and that is why he was chosen for a special task of restoring the balance of Mother Earth.

Agastya was thrilled. He thanked the Lord for the special privilege conferred on him and agreed to proceed south as ordered. Even though he was the most blessed of all, he was still missing the marriage festivities of God Almighty, he felt.

Lord Siva extended His grace to him further and assured that he can still see all the events of marriage celebrations even while staying in the South. After some days, he would be called back to Mount Kailas, He said.

Agastya rejoiced in God's special assignment to him and went down South. As soon as he reached Podhigai mountain, the balance between the North and the South was restored and everyone heaved a sigh of relief.

## 13. Pârvathi's Marriage

Saraswati and Lakshmi gave Pârvathi the ceremonial bath and prepared her as the bride with glittering jewellery and gorgeous silks adding to her beauty. Then they escorted her on either side to the marriage hall and ushered her to the bridal seat. Indrani was preceding her, filling the route with sweet smelling flowers. All the rivers were fanning her and Kalis were carrying the umbrellas.

When Pârvathi approached the Lord, He took her hand in His. All the womenfolk from heaven were immensely happy at the sight. Pârvathi was looking as bright as the Sun shining in his maximum glory.

Himavan and his wife bowed before the Lord and washed His feet with holy waters. As per traditional rituals they offered flowers, sandal paste, kumkum, mangala Akshadai, etc. The other formalities followed. Himavan gave his daughter in marriage amidst Vedic chanting. Brahma and Guru performed the wedding as per age-old practices. All the visitors enjoyed the celebrations. Himavan offered bananas, jack fruit, ghee, honey, milk, etc., to his son-in-law. After Lord's blessing, they were distributed to all the invitees to add to their pleasure. Right at that time, Rathi appeared there and fell at the feet of the Lord.

"Oh my Lord! I have come to remind you of your promise to me at Mount Kailas. When all are rejoicing on this happy occasion, should I alone be mourning? Kindly give back my husband who was instrumental for all these festivities", she said.

Lord decided to grant her prayer. He said "O Rathi! I shall make your husband come back to you as I promised. But he is destined to stay anonymous for some

time. So, you alone will be able to see him in his full form, while he will be invisible for others. Manmatha appeared there at once and worshipped the Lord. While Rathi could see him, the others could only feel his presence. Lord told Manmatha that he will continue to do his job with his bow and arrows, though he would remain invisible.

Soon after, Indra and others took the blessing of Lord Siva and Pârvathi, one after the other. The whole city was indulging in full gaiety with vivid descriptions of the marriage. Everyone felt fortunate to have witnessed the wonderful lifetime event. The sages and the Devas were singing the praise of God Almighty.

After the festivities of the marriage concluded, Lord took leave of all the guests and started his journey back to Mount Kailas with his wife Pârvathi. Parvatarajan and Mena wished them happy journey with tears of joy rolling down their cheeks.

## 14. The birth of Lord Muruga

Devas had gathered at the foot of the Himalayas. They were eagerly waiting for the birth of Muruga, as the wedding of Lord Siva and Pârvathi was already over to their great joy. But the long awaited birth of Muruga was still evading them and they were naturally getting worried about the delay in Lord's ending the atrocities of Soorapadhman. They wanted to make a fresh appeal to God, meeting Him once again at Mount Kailas with Brahma as their leader.

Brahma was not in favour of meeting Lord Siva without an appointment or His prior consent. He suggested that they send a messenger to announce their arrival to the Lord. Who would be the right choice? Manmatha was sent last time and his fate was well known. All Devas hesitated and Brahma had to call Vayu to do the job.

Vayu shuddered at the very thought of going to Mount Kailas to meet the Lord. He pleaded with Brahma. "Oh! Lord of Vedas! Please forgive me. I cannot meet the same fate as Manmatha. I shall not undertake this dangerous task. Please do not compel me." Brahma was seized of his legitimate fears. He tried to convince him again: "Mâruta! You will not meet the same fate as Manmatha. Let me assure you that the situation in Mount Kailas is quite different now. Let us help each other. You will earn good name and fame by your visit."

When Brahma was insisting, Vayu had to yield. As soon as he reached Mount Kailas, he went in gathering all the sweet smell of the divine flowers, as pleasant as the soothing Southern wind. Nandideva stopped him at the second gate and questioned him for his unauthorized entry. Vayu begged his pardon for coming in without his permission and wanted him to forgive him.

"Okay! But please run away from here at once,"
Nandideva said. Vayu went straight to Devas and apprised
them as to what happened. Devas decided to go together
to Lord Siva and make a fresh request. Accordingly, they
chanted prayers to Lord Siva and went to Mount Kailas.
Nandideva informed the Lord of their arrival and with His
permission, allowed them in.

Devas now presented their case in one voice and asked
Him to redress their grievances.

"O Lord of Kailas! How long are we to live in fear of the
devil Soorapadhman? Kindly give us your son, equal in
power to you, to mitigate our sufferings." Lord Siva
acceded to their prayer and agreed to do the needful. Right
in their presence he stood with six faces. Eesânam,
Tatpurusham, Vâmanam, Aghoram, Sadyojâtam were the
five faces and the sixth one "Adhómukam" was visible only
to the enlightened. Devas were stunned at his majestic
figure with the six faces. Six sparks were emitted from the
six eyes in the foreheads of the six faces. The sparks were
so powerful that they spread a lot of heat all around. Devas
ran hither and thither, unable to withstand the heat.
Pârvathi, who was sitting next to Siva, also ran inside with
her anklets tinkling.

Was it proper for Devas to run away from the Lord?
They gathered again before Him and pleaded "We wanted
a son from you to annihilate the Asura and protect us.
The sparks emitted from your eyes are producing so much
of heat all over the place and we are unable to stand it. If
you do not take pity on us, we will just get reduced to
ashes. Who else can help us if not you?"

Lord Siva changed his form and gave darshan with just
one face. All the sparks were called back by Him. He called
Vayu and Agni to take the six sparks to the Ganges river,

who in turn, was to take them to the Saravana Lake in the South."

Vayu and Agni expressed their apprehension whether they would be able to carry the sparks at all as they emanated so fiercely from Lord Himself. Lord gave them adequate courage to take up the task and also assured them that they would have the divine power to do it successfully.

Both took leave of the Lord and Devas felt quite relieved mentally. "Oh My Dear Devas! The six sparks, as soon as they reach Saravana lake, will unite and become my son. He will kill the Asuras and take care of your welfare. Now, you may get back to your places." Lord said.

Devas did not return to their kingdom. They wanted to witness the great event of Lord Muruga's birth on Earth. They followed Vayu and Agni. When Vayu carried the sparks, the heat was unbearable for him. Agni took them to River Ganges. Because of the excessive power of the sparks, the water in the river Ganges began to evaporate. On being briefed about her part of the job, river Ganges took the sparks to Saravana lake. God's grace protected the water in the lake and all the Devas stood around the lake, singing His praise.

The six sparks, which floated in the lake, got united into one big column of fire. Amidst the bright light spreading its rays all around, a divine figure could be seen which was formless, beautiful, endless, unique, multifaceted and supreme.

Lord Muruga was there with six faces and twelve hands and Devas felt happy that they need to fear none hereafter. They worshipped the winsome child seated on the lotus flower, saying that He alone will be their saviour. Lord

Siva called the six Krithika girls to take care of the child. As soon as they drew near the lotus, Lord Muruga transformed himself as six children. He was to be fed and brought up by the six girls. One could see six different childish pranks in the six children brought up by the girls.

One was smiling and taking milk. The second one was still sleeping. The third one had just woken up and enticed them with his first sweet words, the fourth was playing, while the fifth was weeping. When one was crawling, the other was trying to stand. When one was sitting on the banks of the lake, the other was playing in the water.

The different milestones and stages of a little child's growth could be seen there to the enjoyment of everyone. The Krithika girls were sometime worried when they saw the children going all out to play. They, in fact, were worshipping them as God incarnate.

At the time when Lord Muruga was born in the Saravana lake, the Asuras like Soorapadman, Singamukhan and others were having their bad dreams!

## 15. Nine warriors were born

When Pârvathi ran from her seat, unable to bear the heat generated by the six sparks emitted by the six faces of Lord Siva, her anklets hit against each other and sounded sweet. Nine gems rolled out of the broken anklets. In each one of them, Devi's figure could be seen. Lord Siva looked at them with love and nine 'Shakthis' were born. All of them bowed before the Lord and wanted to unite with Him. By God's grace, all of them became pregnant.

When Pârvathi returned to her seat, relieved of her fears, she learnt that God had created a son extraneously in deference to the wishes of the Devas and she had lost an opportunity to bear him. She was so angry that she cursed all the Devas not to get children by their wives.

When she looked at the nine Shakthis, who looked like her, but were somewhat different in their state of pregnancy, she got so wild with them also and cursed them saying that they shall not deliver their babies for a long time.

They were so startled that they sweated profusely. A lakh of warriors were born out of the sweat and they all worshipped Lord Siva. God blessed them by saying that they will help Lord Muruga to fight the Asuras. Immensely pleased, they praised Him. All the nine Shakthis were doing all errands for Devi Pârvathi. The babies belonged to Nandideva's clan but because they were not delivered, they became big bulls inside the wombs. They were praying to Lord Siva from the wombs and nine Shakthis were reeling in pain due to their weight.

When Lord requested Devi to show pity on them, she agreed and withdrew her curse on them, making them deliver their kids. They were the nine great warriors, blessed by Pârvathi.

Veerabhâhu was born to Manikkavalli
Veerakesari was born to Muttuvalli
Veeramahendran was born to Pushparâgavalli
Veeramaheswaran was born to Komethagavalli
Veerapurandaran was born to Vaidooryavalli
Veerarakshasan was born to Vajravalli
Veeramârthândan was born to Maragathavalli
Veerântagan was born to Pavazhavalli
Veeradheeran was born to Indraneelavalli

Just as Nandideva resembled his Mother Earth, these nine warriors were like their mothers in colour. Fully grown in size they came through the navel like Lord Brahma. Clad in golden silks, they bowed before Lord Siva. "They are all handsome and intelligent sons for us", said Lord Siva and Pârvathi also blessed them. Lord gave each one of them a dazzling sword and asked them to serve His son Lord Muruga, with the lakh soldiers already born.

The nine warriors took leave of the Lord and reached the abode of Lord Muruga taking his service as directed. Nine Shakthis continued to serve Pârvathi as before.

## 16. The divine couple at
## Saravanam with their son

After the nine warriors left, Lord Siva told Pârvathi that He wanted to bring their son Muruga to mount Kailas. "In order to redress the grievances of the Devas, I had created

Muruga out of the sparks from my forehead eyes. He is now at Saravana lake and the six Krithika girls are taking care of him. Let us go and get him here." Pârvathi readily agreed and both left for Saravanam with their celestial group of men.

Lord Siva asked Devi to bring their son to him. **She happily took the six children playing around the lake and now there was one lovely child with six faces and twelve hands. As six forms were made into one form, he was named "Kandhan"** (Tamil version of "Skandhan" which means united by Lord Siva).

When Devi hugged the child with all her love, milk was flowing from her breasts. She collected it in a beautiful bowl and fed the child. She took him to Lord Siva, who blessed him.

God took the child on his lap and made Devi sit on his left side. This posture is called *"Somâskandamürtham"*. All Gods and Devas enjoyed this darshan of the divine family and showered flowers on them.

Lord called the Krithika girls and told them, "As our son was brought up by you, he will be called 'Karthikeyan' and anyone who worships him on the day of your star "Karthigai", will be blessed by him for all their desires."

When Devi fondled Muruga with joy, her breasts began to secrete so much of milk that it was flowing into the Saravana lake. Six sons of sage Parâsara were living as fish in that lake due to a curse of their father. When they drank Devi's breast milk mixed in the water, they got liberated from the curse. All of them got back their human forms and reached the banks of Saravana. When they bowed before Lord Siva, He blessed them and asked them to proceed to Tirupparankunram. They were told that Lord

Muruga will come there to give them guidance to attain salvation. Lord Siva then reached Mount Kailas back with Devi and Murugan. The nine warriors and the lakh soldiers also followed them to Mount Kailas to serve the Lord.

## 17. Dévasénâpathi

At Mount Kailas, Kandhan was happily playing with his brothers. As he ran hither and thither, his anklet bells sounded sweetly and his ornaments were glittering on his chest. He will go into the lakes and take lotus flowers from there. Next moment he will climb the peaks of the mountains and play 'hide and seek'. Devi was enjoying his funny childish pranks and asked the Lord, "O my Lord! Even as a child, Muruga is so much interesting and thrilling. I would like to know more about his greatness and glory."

"My dear Devi, Muruga has been born from the sparks of my eyes. Hence he will be as powerful as I am. As he was carried by River Ganga, he will also be known as Gângeyan. As he took a definite form at Saravana lake, his popular name will be "Saravanabhavan". As you had united the six forms into one, "Kandha" befits him admirably. All my six

faces have become his now. Hence, he get's the name as Shanmugkan or Arumugkan also. My Panchakshara (Five syllables - Na Ma Si Vâ Ya) and the Târaka Mantra (Om) have united to become Shadakshara (Om Sa Ra Va Na Bha Va) for him. He is none other than me. He will also be omnipresent. He can take any form. He will protect all those who surrender unto him. He will annihilate Soorapadman and all other Asuras in order to help Devas."

Muruga's playfulness crossed the frontiers of Mount Kailas. His pranks could be seen all over up and down. Mountains were pushed aside without any effort. He will stand on Meru, which will start shivering. All the seven seas will flow into one another. High peaks will sink low. Vâsuki and the other snakes were his toys. Ganges and other rivers suddenly used to stand still! All the eight guard elephants, Ashta Diggajas, will fight with each other. Sun will travel to the region of the Moon and vice versa was also true.

All these were child's play for Muruga. Though they were harmless, people in all the three worlds were greatly astonished. Devas could not decipher whether they were mere transitory pranks of the child Muruga or the tricks of the wicked asuras!

If they were the handiwork of asuras, they would have harmed Devas, but it was not so! Târaka and other asuras on earth were confused as they were beyond the capacity of Devas.

Muruga had a lot of fun doing such mischief, staying away somewhere, invisible for all.

Though Devas knew pretty well that asuras had not been doing these acts, they could not rest in peace. Highly inquisitive, they proceeded to Mount Meru to check the facts with Indra. As he did not know the answer, all of them went to see Lord Brahma.

There they saw a boy, who caught the peaks of Mount Meru as if he was plucking flowers from a garden. This was the boy they very much wanted to meet. But can a small boy do such things? Is it some illusion created by Asuras? If so, they wanted to fight the boy. So Indra called his elephant Airâwatam, got on its back and aimed his arrows at the naughty boy.

None of the Devas could identify Muruga who wanted to prove his prowess to them and allay their fears. With all their anger they attacked the little boy from all the four sides. The arrows fell as flowers on him! Even then Indra could least imagine that this was the divine child who has been sent to rescue them from the clutches of Asuras. With doubled anger, he pushed forward Airâwatam and attacked the boy. Saravanan thought of a bow and arrow. When he returned the fight and shot an arrow, it went straight to pierce the trunk of Airâwatam, which fell down with a thunderous noise. Muruga's next arrow made Indra fall down on Earth. Devas were aghast with fear. They still did not recognize the small boy as to who he was. Varuna, Yama, Vayu, Chandra, Agni and their soldiers crowded there. Saravanan encountered them with a smile. He hit them all together with five arrows and all of them fell flat! Rest fled the scene and Muruga stood there all alone, with none to fight with.

Sage Narada heard the news and ran to Devaguru Bruhaspati. "O Bruhaspati! Devas have not recognized Muruga who has been created by Lord Siva to alleviate their sufferings. Hence they are fighting with him and the result is Indra, Vayu, Varuna and others have been struck down by Murugan. You should rush there before things become worse."

**On hearing Narada, Bruhaspati rushed to Meru mountain and fell at the feet of Muruga. "My Lord! Kindly forgive the Devas for the stupid mistake they have done. In fact they were happy that you have been born to save them from asuras like Târaka, Singamukha and Soorapadhman.** They are always thinking of you only. They are not your enemies. Due to their ignorance, they have not recognized you. Do parents ever punish their own children? You can point out their foolish mistakes and correct them. Kindly forgive them and do not harbour anger against them. Please pardon them gracefully and turn your anger against the asuras" he said.

Kandhan, who was the embodiment of kindness, smiled. Devas who were dead, came back to life with wisdom

dawned on them. They recognized their saviour in
Kandhan. They regretted their mistakes, fell at his feet and
begged his pardon.

Kandhan talked to them soothingly. "My dear Devas! Do not fear anyone from now. Asuras will be done away with, in no time. You thought I was a small boy and hence came to fight with me. I will show you my true self now. You can be rest assured of my strength."

Next moment, Muruga took his gigantic form, which was so fearful for Devas. They begged of him to change his 'Viswaroopam' to a pleasant form. Kandhan gave them the wisdom to see him fully. They saw in Him the entire universe, the eight directions encompassing the seven worlds, the mountains, seven oceans, Chakravâlagiriyam and all the rest of the things were clearly visible. Struck with great wonder, they praised him.

"My Lord! We have seen the entire universe in you. You are formless and also the unique form embracing the infinity. We have seen you from head to toe. You are the only one who can save us from Asuras. You had made many things topsy-turvy to prove your prowess to us. Kindly restore them to their places."

Kandhan granted their prayers. Indra approached him now and said, "We want to formally worship you. Kindly give us permission." Kandha agreed. Immediately Viswakarma erected a beautiful temple on a mountain peak, where there was a huge hall, glittering with gems and an exquisite royal seat. Kandhan was made to sit there after a ceremonial bath, duly decorated with gorgeous silks and precious jewellery. They garlanded him and offered their ritualistic worship. Indra, as the representative of Devas, asked him to accept all of them as his subjects and also rule the entire world, duly crushing all the evil asuras.

Kandhan gave back the kingdom to Indra and asked them again not to worry about asuras. Indra bowed before him and said, "You are our master. We are your soldiers. You shall guide us through any fight to suppress the evil forces." So praising the Lord, they worshipped him from then on. Kandhan became their commander-in-chief, **Devasenâpati**. The mountain where Kandhan was worshipped was known as Kandhagiri from then on.

## 18. The goat becomes the vehicle

Sage Narada performed a yâga to appease Lord Siva. Devas, Sages and Brahmins gathered there to conduct the yâga with due reverence, while a goat suddenly sprang up from the Vedic fire. It was so fierceful that everyone was struck with great fear. It poked the Earth with its horns and there was hectic dust all over the place. It made a thunderous noise and Devas began to attack it with arrows. The goat brushed them aside and fell on the crowd. Many fell a victim to its attack and none could control it. As goats are usually sacrificed in the yâga fire, it looked as if it was taking revenge on the performers of the yâga, on behalf of its species. Even the mountains were shaken and the goat was jumping all around as if it is out to destroy everything. Devas and sages ran for their lives and the goat was chasing them.

When Devas and Narada ran to Mount Kailas to take refuge in Lord Siva's feet, they came across Muruga, who was playing with his one-lakh friends. When Muruga has been born to protect them, Narada and others thought that they could as well take the help of Muruga, instead of going in search of Lord Siva. They cried aloud to Muruga.

"O Lord of the Lords! The goat, which came out of the yaga fire, is behind us. We are unable to counter its anger. You must come to our rescue by controlling it somehow". Karthikeyan promised to help them and ordered Veerabhahu to fetch the ferocious animal, wherever it is.

After ransacking the whole earth, the goat had reached Brahma's world, causing terror there. After a thorough search of the Earth, Veerabhahu reached Brahma's abode and took hold of the goat. When it was caught firmly by the horns by Veerabhahu, its anger subsided and Muruga

now asked the Devas to resume their yâga and conclude it without fear.

Devas pleaded with Muruga thus. **"O Kandha! Please do not allow the goat to go scot-free. Kindly keep it under check and make it your vehicle.** Muruga agreed and over powered the goat immediately. He made it his mount and Devas, amply relieved, went back to complete the yâga.

## 19. Brahma gets imprisoned

Once it so happened that Brahma and Devas came to Mount Kailas to worship Lord Siva. They were very happy at His darshan and returned with great joy. Muruga met them on the way and greeted Brahma specially. Engrossed in thoughts about Lords Siva's grace, Brahma forgot to take notice of Muruga or acknowledge his greeting with due respect. Casually smiling, Brahma approached Murugan and announced that he was just returning after seeing his father.

Instead of saluting him, Brahma had just looked upon Muruga casually as a small boy. This triggered anger in Muruga who wanted to teach Brahma a lesson for his pride as the creator of the world. "Oh Lord of the Vedas! May I know about your assignment?" Muruga asked.

Brahma said, " By God's grace, I am the creator of the entire world."

Muruga replied, "Well, You say that all creation is your responsibility. Could you tell me the meaning of Pranava which is the basis of all Vedas?"

What can Brahma say? How can we explain the meaning of Pranava to a small boy like Muruga?

Even great scholars find it difficult to acquire full knowledge about Pranava and it is no easy task to attempt a simple explanation to befit comprehension by a child like Muruga. Hence Brahma was in utter confusion.

Muruga laughed aloud and said, "O Brahma! So you are not competent to give me the meaning of Pranava, Okay! Let me tell you that Pranavam is the very seat of Lord Siva. All species are born out of Pranava. It is the basis and root of all Vedas. Lord Siva chants Pranava into the ears of all dying souls in Vârânasi. All that you do is futile, if you do not know the simple but lofty meaning of Pranava"

Muruga hit Brahma on his head and asked his soldiers to take him to the prison. While Brahma was imprisoned thus, Muruga took upon himself, the task of creation. He took a Japamala in one hand and a Kamandalam in the other. He blessed the souls with the other two hands. All Devas ran away from there, once they saw Brahma's sad plight in the prison.

A few days passed by. Brahma was suffering in prison, doing penance for not saluting Muruga. Muruga did the job of creation so well that none felt the absence of Brahma. Mahavishnu who rests on the ocean of milk took upon himself the task of getting Brahma released from prison. He led a group of Devas to meet Lord Siva.

All of them apprised the Lord of what happened in Kandhagiri. "O my Lord! Your son Muruga asked Brahma to explain the meaning of Pranava to him. As he could not do it, Muruga has put him in prison in Kandhagiri. He has been doing Brahma's work from then on. Please take pity on Brahma who is languishing in jail for a long time now."

,

Lord Siva called Nandideva and ordered him to go to Kandhagiri to get Brahma released and present him in his court. When Nandideva carried this message to Kandha he became furious. "I shall not release Brahma. I shall put you also in prison if you stand here for a minute more," He said.

When Nandideva came back to Lord Siva and told him about what happened at Kandhagiri, Lord Siva smiled and started to go to Kandhagiri. Devas and Vishnu followed him.

Muruga worshipped at his father's feet and said that he could have sent word for him. Lord Siva said " Muruga! Brahma is in charge of creation. You have imprisoned him for some reason. I sent Nandideva to fetch him to my court. Because you got angry and refused to do as I wanted, I had to come myself."

Muruga, at once, ordered the release of Brahma, who appeared before Lord Siva in a famished state. When Lord Siva commented on his state of poor health, Brahma replied, "Your son had imprisoned me which made me shed my pride and do penance for my misdeeds."

Lord smiled and asked Brahma to resume his duties. He took Muruga on his lap and asked, "My dear son! Brahma failed to explain the meaning of Pranava to you when you asked for it. I suppose you know it. If so, why don't you tell me?"

Kandhan laughed and said "O Father! Did you not impart that knowledge about Pranava to Devi secretly? It is not something that can be made public. You should follow the same rules, as prescribed, to acquire such knowledge."

Lord was delighted to hear his son's words. He put down his son from his lap and gave him a high seat nearby. He sat

on the ground with all humility, befitting a learner and then asked Muruga to teach him, if he was pleased to do so.

**Muruga happily gave the meaning of Pranava Mantra to his father in his ears. It was indeed a great sight to see the son as the teacher of the father.** He was hailed for the Divine teacher status by all Devas and others. With celebrations going on all around, Lord returned to Mount Kailas.

When Agastya learnt about this incident, he came to Kandhagiri and requested Muruga to impart that knowledge to him also likewise. Muruga obliged sage Agastya and gave him the gist of Pranava. The world worshipped him from then on as "Guruguhan".

## 20. Mahavishnu gets two daughters

When Mahavishnu was extremely happy to see Muruga's great darshan at Kandhagiri, he shed tears of joy. Two girls were born from those tears of joy. They were named Amirtavalli and Sundaravalli and both of them wanted to marry Muruga. They came to Saravana lake and sat in prayers chanting the six letters "Shadakshara". Greatly pleased, Muruga gave them darshan. The girls requested him to accept them as his wives, so that they could serve him always.

Saravana did not agree to their desire immediately. He wanted Amirtavalli to be born as Indra's daughter and Sundaravalli to be born as Sivamuni's daughter on Earth. He promised to marry them at the right time, and so they left the place. Amirtavalli took the shape as a small child and went to Indra in Mount Meru. "O Lord of Devas! I was born as daughter of Mahavishnu, your co - brother. You are like my father and I request you to bring me up."

Indra was immensely happy to get her as his daughter. He carried the little girl in his hands and gave her to the divine elephant 'Airâvatam' to help bring her up.

He thought she would bring them all good luck. Airâvatam took the child to Amaravati, Indra's capital and took care of her fondly. As she was brought up by the divine elephant, she was known as "Deivayânai." She was meditating on Muruga all the time, with a keen desire to marry him and so did, Sundaravalli also, growing at the Valli valley in Thondaimandalam.

## 21. The army marches on

Once Muruga had gone with his soldiers to Mount Kailas to see his parents. When Lord Siva was happily engaged in conversation with his son, Brahma, Indra and Devas called on them.

"O mighty Lord of the universe! You had promised to allay our fears of asuras and accordingly gave us Muruga. But still we live in constant fear and no end is in sight for our sufferings. Can you take pity on us now?" they prayed sincerely.

Lord addressed his son immediately. "My dear Saravana! Devas are being tortured by Soorapadhman and his asuras for a long time now and it is high time you annihilate them to restore Indra's kingdom to him."

Muruga took his father's command and started on the job. Lord made Ekadasarudras as his son's weapons. Ekadasa rudras became eleven powerful weapons. They were Tomaram, Flag, Sword, Kulisam or Vajrâyudham, Arrow, Angusam, Ghantâmani, Staff, Bow and Mazhuni. They adorned Muruga. While lakhs of soldiers came as his escorts, a divine chariot appeared there to carry Lord Muruga.

Muruga took leave of his parents and Lord Siva asked all Devas to follow him. When Muruga was leading all of them to the battle field, Lord Siva called Vayu and made him the driver of Muruga's Chariot. Vayu prayed to Kandhan to mount the chariot. There was hectic cheering all around. "Soorapadhman has fallen", shouted everyone. Sankha, Bheri and Murasu started playing loudly and the army marched on. The dusty wind that rose signalled the dark clouds for asuras.

Devas went near Krounchagiri. Narada came there and prayed to Muruga. "My dear Muruga! Once upon a time,

this Krounchagiri was a mighty king of mountains. Due to sage Agastya's curse, it is lying low now. Mâyâpuri is nearby and Soorapadhman's brother Târakan is living there. I shall tell you about his prowess. Once he went to fight with Mahavishnu. Unable to kill him with any of his weapons, Vishnu hurled his wheel at him. Târakan took the wheel in his hand and made it his ornament. You should kill Târakan first, so that you can win over Soorapadhman easily", said Narada.

**Muruga called Veerabhahu and ordered him to kill Târakan. Viswakarma was summoned to provide suitable chariots to Veerabhahu and his brothers. Viswakarma acted accordingly and Veerabhahu took the blessing of Kandhan and started off with his brothers on chariots.**

## 22. Asura creates the illusion

Before Veerabhahu and his soldiers could reach Mâyâpuri, Târakan had known about their coming through his spies. So he was angrily awaiting their arrival, right at the entrance to the city.

There was a fierce fight between the two armies. Asuras killed Veerabhahu's men left and right and Devas also pounced on the asuras in great numbers. Veerakesari sent hundred arrows on Târakan in one go. His crown fell down on the ground and he, as a wounded tiger, sent his Dandhâyudham on Veerakesari. Veerakesari could not stand it and hence fell flat in the chariot. Veerabhahu got wild with anger, stood before the enemy at once and showered arrows on him. Târakan's bow broke into two and so he aimed his "Soolam" at Veerabhahu. His strength was stunning and his men had already caused great havoc on Veerabhahu's army. Looking at the helpless sad plight of the enemy, Târaka roared in laughter. Veerabhahu warned him of a change of scene very soon.

Târakan raised his hand and started proclaiming aloud. "Who do you think I am? I had defeated even your Vishnu. Look at this chakra adorning my neck as an ornament!" he started pouring his arrows on Veerabhahu, which were met half-way itself before they could reach the target. When he sent Agneyastram, Veerabhahu countered it with the same weapon. Now Târakan employed another strategy. He created an illusion of himself at several places and fought Veerabhahu from all the four sides. Veerabhahu sent his Veerabhadrastram and his magic was totally dispensed with. Târaka went and hid himself in Krounchagiri. **Veerabhahu vowed to catch him by all means possible, so that he can take him captive to Shanmukha. He then entered Krounchagiri.**

Târaka had kept Krounchagiri totally under his control.
Because of his magical spell, the whole place was dark
and Veerabhahu could not see anything in the darkness.

He became unconscious by the Magic spell and fainted there. When Veerabhahu did not return even after a long time, his soldiers grew suspicious. They also entered Krounchagiri to check whether he was in danger. But because of the magic spell all over, they also fainted. Târaka thought that they were all dead and so came out of hiding. He got on a new chariot and renewed his attack on the Devas, who were absolutely unequal to his fury. When the situation became pretty bad, Indra ran to Muruga.

"O Lord! Veerabhahu and his men went into Krounchagiri and have not returned. Târaka must have killed them. Devas have been completely shattered," he said.

Shanmukha himself started for the war with the asuras. Vayu took the chariot faster, to match his angry mood. When he reached the spot, Devas regained confidence and were ready to fight the asuras with renewed strength. Târaka kept his forces under check and proceeded to face Muruga. "We have nothing against Lord Siva. How is it that his son is here?" He asked Saravanan, knowing him to be Lord Siva's son.

"Târaka! I too have nothing against you, but you and your men are giving hell of a trouble to Devas. In order to wipe out their suffering and establish righteousness on earth, I have come. If you can promise that all of you will refrain from such evil acts against Devas, I shall go back" Shanmukha said. Târaka ridiculed him by saying thus "You do not know who I am. You may please check with Vishnu first."

"Târaka! I do know that story. You want to show me Vishnu's wheel adorning your neck as an ornament. Don't think of my "Vel" lightly. You can watch its power right away" Muruga said. Târaka ignored his words and started sending his arrows. Muruga also fought with his bow and arrows. Târaka's arrows were destroyed. His chariot was reduced to dust. A thousand arrows attacked his fore head at the same time. All his armour went to pieces. Blood was flowing out of his wounds. He fainted on the spot. Asuras saw their leader fall and so fought more fiercely. But Devas maintained their stand well. The battlefield presented a horrible scene with heavy losses for the asuras.

After a short while, Târaka woke up. He was shocked at his inability to stand against Muruga. By hook or crook, he wanted to win. He started afresh with Brahmâstram, Nârâyanâstram, etc. They went round Muruga and fell at his feet as garlands. Pâsupatâstram was next deployed. Devas shouted "Hara Hara Sambho". Muruga was least bothered. He took it in his hands respectfully and worshipped it. It settled down on his hand as a beautiful flower. The asura now realized that no weapon would really be of any help. He prayed to Krounchagiri to help him with all its magical skills. Krounchagiri took the shape of three big forts from skies and landed on Devas. When Muruga saw this, he sent an arrow to save his men. Alas! The three forts were burnt to ashes in a jiffy. Krouncham came over the entire area as a vast dark cloud. The asura roared like thunder. It was pitch dark everywhere and Târaka made terrific noises. When Krounchagiri became a gale, the asura stood there as a big column of wild fire.

One after the other, magical illusions and false images created by Târaka and Krounchagiri caused panic among Devas. Muruga took his "Vel" in his hand and gave a command. "Let Krounchagiri be broken into pieces and Târaka be torn apart. "The Vel began its work emitting fierce sparks all around. Krounchagiri went to pieces.

Veerabhahu and his men woke up from their magical spell. They renewed their attack on Asuras. The next target for the Vel was Târaka. Before he could think of catching it, The Vel passed through his chest. He fell down like a broken branch of a tree.

Devas shouted slogans of victory. Flowers were raining from heaven. Vel went to Ganges, cleansed itself and got back to Muruga. Sages and others sang Saravana's glory in glorious verses. Devas prayed to Muruga to give life to the soldiers who were killed in the war and Muruga obliged them. He also honoured Veerabhahu with Pâsupatâstram, confiscated from Târaka.

Muruga then proceeded southwards with his soldiers. Beyond Himalayas, when they reached Devagiri, the Sun had set. Indra came there and submitted that they wanted to worship Muruga at that place. Muruga conceded to their prayer and asked Viswakarma to establish a beautiful city there.

Accordingly, Viswakarma built a city with all comforts there. At its centre, an excellent temple was also erected. Muruga was seated there on a throne studded with nine gems. He was given a holy bath with Ganges water brought along the air route. He was greeted with all scented stuff and worshipped with sweet smelling flowers. Devas' hearts were filled with great joy.

After the day dawned, all of them left Devagiri to go further South.

## 23. Asurendra at Mahendrapuri

News of Târaka's end reached his wife Souri at Mâyâpuri. She came to the battlefield and started lamenting his unbelievable demise: "You have fallen on the ground unconscious, perhaps because you are tired after the war or you are taking rest. Devas who will be afraid even on hearing your name, clap their hands happily at your fall now. Is there anyone who can really defeat you? You have earned several boons that protect you. Have they all failed today?"

Târaka's other wives also joined her. His son, Asurendran, who had gone to the city of Singamukhan had returned by then and he joined his mother at the battlefield. After mourning his father's death for quite sometime, he gathered himself and consoled his mother. He duly performed the last rites for his father. Souri, his mother, and the other wives wanted to join Târaka at the funeral pyre. Despite persuasion, which proved futile, all of them died with Târaka and Asurendran performed last rites for them also. He then went to Mahendrapuri, the city of Soorapadhman.

As soon as he saw Soorapadhman seated in his court with his ministers, he fell at his feet and cried bitterly. Soorapadhman asked him as to what happened. Asurendran said "Some small boy called Muruga has led Devas to fight my father and has also killed him in the war. Krounchagiri has been split into two parts."

Soorapadman laughed aloud and asked "Are you joking? Do you want us to be misinformed? Why do you unnecessarily cause tension for me? Who can win over Târaka? Stop that nonsense and tell me the truth".

Asurendran fell at his feet again and cried. "Please believe me, your brother Târakan is dead. It is a blatant fact. He had fallen like a big mountain. I have just cremated him. My mother and all other women have also given up their lives. Devas and that little boy are coming down South", he said.

Soorapadhman rose with anger. He could not digest the news of his brother's death. He cried bitterly. "How incredible! Târaka, who was a terror for Devas, has been killed! How could this happen?" he lamented. **After sometime, he called his guards and asked all the four sections of his army to get ready.** Elephants, Horses, Chariots and Cavalry started getting ready. He also put on all his armour. "Let me go and kill that boy who killed my brother", he said. Anger on one side and sorrow on the other, drove him mad and furious. He was fierce like wild fire, spreading all over, to destroy everything. One of his ministers, Amoghan, tried to pacify him, so that he does not act in haste.

"Kindly do not get angry with me for interfering with your decision. I.want to do my duty as your minister. Asurendran has just lost his father and so is in great distress. Devas have suddenly attacked us, taking the help of some small boy. I can realize your agony. You want to take revenge for your brother's demise. Of course our army is ready. But before we take any concrete step, we have to analyse many aspects. I am not finding fault with Asurendran. But still, we cannot rush to any conclusion just by taking his words alone. It is not that he has told us anything untrue. But it is perplexing that the Devas, who were shivering before us, have made bold to attack us all of a sudden. So, it is necessary that we get to know their new strength now. You are certainly greater than all of them. But let us send out our spies first. You shall not go straightaway personally. A full knowledge of the enemies' actual power has to be ascertained by assessing them

afresh and getting the latest report on their movements. We are interested in your welfare. We shall deal with them suitably. If Târaka had died in warfare, he had no special boons like you. Hence Devas have defeated him. It cannot happen to you. Still, let us take a measured step and not act in haste."

When Amoghan gave a sound advice, Soorapadhman agreed with him in toto. He called his special spies Bhakan, Maayuran, Seran and the others and sent them out to get the correct picture. They also started out on their job immediately.

## 24. Vadivelan reaches Sendhil

As the day dawned, Muruga left Devagiri and reached the sacred city of Kedara.

Sage Bhrungi was a great devotee of only Lord Siva. He was not in the habit of worshipping Him with Devi. In order to correct his attitude, Lord Siva appeared before him along with Devi. But, sage Bhrungi took the shape of a bee and went round Lord Siva alone going through the small gap between the two. Devi felt very sad at being ignored by the sage and wanted to become a part of the Lord. So, she came to Kedaram and meditated hard to achieve her goal. Lord was pleased to grant her prayer and gave darshan as 'Ardhanâreeswara', taking Devi on the left side of his body. Muruga worshipped Lord Siva in this form and left Kedaram to proceed further.

Once upon a time, there was a debate in the assembly of sages, where, sage Vyasa tried to establish that Vishnu was the supreme God. When he raised his hand to affirm his argument, Lord Siva wanted him to realise his mistake and saw to it that his hand was immobilised. When sage Vyasa felt sorry for his folly and approved the supremacy of Lord Siva, his hand was restored to normalcy. This incident happened at Kâsi, now known as Vârânasi. Hence Muruga worshipped Lord Siva at Kâsi also and then resumed his journey.

Next he reached Srisailam. This place was called 'Tirupparuppadam' or 'Mallikarjuna Kshetram'. Nandideva, son of sage Silâda, wanted to carry Lord Siva on his head. Lord Siva, pleased with his prayers, granted his request. Nandideva became a mountain and Lord Siva had his temple on its peak. Muruga offered prayers to Lord Siva here also and proceeded.

Next place of halt was 'Tiruvenkatam'. Once Muruga was angry with his mother when he did not get a mango even after going around the whole world. So he went to the under world and came out through a cave. Vishnu and Devas were very happy to see him again. They worshipped him with flowers.

Muruga was delighted to pass through this place and reached the city of 'Tirukâlathi' mountains. This was another holy place where a spider, a snake, an elephant, Sivakosariar, Kannappa Nayanar and Nakkeerar attained salvation. This is hailed as 'Dakshinakailâsam' (Kailasa of the South).

'Tiruvâlankâdu' was the next place of visit. Once, Kali Devi got very angry and started out to destroy the whole world. Brahma and others got so terrified that they prayed to Lord Siva who gave them refuge. In order to put down the conceit of Kali, he danced at Tiruvâlankâdu and saved the world.

Then Muruga reached Kanchipuram, which never gets washed away even by the great deluge (Mahapralayam), which happens at the end of the ages. Vishnu and Brahma also have temples here. After worshipping at this holy city, Muruga resumed his journey.

Once Vishnu and Brahma got entangled in an argument. Each one claimed that he alone was superior. When they were quarrelling with each other on this issue, Lord Siva stood like a big column of fire. While Brahma and Vishnu set out to see His head and foot respectively, they failed miserably. It proved that Lord Siva was the greatest of all. On realizing this, they worshipped Him at the place called Arunagiri, otherwise known as Tiruvannamalai, where He gave them darshan. After worshipping the Lord at this place, Muruga next proceeded to Tiruvennainallur. Here, Lord Siva came in disguise of an old Brahmin, showed a manuscript to prove Sundarar, one of the four saivite seers, that he was His slave. Sundarar refrained from marriage and entered Lord's Service. Lord Siva took Sundarar in his fold only at Tiruvennainallur. After prayers here, Murugan reached Vriddhachalam.

The 'Old Mountain' or 'Vriddhachalam' witnessed another feat of Lord Siva. He takes charge of all the innocent souls, keeps them on his lap and gives them the true meaning of 'Panchakshara', which ensures their salvation. There comes Devi to help the Lord get some fresh air by means of fanning with her saree. As Lord Siva helps the souls here, as he does in Vâranasi, this holy city has the same sanctity. After having darshan of the Lord here, Muruga proceeded to Chidambaram.

Two sages Patanjali and Vyaghrapâda saw the Lord's darshan to their heart's content, as He showed the greatness of cosmic dance as Nataraja here. Muruga worshipped the Lord here also and was thrilled at His kindness.

Next they reached the banks of Manni river. The sun was about to set in the West. Brahma and others wanted to pray to Muruga at that beautiful spot which was full of sandy hills and green gardens.

Muruga agreed and Viswakarma immediately erected a wonderful city there. Devas worshipped Velavan at the temple here and this place was later known as Kumarapuri. (Presently the name is said to be Tirucheinallur).

When Devas were camping at Kumarapuri for the night, a Vanadevatâ (Maiden of the forest) came to meet Indra there from the nearby Seerkaazhi town. Indra stayed in exile at Seerkaazhi, while he had to live secretly in fear of Soorapadhman. He had then bundled up the ornaments of his wife Indrani and had given them to Vanadevatâ for safe custody. When she brought them to Indra now, Indra remembered his wife and spent a sad night there.

As the day dawned, he was ashamed of himself for having thought of his wife at this juncture, when Muruga was also there on a mission for him. Muruga wanted to worship Lord Siva at this place where Brahma, Indra and others had prayed to him. Viswakarma established a temple at once for Lord Siva and Indra brought all the requisites for the Puja.

After the holy bath at the nearby river, Muruga prayed to Lord Siva, who gave him darshan with Parvati and Nandideva. He gave his son a mighty weapon - Pâsupatâstram, which can destroy the whole universe. "Velava, this weapon is mine. Brahma and Vishnu do not have it from me. You are the fittest to wield it. You may destroy Soorapadhman's army with the help of this most powerful weapon", he said and disappeared.

Then they passed through Tiruvidaimarudur, Mâyavaram and Tiruppariyalur and worshipped Lord Siva in his various forms. Then they reached Tiruvarur, where Lord gives darshan as Veedhivitangapperuman and Vanmeekanathar and offered worship as required. These places were usually very dry and hot too. When the son of the Lord and Devas travelled through this area, the place became cool and fertile, becoming comfortable for everyone.

**Six sons of sage Parâsara - Tatta, Ananta, Nandi, Chaturmukha, Chakrapani and Mâli - were sitting in mediation at Tirupparankunram. They could perceive with their inner vision of wisdom that Saravana was approaching their city. They greeted and welcomed Muruga saying that they were waiting for his grace all along.**

Indra addressed Muruga with all humility and said "O King of Devas! These sons of sage Parâsara were playing in Saravana lake, when they caught hold of fish and playfully threw them on the banks where they cannot naturally survive. The sage who came there saw this harmful play and cursed them to live as fish in the lake. They realized their mistake and asked for reversal of the curse. He foretold them that you would be born there as the Son of God and when Devi takes you in her hands, her breast milk will flow into the river. On drinking the water mixed with the divine Mother's milk they would get their human form again. It happened exactly the same way and from then on, they are here mediating and awaiting your arrival here. Lord Muruga smiled and took all of them along with him.

They worshipped the Lord at Tiruchendur and then reached Sendhil town. As Muruga desired to stay there,

Viswakarma erected a unique temple there. Muruga
reached his abode equipped with all comforts. He then
asked Indra to narrate the entire story from the birth of

Soorapadhman, how he acquired his skills and strength and what all he had done to Devas, causing them hectic suffering.

Indra requested Bruhaspati to give the sequence of events, as required by Muruga. Bruhaspati worshipped at the feet of Muruga and said. "Oh Lord! You are omnipresent and so you are aware of the whole story. Your question must be for a purpose, not clear to us. I am not going to tell you anything new. Perhaps to refresh us after the long journey, you want me to narrate the past history. I shall attempt it to the extent that I know."

The narration regarding the asura's birth, growth and actions began.

## 25. The birth of Asuras

Sage Kashyapa gave birth to six crores of asuras. Asurendran was their leader and he married Mangalakesi. They got a daughter who was named Surasai. Sukrachariar, the teacher of asuras, gave her the knowledge of all magic. As she was an adept in that art, he called her Mayai, which meant magic.

One day he called Mayai and said thus: "Vishnu, Indra and sages have already killed countless Asuras, your father is incapable of fighting them. You alone have to save the clan. You may take the form of a beautiful girl and entice sage Kasyapa. You can then give birth to a number of Asuras".

Surasai took leave of her father and the teacher and left for Mount Mahameru where sage Kashyapa was in meditation. She first converted the forest area into a beautiful garden. Kashyapa wondered at the miraculous change of the surroundings, but could not decide whether it portends good or evil.

When he saw Surasai on his way to meditation, her exquisite beauty attracted him. He forgot his meditation and approached her.

**"O! Who are you beautiful girl? What is your name? Who are your parents? Who are your ancestors? Which place do you belong to? I have not seen such a beauty like you so far in my life."**

Mayai smiled at him and said "O Sage! Have you forgotten your status? When you are an ascetic, you should concentrate on mediation to achieve your goal. It is shameful that you think of a girl like me. Kindly mind your work." The sage was further tempted towards her. "O sweet girl! We do penance only to attain what we want. I have prayed so long only to get you. At last you have come, why sit in prayer now? Please come with me. Let us go to my hermitage and live happily", he said.

Mayai laughed aloud and said "O Sage! Why are you speaking something that is not true? Were you sitting in prayer for my sake?

The sage reiterated. "Yes my dear! I say nothing but truth. I meditated with a desire to get you only. That is why I have been able to see you."

"O Sage! I live in Uttamapuri and I am on my way to take a holy dip in River Ganges. Please do not stop me." The sage was mad with lust. "Please listen to me. I can get you all the seven holy rivers here for you to bathe. Whatever you want I can fetch it right away here. If you want to get good children, I can bless you. Even Rambha

or any maid from Devas' kingdom can be brought here to serve you. Please do not delay now. Let us go now."

"O Sage! You behave so badly with me thinking that I am alone. Let me run away." Mayai started running and soon vanished from his sight. The sage searched for her all over the place and by dusk, he stood there fatigued. Mayai appeared there again. The sage was happy and again pleaded with her, "O dear girl! At last you have pity on me. Come, let us not delay."

Mayai now said, "O great Sage! I shall fulfil your desire. First of all, you should change your form to match my beauty. Later you should take different forms to suit my different tastes and needs."

The sage took a beautiful form. Mayai created a mansion by her magic and took the sage in. In the early evening, Mayai got a son through the sage and that was Soorapadhman. From the sweat of their bodies, thirty thousand asuras were born. She left them all there and took the sage to another place.

In the second stage, they took the form of lion. Singamukhasuran was born by their union with thousand faces of lions and two thousand arms. From their sweat, again, forty thousand asuras with lion faces were born.

In the third stage, Mayai and the sage gave birth to Târakâsura, with an elephant's face and four tusks. From their sweat, forty thousand asuras were born with elephant heads.

During the fourth stage, both the sage and Mayai took the shape of goats. There was born a girl with the face of a goat called Ajamukhi. Thirty thousand asuras were born now with goat's face.

In the early hours of the next morning, they went on and on with more creations like Yali, Tiger, Horse, Deer, Cow, Bear, Pig, Kooli, etc. Sixty thousand asuras were born thus.

When the day dawned, Mayai and sage Kashyapa resumed their original form. They were happy to see their three sons, a daughter and lakhs of asuras.

The sons bowed before their father and asked him to tell them what they were supposed to do for him.

"My dear children! Those who are endowed with wisdom will always like to meditate on God Almighty. They would desire to attain the feet of the Lord and get salvation. When you meditate you should not harm anybody. Once you indulge in causing pain and suffering to someone, your whole meditation will be of no avail. You will again be caught in the endless web of birth and death. Hence, give up your evil designs and start meditating on Lord Siva. You should do penance following the prescribed rules and regulations and observing the necessary physical restrictions. You will certainly acquire the highest place on Earth only by this method. Let me illustrate this doctrine with a story." The sage began to narrate a story in order to drive home what he said.

## 26. Chiranjeevi Mârkandan

There lived a Brahmin by name Kuchchaga in a place called Katakam. He had a son named Kausika who was well versed in all Vedas. He meditated on God Almighty to attain liberation from the worldly ties. He sat motionless and concentrated only on Panchakshara japam, without caring about what happened to his body. The animals that passed by used to rub their bodies on him but he would never realise that, as he was so engrossed in his prayers.

Lord Vishnu was immensely pleased with his ardent prayers that he appeared before him with Devas. He patted his body and said, "Kausika, the animals were rubbing their bodies on your motionless figure and you were totally unaware of it. You had been so immune to physical feelings and sat in meditation with undisturbed concentration. Hereafter, you will be known as Mruga Kandooyan".

Kausikan opened his eyes and saw Mahavishnu before him to his great delight. With tears of joy, he worshipped at his feet.

Mruga Kandooyan returned to his father and reported as to what the Lord Vishnu said. Kuchchaga was extremely happy and asked him to put on end to his Brahmacharyan (state of celibacy) and enter married life known as Grahasthasramam.

Miruga Kandooyan replied " My dear father! I had liberated myself from all my bondage and then went for meditation. Why do you want me to get married? When clear water is before us, why should we take bath in muddy water? Woman is the repository of all sins. Love of woman can lead one to hell. Indra went crazy for Ahalya and was condemned by one and all. Even Brahma fell in love with

Tilottama and did he not end up with four faces? I desire to follow the path of meditation only and that is the only permanent treasure."

Kuchchaga was not happy with the answer from Kausika. "My dear son, meditation is certainly great. I do not deny that. But before one undertakes the line of meditation, he has to run a home also and get children. The scriptures have prescribed that married life is just not for mundane pleasures alone. In order to do your duties to your forefathers and also to go to heaven, one has to have children. We have to climb step by step to reach heights. If one does not follow the rules as a good householder, there is no penance for it. Lord Siva also has married Devi Pârvathi, only to guide the souls aright. Please do not oppose me and you will not come to grieve."

Miruga Kandooyan conceded to his father's advice but stipulated certain qualifications for his bride to be. "My dear father! The girl has to have a good parentage, kith and kin, and look beautiful. Coming from a decent family, she should not be physically handicapped. She should be modest and brisk. She should not have a lust for men or possess manly qualities. She shall not be angry or bad tempered. She has to be born in a different lineage than ours. A pious girl who is devoted to the service of sages and seers would be an ideal wife. Soft spoken, good-natured in word and deed and a girl with good features alone can make my life pleasant. If you can find such a flawless companion for me, I am willing to marry, so that I can lead a peaceful and purposeful life."

Kuchchaga searched for a suitable girl for his son. Getting information from some sages, he met another sage named Uchathya in the forest called Anâmayam. The sage welcomed him and asked about the purpose of his visit.

Kuchchaga said that he had heard a lot about his daughter and he felt that she would make a good daughter-in-law for him.

Uchatya also felt happy to give his daughter Vrutha to Miruga Kandooyan, who had been greatly blessed by Lord Vishnu. Kuchchaga stayed with sage Uchatya for some time before returning home.

One day Vrutha went to the river to take bath and when she was returning an elephant chased her. When she ran in fear along with her friends, it so happened that she fell into a well, covered by bushes and died. The friends reported the matter to her mother Mangai, who in turn told her husband. Uchatya rushed to the forest, saw his daughter's ornaments on the way and finally got her dead body also, from the nearby well. He brought the body home. Vrutha's mother and all others wept bitterly.

Kuchchaga came to the sage and said "O Sage! You are an enlightened scholar! You shall not grieve so much for what has happened according to destiny. Any how, I have a vision that she can be saved. Please preserve her body applying oil on that and tomorrow she will come back to life. I will accept her for my son."

Uchatya felt consoled to an extent and accordingly embalmed his daughter's body and preserved it. Kuchchaga went to a pond nearby, went under water and started meditating on Yama. The same elephant, which chased Vrutha came there and put its trunk inside water. The elephant caught hold of Kuchchaga and took him on its back and started running. Kuchchaga tried to see the reason behind this event.

There was a trader by name Devadatta in a place called Haripuram in Kalinga country. He had a son called

,

Dharmadatta. As they were great philanthropists, they were quite famous in the country. As they became old, both Devadatta and his wife passed away. Dharmadatta stayed indoors for a long time, mourning the death of his parents.

One day a magician came to his house and said he knew a special feat by which anything can be turned into gold. "Lord Siva has taught me this art of magic. I can talk about this only to those who respect their teacher or who are absolutely innocent. You are the fittest one to know this secret", he added.

Dharmadatta felt happy to hear this and brought all the things that he had. The magician laughed in ridicule and said "You are a great trader. Do you want me to believe that you have only this much of wealth? Come with me and I can give more things."

Dharmadatta did not want to displease him and so sold away all his property and brought all the money before him for conversion into gold. The magician melted the entire lot and added a chemical to make it into a round ball. He then put it in a mud pot. Closing the pot with mud again, he heated it 108 times. He then said that, at the last stage, he had to add one more chemical and store it in an airtight place.

Dharmadatta showed him a room suitable for the job and both went inside. The magician lit a fire there and put the mud pot on it. When the room was filled with thick smoke, they could not see each other. All the things inside the pot were taken away in the dark by the magician and he put something else inside which he had brought.

Soon after he came out the magician told Dharmadatta that he should not eat for the next three days, nor talk to anyone and think of him only. "I am going to the forest and will do yâga for Kâlidevi there. When I return on the fourth day, you will get what you wanted", he said and left.

For three days Dharmadatta rigidly followed the rules, but on the fourth day the magician did not return. He went to the Kali temple and searched for him in vain. When he returned home and saw inside the mud pot, there was nothing but an iron ball! As he thought of his foolishness and greed, he was shocked and died immediately. Just to get a lot of gold he had sold away not only his properties but also the fruits of all his philonthropic acts. So it is that he was roaming about the forest, born as an elephant now. Kuchchaga took pity on him and gave him the blessing earned by his one day's meditation. Dharmadatta got back his beautiful form and reached heaven in the celestial vehicle after thankfully taking leave of Kuchaga for all the help he gave him.

Kuchchaga went back to the pond and resumed his meditation. Yamadharmaraja appeared before him and asked him as to what he wanted. "I came to ask for the hand of Vrutha, the daughter of sage Uchatya, for my son. Unfortunately she has passed away yesterday. You must kindly get her back to life." Kuchchaga pleaded.

Yamadharmaraja granted his prayer. Vrutha got back to life, as if she was sleeping all along. The sage and his wife were very happy. They looked upon Kuchchaga as God, when he reached there.

Mruga Kandooyan and Vrutha got married on an auspicious day. They got a son and he was named Mrugandu. When he was six years old, Mruga Kandooyan performed his Upanayanam and asked him to pursue the life of a Brahmachari. He then left for the forest to start his life of mediation.

Mrugandu learnt all the sastras and became a great scholar. He then married Maruthuvati, the daughter of a sage. They did not get a child for a long time and hence they went to Vâranasi. After bathing in the Ganges, they worshipped Lord Siva at Manikarnika temple. Then he sat beside the same temple in meditation.

When Lord Siva appeared before him and asked about his desired goal for meditation, Mrigandu asked the Lord to bless him with children. "Do you want to have a son who will be a wretched fool, handicapped in sight, hearing, speech and limbs, sickly, but having longevity for hundred years or a son who will live only for sixteen years, as a bright and beautiful boy with absolute devotion for me?" the Lord asked.

Mrugandu thought for a while and said, "Please give me an intelligent son who would be your devotee." Lord granted his prayer accordingly and disappeared. Mrugandu got a son on an auspicious day. He and his wife were very happy and gave away lots of gifts and presents to many people, who blessed the newborn child.

Brahma named the child Markandeya. At the age of five, the parents performed Upanayanam for him. He was well versed in all arts and worshipped Lord Siva everyday with great devotion.

Markandeya was nearing his sixteenth year of age. Mrugandu and his wife were sad to think of his approaching end. One day Markandeyan asked his parents as to why they were looking sad. Mrugandu was in tears narrating God's grant of a short life of sixteen years only, for him. Markandeya consoled his father and said, "My dear father! Do not grieve for my end. I shall pray to the omnipotent Lord Siva and win over Yamadharma. I will come back home soon. Please bless me."

After taking leave of his parents, Markandeya went to Manikarnika temple and prayed to Lord Siva. He chose a place in the southern quadrangle of the temple itself and installed a Sivalinga there, he prayed to the Lord with such devotion that he appeared before him and asked for his desire. Markandeya requested the Lord to save him from the clutches of Yamadharmaraja. Lord was pleased and gave him refuge from Yama. He continued his puja there with devotion.

Markandeya completed sixteen years of age. Messengers of Yama came to take his life away. As he was engrossed in Siva puja, they were afraid to go near him and so apprised Yama of their inability. Yama got angry and called his minister Kaala to get. Markandeya's life.

Kaala went near Markandeya and saw him in deep worship of Lord Siva. He politely announced his arrival and told him,

"O Markandeya! I am Kaala, messenger from Yama. God has given you a life span of sixteen years only. I have, therefore, come to take you. Kindly come along with me. As you are a devotee of Lord Siva, you will not fear Yamadharmaraja. He will also welcome you and treat you very well."

Markandeya heard him and replied firmly, "Devotees of God desire His feet only and nothing else. Even Indra's abode will not please them. They aspire only to go to Lord Siva's abode. I am God's slave. I shall not go anywhere or with anyone else except Him. Please leave this place fast."

Kaala was hesitant to approach Markandeya and so returned to Yama to narrate what happened. Yamadhar maraja's anger knew no bounds. He took his armour of staff and Soolam and got on to his vehicle, the buffalo. His soldiers also followed him.

Sighting Yama at his side, Markandeya prayed once again, "O mighty Lord! Yama has come to take me. Please protect me." Yamadharmaraja roared in laughter. "Markandeya! All those who are born are necessarily to die one day or other. None can escape it. Even Indra and Devas, Brahma and Vishnu, none is an exception to this rule. All of us have to die one day. So I cannot return without you", he said.

Markandeya said, "Devotees of Lord Siva do not die. Even if they have an end, they will go straight to Lord Siva's abode and not to your place. There is no difference between the Lord and his devotee. So, if you want to save your life and position, better go away."

**Yamadharmaraja roared like thunder and threw his rope over Markandeya. When Yama's powerful rope called Paasam was pulling his neck, Markandeya called out "Sankara! Sambho!" and hugged Sivalinga. "My dear child! Do not fear", a divine voice was heard. Lord Siva came out of the linga and kicked Yama with his left foot. Yama could not take it and so fell down dead from his buffalo. The soldiers who accompanied him also died out of sheer fear of the Lord.**

Lord Siva blessed Markandeya and said, "My dear child! Your steadfast devotion for me was superb. You shall live forever and have no end at all." He then disappeared. Markandeya was thrilled at God's great boon granted to him. He returned to his parents and narrated what all happened. For sometime, he continued to stay at Manikarnika City to pray to Lord Siva. Then he visited the other holy places and prayed to the Lord.

As Yamadharmaraja was dead and gone, there was no death on earth. Everyone lived long. Bhoomadevi was

burdened with great pressure. She appealed to Lord Vishnu, who in turn went to Mount Kailas with Brahma and Devas and asked for Yama's life. "O Mighty Lord! Yama got killed because he did not realize your grace. Because of his demise, there is no death for anyone. Bhoomadevi is unable to bear the excessive weight on Earth. Kindly relieve her of the burden by pardoning Yama and getting him back to life."

Lord Siva agreed to his plea and Yama was once again back to life and work. His men also woke up and all of them prayed to Lord Siva and sang His praise. Lord enlightened Yama thus: "Remember hereafter what I tell you now. My devotees are not mere mortals. There is no difference between them and me. Those who wear the sacred ash and Rudraksham and pray to me with devotion have always got to be spared by you".

## 27. Mayai's advice

Sage Kasyapa gave the story of Markandeya to his sons and told them, "My dear sons! You would have now known the value and merits of meditation. So, follow only the best path of meditation at any cost."

Mayai, who was nearby, looked at him in ridicule. "O Sage! This entire sermon was required only for sages who seek salvation. These young children need to be told the ways and means to acquire wealth, victory and happiness and longevity." Kashyapa was not happy. He turned to her and said, "All right. If that is what you desire for your children, you may give them suitable instructions yourself."

Mayai addressed her children thus. **"Look children! Leave aside all the philosophy the sage told you. If you do not get the wisdom and wealth required for this life, why should you live at all? There are many kinds of wealth. You should work hard to acquire all that.** As you were born in the night, you are asuras. Devas are your enemies. They have worked and managed to get high positions. You should excel them in everything. There is a place called Uttarabhoomi in the North, which is suitable for asuras. You go there and worship Lord Siva, offering Him blood and meat. I shall give you whatever you need. When Lord Siva appears, you can ask Him for everything you desire."

She taught them the rules and mantras for the yâgas. Soorapadhman went North accompanied by his brothers and others. As soon as they went, Mayai left the sage. Kashyapa pleaded with her not to go.

"O Sage! I came in search of you, to get children only and not to live with you or serve you. I cannot stay here any longer. Please try to understand that I am Mayai." So saying she left the place. All things created by her magic also disappeared. Kashyapa was very much upset over what all had happened.

Brahma came there and asked Kashyapa as to why he gave up his meditation and fell into the trap of a cunning girl. When the whole story was narrated by Kashyapa, Brahma was sorry for him and said, "My dear son, I am ashamed of your weakness". Even after having mastered all the sastras, you could not win over lust for a worthless girl. Liquor and lust are two bad temptations. When you drink liquor, you lose your senses. When you think of a woman, that lust alone will suffice to kill you. Foolishly enough, you fell a prey to a wretched woman. By

associating yourself with her, you have done undesirable things only. To atone for your sins, you would do well to resume your meditation."

Kashyapa was now clear as to what to do next. As advised, he forgot Mayai totally and resumed his meditation.

## 28. Asuras perform yâga

When Soorapadhman travelled north, he asked his two brothers to escort the two lakh asuras. When they were all moving, the Earth was quaking and the mountains were shaking. Devas were startled.

There came Sukrachariar, the teacher for asuras. He was surprised to see the asuras' army and the three brothers marching along. He thought they will be the fittest to encounter Devas. If they perform yâgas and acquire great boons and weapons, undoubtedly they would conquer Devas. So he wanted to prepare the three brothers for this task. He desired to meet Soorapadhman. As he was walking in the centre, he tried to reach him through his mystic powers of going in between the asuras. They identified him and took him to their leader. He blessed him and said, "You will be greater then Indra and Devas. You will be the right choice to put an end to the troubles of the asuras."

Soorapadhman bowed before him and said, "O Respected sir, may I know about you? Where are you coming from? I feel so happy to see you. I have been fortunate to have you here by my good deeds of the past."

"I am Sukra, the teacher of Asura clan. I have come here to do good things for you", he said. Soorapadhman was extremely happy and felt that he will have no problems as a blessed student of the Guru.

Sukrachariar called him to his side and said, "I congratulate you, as you will be the leader of asuras. When you perform your yâgas, enemies are bound to give you all troubles. I will teach you a mantra, by which you will come out of all hurdles." He initiated him into Mruthyunjaya mantra to be the winner over death. Then he said, "My dear asura, chant this mantra every day. Give up all evils like murder, dacoity, lust and falsehood. Do exercise full control over your five senses and start your meditation."

On reaching North, Soorapadhman chose a forest of banyan trees. He then levelled the ground for an area of ten thousand units and kept mountains as the compound walls. Chanting appropriate mantras, he fetched brave women as gatekeepers. Around the fortified area, asuras stood guard. All evil spirits and Kali were asked to protect the Yâgasalai. At the centre, he made a big pit of thousand square units for the main Yâgakunda, around which 108 smaller ones were also established. In the second round, then were 1008 yâgakundas. Then he thought of his mother Mayai who appeared there. Very soon, there were all the things required for the yâga namely lion, tiger, bear, yaali, cows, rice, paddy, flowers, kasturi, nine cereals, darbhai grass, popcorn, poisonous twigs and the vessels. Vajra staff was installed at the centre of the pit.

Soorapadhman then prayed to the women gatekeepers and the guarding asuras and satisfied them with ample meat etc. He lit the fire in all the yâgakundas and gave offerings in the fire, in order to please Lord Siva. Târaka was ordered to keep the fire ablaze in all 1008 yâgakundas.

Singamukhan was asked to take charge of 108 inner ring of yâgakundas. Then he went to the main pit at the centre, chanted mantras and offered various things one by one, to appease Gods. The fire was so huge in the whole area that the heat could be felt even in the heaven. The yâga went on and on for ten thousand years. God did not appear. Soorapadhman got dejected. **He rose high in the skies and started offering his own limbs in the sacred fire. His blood poured into the fire like ghee. But God did not still come there. Soorapadhman grew more and more annoyed. He went on offering all parts of his body. But they started growing afresh. Another thousand years elapsed but still with no avail. He threw himself on the central staff and got burnt completely.**

Singamukhan could not stand this sight. Târakan was rolling in the ground in grief for his brother. All the rest of asuras were wailing in mourning. Singamukhan did not want to live after losing his brother. So, he cut down all his thousand heads and threw them into the fire. But alas! They were growing again and again. Târaka also followed suit. His head also reappeared. Many asuras also sacrificed their lives.

Singamukhan got ready to kill himself by jumping into the fire. There appeared a Brahmin, who was none else in disguise then Lord Siva himself. He asked all of them as to why they were all crying so much. Singamukhan narrated the whole episode from the start.

The Brahmin consoled him and said that he would bring back his brother to life. River Ganges was made to flow into the yâgakundam and Soorapadhman came out shouting. All were in great spirits when they saw their leader come back alive. Devas who were happy that the Asuras were dead, felt miserable now on seeing them alive again.

Lord Siva gave up His disguise and was on his Rishabha vahana, along with His consort Pârvati. Soorapadhman fell at His feet with his brothers and others and sang His praise. Lord Siva was ready to grant him any boon.

Soorapadhman prayed thus "O My Lord! I should become the sole commander of the whole world. All of them must be under my control. I should be able to travel anywhere as I wish for which I require a special chariot. I should never meet with my end and should conquer Vishnu and all Devas."

Lord Siva made him the supreme commander for 1008 worlds out of the 1000 crores of worlds, for a period of 108 yugas. He was given a chariot called Indragnalam to travel anywhere in the vast area under his control. He gave him an Aagnachakra, an all-powerful wheel, lion mount, Pâsupadam and other weapons to win over Devas, besides blessing him with enormous strength of muscles. He then made river Ganges flow into yâgakundam, from which ten thousand strong army with four sections were created. Soorapadhman had a lavish gift of all that he wanted and much more.

Târaka and Singamukhan also worshipped Lord Siva. They were also given powerful weapons and were blessed to live long like the two shoulders of Soorapadman. Lord also gave the boon that all the three will not be over-powered by anyone other than his own self.

The news of Soorapadhman getting countless favours from Lord Siva spread to all directions. Asuras gathered there and made him their leader. Soorapadhman appointed suitable asuras as commanders of the four sections of the armies. He then met his father sage Kashyapa and gave him details of Lord's special blessings bestowed on him.

When he asked for his assignment now, Kashyapa could foresee bad times for Devas. He concealed his real thoughts and asked him to meet their teacher, Sukrachariar. Soorapadhman took his blessing and went in search of the asura guru. He had anticipated him and so welcomed him to his mansion. Soorapadhman left his armies to take positions outside and asked Târaka to take care of them. He then went to see Sukrachariar, accompanied by the other brother, Singamukhan.

## 29. The great world

Sukrachariar asked Soorapadhman to spell out his intentions in visiting him. Soorapadhman detailed as to how he completed the yâga and obtained precious boons from Lord Siva. He wanted his teacher now to give directions for his next assignment.

Sukrachariar taught him the Maya philosophy, "Pati, Pasu, Pâsam". These three concepts denoting the Lord, the soul and bondage are all myths. The Lord and the soul are not two separate entities. They are only one. The Lord who has no birth or death manifests himself by "Maya" or illusion as the soul in all the creatures of the world. When the bodies perish, He, the soul within, remains permanent as before. "Maya" is only God's play. Good and bad, happiness and suffering all are myths. They say that there is a goal to be reached at the end and that is Liberation or Mukti and everyone should strive to achieve it. This concept which prevails is also wrong. It is also said that if you commit a sin now, you will suffer in your next birth. This is another lie, as there is no re-birth. We can do anything, good or bad, taking it to be God's acts. When one dreams of good or bad, he does not get happiness or suffering in reality. So, the doctrine that, what we sow in this birth, we reap in the next birth is also a falsehood.

You have got a big kingdom, which is difficult even for the Devas to attain. So you are none but God himself. Do not worship Brahma or Devas. They are your enemies. Indra has already killed countless asuras. To take revenge for that, you enslave as many Devas as possible and put them in jail. Enjoy every pleasure in this birth itself. Visit all your thousand and eight worlds, appoint your representatives there and rule your kingdom like an emperor".

Soorapadhman was extremely happy to hear his sound advice and said, "Acharya, I shall just do as per your directions". I am eager to know about the 1008 regions given to me by God. Let me know what they are ", he said.

Sukrachariar gave a detailed account of them. "Bhâratavarsham" (Presently known as India) is a place where both good and evil exist. People who live here have many avocations. Vegetables, fruits and roots are their main food and they live happily or otherwise, depending upon their deeds, good and bad. Sages and Devas congregate in this country to meditate upon God.

Bharata had eight sons - Indran, Kasaeruthi, Tamiravarna, Gabasti, Natha, Sowmya, Gandharva, Varuna and a daughter named Kumari. He divided his kingdom into nine and gave it to them. Of all the nine, Kumarikkandam is the best of all. Ganga, Goutami, Yamuna, Kumari, Saraswati, Kaveri, Narmada, Tungabhadra, Panchali, Sarayu, Veni, Porunai, Pennai, Pâlâru are the rivers flowing in Bharatavarsham. Mahendram, Podiyam, Sahyam, Saktimaan, Vruksham, Paariyatram, Vindhyam are the seven mountains here. Holy cities which afford salvation to souls are also seven and they are Kaanchi, Kasi, Ayoddhi, Madura, Maaya, Avanti and Dwaraka. Besides, this country is blessed with

1008 centres of worship for Lord Siva. Beyond Jambudweepam, there is the salty sea. Beyond that lies the Sâkadweepam. Milky oceans surround this island. Medhadi was the king of Sâkadweepam. He divided his kingdom into 7 parts for his 7 sons viz. Santhavayan, Sikiran, Sodayan, Anandan, Sivan, Kemakan and Dhurvan. Each part was known by the name of the respective king. Sâkadweepam had seven mountains, viz. Chomakam, Samanam, Chandram, Tundumi, Vaprasanam, Naradeeyam and Komedhagam. The seven rivers of this island were Sivai, Vibhavai, Amirtai, Sukhirtai, Manudattai, Chitthi and Kiramai. The people of this land were known as Aryar, Vindar and Kukkurar and they worshipped Vayu as their God.

Beyond Sâkadweepam is situated the Kuchadweepam. Ocean of Curd surrounds this island. The king of this country, Vapushtu, also had seven sons viz. Kapratan, Karagitan, Dheeran, Mukhan, Suvetagan, Siddhiyan and Vaythitan. The seven parts ruled by these sons were known by their names. Unnadam, Kumudam, Kumaram, Megham, Chandram, Mahisham and Dronam were the seven mountains here. Sonai, Velli, Mathi, Tomai, Nendirai, Vimochanai and Virutti were the names of the seven rivers flowing here. People who live here were known as Darpakar, Kapiyar, Charanar, Neelar, Dandar, Vidandakar and they also worshipped Vayu.

Beyond Kuchadweepam was Krounchadweepam. The ocean of ghee surrounded it. The king of this place was Jothishtu and he also had seven sons viz. Saranan, Kapilan, Kruthi, Keerti, Venuman, Ilambakan and Urpitan. The country was divided into seven regions bearing their names. The seven mountains here called Kuchesayam, Ari, Vidurumam, Pushpavarutam, Imam, Tudiman and Mandaram. The seven rivers here were known as Sivai, Vidhutapaanam, Imai, Punitai, Pooranai, Akilamaayai and Tambai. Four sects of people called Tâpadar, Chadavatar, Mandekar and Anekar lived here and their God was Brahma.

Chânmalidweepam was the next island to Krounchad weepam. Ocean of cane juice surrounds this island. Tudimân was the ruler of this place and his seven sons were Cuchalan, Veyyan, Devan, Muni, Andhakâran, Manorathan and Dundubhi. They ruled the seven regions of the same names.

Timiram, Surabhi, Vaapinam, Virutham, Dundubhi, Sammiyathadam, Pundareekam were the seven mountains of this place. Kumudam, Kavari, Âdi, Yâmai, Pundarikai, Manobhamai and Sandhyai were the seven rivers here. Pushkalaadhar, Pushkarar, Thaniyar and Sisirar live here and they worship Lord Siva.

Beyond chânmalidweepam lies Komedagadweepam. The ocean of honey surrounds this island. Alliyan is the ruler. He partitioned his country into seven parts and named them after his seven sons, Vimochanan, Mohan, Sakalan, Soman, Sukumaran, Kumaran and Marechakan. Singam, Atham, Udayam, Chalakam, Krounjam, Aambikeyam, Ramyam are the seven mountains here. Ayaathi, Tehnu, Kamathi, Sukumari, Kumari, Ikshaki and Mayai are the seven rivers flowing here. Mandathar, Aamanger, Maagathar and Maasairi are the groups of people who live here and they worship Chandran (Moon).

Pushkaradweepam is the next island. An ocean of potable water called Suddhodakam surrounds it. The king of this country, Chavanan had two sons only. So he divided his kingdom into two regions and gave it to them. Thathaki and Maaveedhan ruled over their parts. Rishabham, Mahendram, Varunam, Varaham, Neelam, Indram and

Mandriyam are the seven mountains here. Kudilai, Sivai, Umai, Dharani, Sumanai, Singai and Kumari are the seven rivers. Narakas live here and their God is Surya (Sun).

Beyond Pushkaradweepam, there lies a mountain called Mânasóttaram at a distance of fifty thousand yojanas. This is in the shape of a wheel and there are eight guards on its eight sides.

Swarnabhoomi surrounds Mânasóttaram mountain. Beyond that is the red coloured Chakravaalagiri mountain. It has bright light inside and the outer wing is dark. Yakshar, Rakshatar and demons live there.

Beyond Chakravaalagiri lie the vast ocean and the dark country. At the end is the compound wall of the continent. Fools and those who committed suicide are the habitants here, suffering for existence.

Above the Earth, Sun's region is there at a distance of one lakh yojanas. Thirty-three crore Devas live here. Between the Suryamandalam and the Earth, Kimpurudar, Garudar, Siddhar, Vidyadharar and Yakshar live in various regions.

Above the Suryamandalam, one lakh yojanas have to be crossed to reach Chandramandalam, the region of the Moon. Beyond is the region of stars again after a lakh yojana distance.

Above the region of stars, Budhalokam is situated at a distance of two lakh yojanas. Further beyond at a distance of another two lakh yojanas live Sukran. Bruhaspati's region is further beyond by two lakh yojanas. Saturn's kingdom extends further at two lakh yojanas.

Beyond the Saturn's region at a distance of two lakh yojanas is the habitat of the seven sages. Dhruvaman dalam is above this region. The whole expanse is known as Bhuvarlokam and its area covers about fifteen lakh yojanas.

Above Bhuvarlokam, beyond another eighty-five lakh yojanas is Swargalokam or Devalokam where Indra lives with his Devas.

Beyond Devalokam, it is another long way to go for two crore lakh yojanas to reach Makalokam where sages like Markandeyan live.

Janalokam is situated another two lakh yojanas beyond Makalokam. Our forefathers live here.

Tavalokam is the next at a distance of twelve crore lakh yojanas and sages like Sanaka live here.

Beyond Tavalokam, one has to go another sixteen lakh yojanas to find Satyalokam. Further beyond three crore lakh yojanas, Brahma's abode, Brahmalokam can be seen. Even beyond this one has to traverse three crore lakh yojanas to reach the abode of Vishnu. Another four crore lakh yojanas to go for Siva's abode, Sivalokam. The shell covering the entire expanse is further away by crore yojanas.

Knowledge evolved from the expanse of nature. It gave rise to pride. This led to the five senses. Out of these were born the five elements. From Prithvi, one of the five elements, thousand crore continents were born. Out of these, Lord Siva gave 1008 continents only to Soorapadman.

The very tiny atom seen in the sunlight is the origin of our measuring unit. 24 atoms make the tip of a hair. Eight such tips make a germ; Eight germs make a louse; Eight lice make a grain; Eight grains make an inch; Twenty four inches make a muzham; Four muzhams make a dhanu; Two dhanus make one dandham; Two thousand dandhams make one krosam; Four krosams make one yojana. Hundred crore Yojanas wide and high is an andam. Above the surface of the Earth, fifty crore yojanas high, and down below the surface, another fifty crore yojanas deep is called andam or continent. On all directions of Meru mountain, there is a distance of five crore yojanas up to the end of the andam. The frontier is called Andakadaakam (Boundary of the continent).

Down below the earth, the shell of the base is there. Just above that is Rudralokam. Next layer has twenty-eight crore cities in it. The next layer is called Kurmanda Rudralokam. Above that are the seven underground worlds. They are known as Pâtâlas. Above that is the world of Aadagaserudrar. Only above this is the Earth supported by eight elephants on the eight directions and guarded by the big eight snakes.

The Earth consists of seven islands viz. Jambudweepam, Sâkadweepam, Kuchadweepam, Krounchadweepam, Sânmalidweepam, Komedagad weepam, and Pushkarad weepam.

These islands are surrounded by the salt sea, milk sea, curd sea, ghee sea, cane juice sea, honey sea and sweet water sea respectively. Jambudweepam has an area of lakh yojanas. The salt sea, which surrounds it, also has the same area of a lakh yojanas. The rest of the islands and the seas have double the surface area each. All the seven islands and seven seas put together have a total area of two crores and fifty four lakh yojanas.

Beyond these islands surrounded by seas, golden sandy soil is spread over ten crore yojanas. Chakravalagiri is situated around that, occupying an area of ten thousand yojanas. Around that is the ocean encircling for a crore and twenty-seven lakh yojanas. The dark region extending for thirtyfive crores and nineteen lakh yojanas is beyond that. The surrounding compound wall is one crore yojanas thick. As such the total width of the whole Earth is hundred crore yojanas.

Priyavratan, son of the Swayambhu, born out of the right shoulder of Brahma ruled over the entire Earth. He had seven sons viz. Agnitran, Medhadi, Vapushtu, Jyothishtu, Tudimân, Avyan and Sâvadhan. These seven sons were given charge of the seven islands and Priyavratan ruled as the chief commander.

Agnitran had nine sons. They were Bharatan, Kimpurushan, Ari, Kethumalan, Bhadrasuvan, Ilaavruthan, Iramiyan, Iranyan and Guru. Jambudweepam was partitioned into nine continents and given to these nine sons, as their territories to command.

Meru mountain is at the centre of Jambudweepam. It is four thousand yojanas deep on the surface of the Earth. Its peak is thirty-two thousand yojanas wide and its base is ten thousand yojanas deep. Hence it looks like a bud of lotus. Meru has three tiers. The upper most tier has many peaks and on its central peak is Brahma's abode, Manovati and other cities. The Western tier has Vishnu's abode, Vaikuntam. Northern side peak has Siva's abode, Jyotishkam. The surrounding eight peaks are the cities of the eight guardians of the directions.

East of Meru is the white Mandra mountain. On the South is the golden coloured Suddhamâdana mountain. West Side has the blue coloured Vipula mountain and Suparsuva mountain with its pomegranate colour is situated on the north. Kadambu, Nâval, Arasu and Banyan trees grow tall in these mountains respectively. At the foot of these mountains, the lakes called Arunam, Mânasam, Asitotham and Mamadu are situated. Sayithratham,

Nandanam, Vaiprasam and Tiruthakkiyam are the beautiful forests here.

As 'nâval' trees grow in the south of Meru, Bharatavarsham is known as island of 'Nâvals'. The juice from the fruits of this tree flows as a river on the northern side of Meru. So it is called Jambunatham (Jambu is the Sanskrit word for 'naval' fruit). Those who drink this juice will have golden coloured skin and live long for thirteen thousand years. Mâliyavân mountain is to the East of Meru. Nishtham, Hemakootam, Himayam are the mountains in the South. Kandhamaadanam is in the West. Neelam, Swetam and Srungam are the mountains situated in the North of Meru.

The region from the Northern Sea to Srungam mountain is called Guruvarsham. The region from Srungam mountain to Swetam mountain is called Iranyavarsham. The region from Swetam mountain to Neelam mountain is called Ramyavarsham. Around the Meru is the region known as Ilâvrutavarsham. The region from Mâliyavân mountain to the Eastern Sea is called Bhadrachuva varsham. From Kandamâdana mountain to the Western Sea is known as Thethumasavarsham. From Nishada mountain to Hemakoota ountain is Arivarsham. From Hemakoota mountain to Imaya mountain is Kimpurusha varsham. From Imaya mountain (Himalayas) to the Southern Sea is known as Bharatavarsham. Kethu malavarsham and Bhadhirachuvavarsham are thirty four thousand yojanas wide each. The other seven varshams or continents are nine thousand yojanas wide each.

The people of varshams except Bharatavarsham are pleasure seekers like Devas. In Guruvarsham, boy and girl of the same mother get married. They live for thirteen thousand years. 'Deva' trees grow in plenty in that region and its fruits give them longevity. They have a green skin. Those who live in North are white skinned Siddhas, Charanas and sages.

Red-coloured people inhabit Bhadrachuvavarsham. They eat vegetables and fruits growing there and live for thirteen thousand years.

The citizens of Iranyavarsham are milky white in colour like the moon. They eat fruits growing there and live for twelve thousand and five hundred years.

The people of Iranyavarsham have deep blue colour of the Kuvalai flower. They eat the Banyan fruit and live for twelve thousand years.

Ilâvruthavarsham people take plenty of cane juice. They also live for twelve thousand years. They are white skinned.

Kethumalavarsham people have the red colour of hibiscus flower. They eat kandasi fruit (Pineapple). Their life span extends to ten thousand years.

The people of Arivarsham and Kimpurushavarsham have longevity of ten thousand years. Arivarsham people have the colour of the moon. Kimpurushavarsham citizens are white in colour.

Mount Kailas is situated south of Hemakootam and north of Himalayas in Kimpurushavarsham. Lord Siva lives here with Devi. During the great deluge at the end of the ages, this mountain alone will not sink in water but grow to great heights above the Earth.

Except the people of Bhâratavarsham the inhabitants of the other varshams have no greying, old age, diseases or suffering. They are ever young and strong. They have no rains there. They have no difference between the good and bad or right or wrong.

Sukrachariar gave such a vivid account of the whole universe and told Soorapadhman to visit all regions personally, for a first hand knowledge of the 1008 continents given to him by Lord Siva.

**Soorapadhman was extremely happy to get the guidance from asuraguru. He took leave of his teacher and set on his long journey with his blessings.**

As soon as he came out, Târaka who was guarding the army came near and saluted him. Soorapadhman apprised him of all that he heard from Sukrachariar and added, "Let us start right away to win over our enemies and take them captive as our slaves".

On hearing his words, Asura soldiers sounded the war cry and marched ahead.

## 30. The Asuras go round the world

Soorapadhman set out with his soldiers to go round the world as advised by Sukrachariar. Maya appeared there and learnt from her three sons all about their yâga, Lord Siva's boons and their meeting with Sukrachariar. She praised them for all their achievements and blessed them for the onward journey.

"My dear children, as advised by our Guru, you win over Indra and Devas. In case you need my help to achieve anything by trick, just think of me and I shall be there", she said.

Soorapadhman and others took leave of her and went straight to Alagapuri, the city of Kuberan. Soldiers were in high spirits when they marched northwards. Soorapadhman got into the chariot Indragnalam, given by Lord Siva. Singamukhan took the chariot drawn by yalis, horses and demons. Târakan went on the chariot drawn by ten thousand horses. All of them laid siege on Kubera's capital.

The news of Soorapadhman's arrival with asura army reached Kubera. He was shocked and knew very well that he cannot oppose Soorapadhman blessed by Lord Siva. He got on to his chariot, 'Pushpakam', and reached Soorapadhman's place.

He fell at his feet and said, "Asurendra, Was it necessary to come and see me? You could have sent word and I would have come to you myself. You are blessed by God and I am your slave."

Soorapadhman was pleased with his gesture of surrender and said "You can rule your kingdom from Alagapuri. But please give away all wealth for my soldiers, as much as they want."

Asuras looted all the riches from Alagapuri. The city lost its beauty and Kuberan was helpless.

Asuras went next to Northeast. As Rudras were living there, they turned East and went in search of Indra. Knowing the strength of Soorapadhman, Indra did not want to fight with him. So he left the city and took refuge in Devalokam. When Asuras did not find Indra there, the whole city was set on fire.

Their next target was Agni's city in the Southeast. Agni got wild and fought with Soorapadhman with great force. Agni's forces could not match asuras and so met with defeat. Agni became furious and burnt down asuras. Târakan saw the onslaught by Agni and took Pâsupata stram to wipe out Agni and his army. Agni realized the impending danger for Devas and decided to surrender. Târakan forgave him and asked him to resume his rule, but under his control. Agni had to agree to obey him, before he returned to his city.

Soorapadhman next went to the city of Yama. Yama had already heard about the all-powerful Soorapadhman and how he defeated Kuberan and Agni. So he did not oppose him and instead surrendered as his slave. Soorapadman then left him in his place and asuras, of course, took away all the wealth from Yamapuri also.

Soorapadhman went thereafter to Niruthi's city in Southwest. He surrendered to Soorapadhman with his soldiers. Even Vayu and Varunan were afraid to stand before Soorapadman. Vayu hid himself in a dark place and Varunan took shelter under the sea. Asuras ransacked their cities.

All the seven worlds in 'Pâtâlaloka' came under asuras' command.

When they went to Nagaloka, Âdiseshan opposed him. But very soon, he was defeated and had to surrender. Soorapadhman stayed there for a day after a truce and thus asuras' flag flew higher and higher wherever they went.

The next target of attack was Lord Vishnu. The soldiers crossed the milky ocean and reached his abode.

Bhoomadevi and Lakshmidevi stayed very close to their Lord in great fear. Vishnu got on his Garuda vahana and opposed the asura. All his five mighty weapons poured a heavy rain of arrows on the asuras. Most of them were killed and blood was flowing all over. Târaka came forward and attacked Garuda and Vishnu. Vishnu destroyed Târaka's chariot and killed his driver in no time. For a long time they fought with each other, deploying various tricks also. Finally Vishnu sent his Chakrayudham to finish him. Alas! The awful chakram, when it came near Târaka who had the blessing of Lord Siva, became powerless and settled in his neck as an ornament.

**Vishnu stopped fighting and told Târakan, "God gave me the Chakrayudham and now it is adorning your neck. The victory is yours and let us give up fighting. We are friends now."**

Soorapadhman heard about this great triumph over Vishnu and was highly pleased. He went to Devalokam in search of Indra now.

Indra escaped from there in fear, in the form of a cuckoo, taking his wife also with him. Asuras were very angry as they could not see Indra there and so tortured all the Devas. Devas came running to Soorapadman and pleaded. "Asurendra! You have won over all the Gods and we are no match for you to fight. Please do not make us suffer anymore. We will take your orders and live as slaves to you" they said. Soorapadhman took pity on them and asked his soldiers to stop chasing them. All the same, Devalokam was also looted completely.

Soorapadhman then visited Janalokam, Makalokam and Tharalokam and got the sages' blessings. Finally he reached Satyalokam, the abode of Brahma.

On hearing about Soorapadhman's arrival, Brahma too was perplexed and went to see him. After showering all praises for his achievements, he said, "Your father Kashyapa was my son. So, I become your grandfather and am happy with you and your brothers. You ask me for any boon and I shall give you". Soorapadhman got various weapons for himself and his brothers. He proceeded to Sivalokam next, to see Lord Siva. On his way, Vishnu welcomed him at Vaikuntam and treated him with great honour. At Mount Kailas, he worshipped at the feet of Lord Siva and took His blessings for himself and his brothers. He then went to Andakolakai and met the Rudras. They guided him to other continents. Soorapadhman went round all the one thousand and eight continents given to him by God and appointed competent Asura leaders to govern them on his behalf. After successfully concluding his tour of all his regions in the entire universe, Soorapadhman returned to Devalokam with a great sense of triumph and achievements to his credit.

## 31. Rudras come to create

While Soorapadhman returned from his Digvijayam (conquest of all directions), Mayai's father, who was the king of Avunars, expressed his desire to the asura guru Sukrachariar to see Soorapadhman. The asura guru brought him along to Soorapadhman and introduced him.

"Soorapadhman! This king is the father of your mother Mayai. He is a great scholar and takes good care of all Asuras. He has fought with Indra several times and having heard about your prowess and victories, has come to see you."

Soorapadhman took the blessing of his grandfather. They hugged each other happily and Soorapadhman returned to Bhoolokam.

Devas were quite nervous to hear about the return of Soorapadhman after his tremendous victories achieved in his Digvijayam. They took Brahma and went to Vishnu who was asleep in the Milk Ocean. They woke him up and asked for a strategy to annihilate Soorapadhman.

**"O Devas! This is your own making as you incurred the wrath of Lord Siva, by participating in the yâga conducted by Dakshan to insult Lord Siva. Soorapadhman has now been blessed profusely by Him. He has been made the king of one thousand and eight continents. Whatever we may do, we can never defeat him. It is better that we maintain good friendly relationship with him. As he has now returned victorious after Digvijayam, let us express our goodwill by calling on him and blessing him" Vishnu said.**

Vishnu, Indra and all Devas accordingly went to Soorapadhman's place and congratulated him. When he saw eleven crore Rudras along with Devas, Soorapadman wanted to know more about them. Vishnu gave the information desired by him.

Once upon a time, Brahma created the three worlds and the creatures. He grew very proud that he was a great creator. He forgot that he could do that only by the grace of God Almighty. He boasted of his supreme power with which he could do any great task.

In order to teach Brahma a lesson, Lord Siva saw to it that the task of creations became stagnant all of a sudden.

Brahma was shocked to see the stunted growth of humanity. He knew that there was some mistake somewhere. When he thought more about it, he realised that he had forgotten the feet of the Almighty who does the five fold task of Srushti, Sthithi, Samharam, Tirobhavam and Anugraham, as easily as if it is all a child's play. It dawned on him that without His grace, his task of creations will not progress. He repented for his mistake and started meditating on Lord Siva. Even after a longtime, God did not appear. Brahma cried bitterly and tears rolled down from his eyes. Demons were born out of these tears and Brahma fainted with fear at the very sight of them.

Lord Siva appeared in his dream and told him that creation has to come to suffer a set back, because he forgot to think of Him. He also said that he was sending Rudras to help him in his task. Brahma came out of his trance and prayed to Lord Siva. Eleven Rudras were born from his forehead. He asked them as to who they were.

"O Brahma! We are a group of eleven known as Rudras and we have been sent by Lord to help you for the task of creation."

Brahma asked them to demonstrate their skill for the creative work. Each one of them created a crore Rudras at once in their own image. Then they took leave of Brahma and went back to Mount Kailasa. All the eleven crore Rudras, were accepted as Devas.

Vishnu thus gave the full account of the Rudras' birth as desired by Soorapadhman.

## 32. The coronation of Soorapadhman

Soorapadhman wanted to establish a capital city for himself. He invited Viswakarma, the architect of Devas, to build a city suitable for his living. Viswakarma respectfully asked him to identify a spot for the city. Sukrachariar chose a location in the Southern Sea. Viswakarma established a city in the centre of the sea for an area of 80,000 yojanas. Big mansions and high towers filled the place. In the central area of the city, an exclusive and exquisite palace was built for Soorapadman. The city was called Veeramahen drapuram. On its eight sides sprang up eight cities called Emapuram, Imayapuram, Lankapuram, Neelapuram, Swetapuram, Avunarpuram, Vamapuram and Paduma puram. For Singamukhan, a separate city named Âsura puram was erected. In the South of Meru mountains came up another city called Mâyâpuri for Târaka. For the army chiefs, separate cities were formed on different islands in the sea.

When Viswakarma reported to Soorapadhman about what all have been done, he was happy and entered his capital city with his forces.

Brahma and Devas wanted to conduct the coronation for Soorapadhman for his having become victorious over all the worlds. They brought holy water from the Milk Sea and gave him a bath. Then he wore gorgeous silks and golden ornaments and came to the main hall with his brothers. Asuras welcomed him with loud cheers. Sages greeted him and Devas sang his praise. Brahma made him sit on a throne studded with all gems and gave him the royal crown.

**All directions resounded with happy music and echoed the instrumental renderings. Asuras bowed before him. His two brothers took their seats on**

either side. Indra was standing with a spittoon and Kuberan was there with the box of betel leaves. Vayu was fanning him and Niruti was standing as guard of honour before him with his sword. The Sun and the Moon were holding the royal umbrella. Varunan and his sons were carrying the welcome arches. Garudar, Gandharvar and Siddhar sang divine songs. Yama and Agni were regulating visitors to the hall with golden staffs in their hands. Devaguru and Asuraguru sprinkled holy water on his head and blessed him. Rambha, Menaka, Tilothama and the other dancing girls gave an amazing dance recital.

When Soorapadhman sat as the emperor of the entire world in all-royal splendour and grandeur, everyone was bowing low before him. He felt on the top of the world and became so self-conceited as to pass funny and autocratic orders to one and all irrespective of their age, wisdom or status.

He called Vishnu and said, "You are my grandfather. So you must be present here at my beck and call."

He summoned Brahma and said "You will come everyday morning and tell me about the planets and stars of the day."

Sun was ordered to cross the city only with moderate heat waves. Moon can enter the city only with full bloom. Agni should take orders from everyone and anyone in the city and attend on them at any time of the day or night. Varuna was asked to sprinkle scented showers on the city everyday. Indra had to report to Soorapadhman everyday to take errands. Devas were thus assigned various jobs as slaves to asuras and they also complied with his commands implicitly, for fear of their lives.

Asuraguru wanted Soorapadhman to get married. He decided on Padumakomalai, daughter of Devas' architect, as his bride. In his extreme fear for the asura King, he agreed for the alliance, hoping that he would at least be spared from harassment after the marriage.

Brahma and others attended the marriage and blessed the couple when it was grandly celebrated on an auspicious day. Singamukhan married Vibudhai, daughter of Yama. Târaka married Gowri, daughter of Niruti. After the celebrations were over, Singamukhan went with his bride to Âsurapuram and Târaka to Maayapuri, accompanied by their forces. The rest of the army chiefs went to their respective islands.

Soorapadhman was ruling the world from Veerama hendrapuram, with his lakhs of soldiers. Army comman ders were posted for guarding the eight cities around the capital. Durgunan, Dharmagopan, Dhurmukhan, Gangabalan, Vakrabalan and Mahishan were appointed as his cabinet ministers.

One day, Soorapadhman called all the Devas headed by Indra. "Devas! You are the younger brothers of asuras. It is your duty to take care of your elder brothers. So, hereafter, you should go to the sea and bring fish for all of them." Soorapadman ordered. Indra was startled. What a fall for Devas! They are ordered to fetch fish for asuras!

But, can anyone flout the orders of Soorapadhman? Indra went to the sea with Devas. Varuna brought all the fish from the sea and put them on the shore like mountains. Devas were carrying them in big platters on their heads to the palace. Asuras ridiculed Devas for this slavish plight of carrying the fish. Devas could not tolerate their taunts and giggles but yet had to put up with all such insults helplessly.

## 33. The Sun gets arrested

As days passed by Padumakomalai became the proud mother of a baby boy. Soorapadhman celebrated the birth of his son by giving gold and gems to all the asuras.

One day the boy was in his cradle. When the Sun went on his routine passage up in the sky, the child could not stand his heat. He jumped up from his cradle and caught hold of the sun as if it was a snake. He brought it and tied it to the leg of the cradle and went to sleep thereafter.

The Sun's arrest by the son of Soorapadhman spread as hot news all around. The world was suffering, as Sun did not travel in his route. Indra and Devas complained to Brahma who appealed to the Soorapadhman for the release of Surya.

Soorapadhman laughed aloud and said " I am surprised at this news. What happened and why was Sun arrested by my son?"

"Asurendra ! When your son was in the cradle, Sun had traversed in his route as usual. As his heat waves were too much to bear for your son, he has brought him down and put him in chains", said Brahma.

"If that is the issue, you better ask my son." Soorapadhman said jokingly.

**Brahma went to the child's place. Rambha and other dancing women tried to make the boy happy with their singing and dancing. Brahma then asked him to release the Sun. The child asked for Brahmastram in return. On Brahma giving it to him, Sun got released. He was also pleased with the boy's bravery and gave him Mohanastram.** From that time the child was known as Bhanugopan (pet boy of the Sun). Bhanugopan was so handsome that

all women took him for Manmatha. After Bhanugopan, Padumakomalai got three more sons viz. Agnimukhan, Iraniyan and Vajrabhâhu. Soorapadhman had also married few other girls. He got three thousand sons through them.

Singamukhan got a son named Atisoora and also one hundred other children. All of them were quite brave. Târaka also got a son who was named Asurendra by asuraguru. He was well versed in all arts and crafts. Contrary to the characteristic behaviour of asuras, Asurendra was different altogether. He did not indulge in misdeeds and he never resorted to any evil act. He was just like a scented stick got out of wild plant or like a lotus from muddy water.

## 34. Vilvalan gets a peculiar boon

Soorapadhman's sister Ajamukhi was loitering around in the forest without any control. She did not marry anyone. She used to enter the hermitages and Yâgasalas of sages and cause havoc all around. If she happened to see any young men, she will torture them, enjoy them and finally kill them and eat.

During her usual rounds, one day she reached the hermitage of sage Durvâsa. He was looking great with his glow of meditation. She wanted to get two sons by marrying him, but he did not agree. "I do not want to lose my power of meditation by accepting you. You are an evil. I cannot agree to what you want. You better go elsewhere", he said.

**Ajamukhi was adamant. She was keen on getting her desire fulfilled. When the sage tried to escape,**

**she hugged him violently and got two sons. Both the sons of the wretched girl were extremely strong and brave. They begged Durvâsa, their father, to give them all the power he had acquired by his meditation.**

He refused to yield and asked them to ask for something else. But, they would not change their stand. Both of them compelled the sage and even threatened to kill him. But Durvasa got out of their clutches by his 'Yogasakti' and cursed them thus, "You wicked creatures, you will behave the same way with all the sages as you did to me and sage Agastya will teach you a lesson."

Ajamukhi's sons were named Vilvalan and Vâtâpi. As advised by their mother, they went to meditate on Lord Brahma to get great boons in their favour.

Days passed by, but Brahma did not appear. Vilvalan planned a strategy. He killed his brother Vâtâpi and offered his meat and blood as food and water in Yâgakunda. All the time, he was chanting the Moolamantra to propitiate Lord Brahma. At last Brahma appeared and asked him as to what he wanted.

The first request was the life of his brother Vâtâpi, who was killed by him to perform the yâga. Brahma brought him back to life in the form of a goat. The second request was to get Vâtâpi alive, whenever Vilvalan had to kill him. This was also granted.

Both of them then called on Soorapadhman and introduced themselves as his nephews and as brave warriors who are capable of killing the sages. Soorapadhman gave them shelter in his palace with love and affection. They both proceeded West and established an Ashram at a junction of four routes. They used to

waylay any sage who passed by that side. Vilvalan would kill his brother Vâtâpi and feed the sage. Soon after he would call him by name and Vâtâpi would come out of the sage's stomach in the form of a goat. Both of them would then eat the flesh of the dead sage. This atrocity was continuing there without a check.

## 35. Indra stands as a bamboo

One day Soorapadhman got angry with Indra. He asked his soldiers to go to Devalokam immediately and fetch Indra and his wife Indrani.

Getting this news in advance, Indra left Devalokam and reached Bhoolokam with his wife. The soldiers searched for him in vain all over Devalokam and even tortured Devas to tell them where Indra was hiding. But alas! None of them knew where Indra was.

When asuras returned to Veeramahendrapuram and reported that Indra was missing with his wife from Devalokam, Soorapadhman got very wild with anger. He reiterated that Indra and Indrani have to be traced and brought to him and so sent his Asuras to search for them in all the three worlds as they would be hiding some where in some form.

Indra's son Jayanta was badly tortured by asuras and so he took refuge in Vaikuntam with Vishnu. After some time, he returned to Devalokam.

One day when sage Narada came to Devalokam, Jayanta narrated the whole story of his sufferings due to Asuras and asked him if there was no end at all for asuras' atrocities and whether they should suffer life long at their hands.

Sage Narada consoled him. "O Son of Indra! Do not grieve so much. Soorapadhman's end is nearing. That is why all these cruelties persist. You start praying to Lord Siva. Your good period will start very soon", he said.

On coming to Bhoolokam, Indra went to Seerkazhi in South India. He created a beautiful garden near Seerkazhi and worshipped Lord Siva there with all good flowers daily. Even Devas did not know his whereabouts.

As Indra was not found in Devalokam. asuras started their search for him in Bhoolokam. They looked for him vigorously in hillocks, riversides, gardens and forests, without an exception. One section of asuras entered the garden near Seerkazhi, where Indra was hiding. Indra saw no escape from the situation and hence stood like a bamboo, worshipping Lord Siva sincerely. Asuras could not identify him in the shape of a bamboo and so left the place, presuming that he was elsewhere. After they went away, Indra took his original form.

When Indra was not traceable anywhere, Soorapadhman went mad with anger. He summoned the clouds and ordered that they shall not rain thereafter. The clouds had to obey his command. There was no rain, resulting in acute water scarcity. All rivers went dry. The crops failed. Indra's garden near Seerkazhi also started withering away. Plants were dying. Indra was very sad.

**"Oh my Lord! We live in such a shameful seclusion because of our fear for Soorapadhman. Even then, I raised this garden to pray to you with flowers. Now, this has also withered away. What do I do next?" cried Indra.**

Suddenly, there was a divine announcement from the sky to say that there will be a river there very soon. Indra felt happy at God's kind response.

## 36. Vindhya's Conceit

Once during sage Narada's sojourn in Bhoolokam, he came to Vindhya Mountains. Vindhya took the form of a Deva and worshipped Narada. He welcomed him and gave him a comfortable stay. But Narada had come there for a different purpose. He told Vindhya, "I feel so sorry for you, Vindhya! Meru is proud of his achievements. When Lord Siva set out to fight the three Asuras who were causing havoc by travelling in the sky like forts, Meru became a bow in His hand. It stands so tall and high that the sky alone is its limit. Sun shines on his peaks daily. Kailas, the abode of Lord Siva, is at his feet. As he is very near God, Soorapadhman does not disturb him. Devas live happily on many of his peaks. He has so many such aspects to boast of and so he always proudly talks about his first position among all mountains. Devi, who is the mother of all creations, had been born in his kingdom only. When he is so great and has many honours to his credit, you are so simple and humble. Are you not worthy of some great things?" Narada asked.

Vindhya replied, "What is there to be proud of in our routine accomplishments? God lives on some of my peaks also. Devas have attained salvation by meditating in my valleys . The sun passes through my peaks . Soorapadhman has not troubled Meru only because he thinks of him only as a mountain. If he is proud that Devi was born in his clan, we also belong to his family only and he is none but our king. Once upon a time, there was a great fight between Vayu and Âdiseshan. Âdiseshan covered Meru with his thousand headed hood, but still Vayu blew three of his peaks away. Is Meru an immortal Deva? Is he Brahma, born on a lotus? After all, he is also a mountain like anyone of us."

"Vindhya! Don't take anything to heart. I was just mentioning whatever came to my mind", said Narada and went away.

But Vindhya took his words seriously and started feeling bad. He wanted to prove that he was in no way lesser than Meru. So, he grew towards the sky, higher and higher, by his power of prayers, till his head reached Brahmalokam.

When Vindhya mountain started growing upwards, the nine planets took it for asuras' magical feat. Sun's pathway was blocked. Bhoolokam faced a lot of problems.

When there was a huge rocky mountain as a big stumbling block, without a gap or a passage, the Sun and others started thinking. They could easily guess that Vindhya was competing with Meru. Jealousy was the root cause of Vindhya's arrogant behaviour. They wanted to teach him a lesson. Sage Agastya who drank the ocean as a drop of water in his palm was the right person to cut him to size, they thought. As Agastya was meditating on God at the foot of Meru, they went and beseeched him to punish Vindhya suitably in order to save that world.

"O Sage! When Gajendran cried in distress from a lake where a crocodile caught him, did not Vishnu rush to his help? When Brahma went crazy after Urvasi, she prayed to Lord Siva. Did He not come to rescue her? When

Vishnu killed the chaste Kyâti, her husband, Sage Brughu cursed Vishnu to be born again and again in Bhoolokam to undergo sufferings. When Vishnu begged for a reversal of his curse, he limited his births to ten and obliged him. When the Devas or the humans suffer, is it not the duty of good people to help them out? Is not helping anyone in need greater than simple meditation?

"When an asura stole the Vedas and hid himself under the sea, Vishnu took an 'avatar' as a fish and redeemed Vedas. When we chased Vrutrasuran, he hid himself in the sea and then you were kind enough to make the entire sea water shrink as a drop on your palm, so that we could know his hiding place. Just because Narada made some casual remarks, Vindhya has suddenly become jealous of Meru and in order to prove his supremacy, he has grown up to the sky, causing hindrance for all of us. We have no power to go past him and the whole world and its creatures are so confused by our stoppage of work. Kindly help us by teaching Vindhya a suitable lesson to come to his senses", they pleaded.

Sage Agastya also knew what had happened through his vision of wisdom and so took pity on Devas. He prayed to Lord Siva at once to give the power to put down Vindhya's conceit. Lord Siva appeared there on his mount of Rishabham. Agastya was thrilled to see Him. When Lord asked Agastya to spell out his wish, he asked for the strength to deal with Vindhya suitably for his arrogance. Lord Siva blessed him and asked him to proceed to Podhgai. Agastya prayed to Lord again and made a request. "Maheswara! I shall obey your orders. But I do not want any interruption in my Pujas to you. So kindly send along with me a holy river to help me for my duties there", he said.

Lord Siva accordingly thought of one of the seven holy rivers in Mount Kailas. Ponni River stood before him in the form of a lady.

**"Dear lady! This sage in going South on my order. You should also accompany him", Lord said. Ponni bowed before him and said, "He may be a great sage, but he is a man. As a young girl, how can I go with him?", she asked.**

Lord smiled and said, "O! lady! He is my devotee and also steadfast in his principles. You may go with him without fear."

Ponni was still hesitant. "Kindly tell me as to when I can leave him."

"The sage will tell you when you can leave. As soon as he permits you to go, you can depart", Lord said. Ponni got ready to go with the sage. Now, the Lord told Agastya thus.

"Do not make her walk all the way. You may take her in your kamandalam, the small puja vessel."

Ponni took the shape of water and went into the vessel in his hand. Agastya took leave of Lord Siva and started off with Ponni.

On his way, Agastya stopped at Mâyapuri, where Târaka lived. An asura by name Krauncha was the bodyguard for Târaka and he was good at magic. He can reverse anything and create illusions viz. Devalokam as Bhoolokam, mountain as sea, Sun as the Moon, one atom as Meru, Meru as an atom, etc. He can create illusions to deceive Devas and sages also. On seeing Agastya and reading his mind for the mission on which he was going, he stood like Vindhya Mountains with all its peaks blocking his way.

There was a forest at the foot of the mountains. The
sage went inside the forest for a distance. There was a desert

after that. He wanted to retrace his steps and go another way. But he did not know the correct route. There was a big fire there and heavy gale also. There were heavy rains accompanied by thunder and darkness encircled the place. The asura who stood like a big mountain surrounded the sage and squeezed him.

Only then the sage realised the truth. He could see that nothing around him was natural. They were mere illusions created by the magic of the asura. He got angry and laughed at the asura. "O Wicked asura! What do you think your magic can do to me!" So saying he hit the mountain at several places with the staff in his hand.

"You can never regain your form. You will stay as a mountain only. The holes that I have made in you will become caves where your magic will disappear. You will meet your end by the Velayudham of Lord's son Murugan." Agastya cursed him thus and sprinkled water on him chanting the mantra. Asura's magic vanished and he stood like a mountain.

The sage then went to Kâsi and had a good darshan of Lord Siva there. Then he travelled South and reached Vindhyas. "Vindhya! I am to go to Podhigai. Please give me a passage." he said.

Vindhya smiled and said. "O Sage! I have not even yielded to sun and the Moon, as I stand so huge. After all, you are so small a person. Should I fear you and oblige you? Please get back and go away. You do not know my enormous power."

**The sage prayed to Lord Siva and stretched his right hand. It grew long and long enough to reach Vindhya's peak. He put his hand on his peak and pressed. The force and pressure were so great that**

**the Earth gave way and Vindhya went right down below the Pâtâlalokam and up to the place where Âdiseshan lived.**

Vindhya had a rude shock by this unexpected jolt and folded his hands before Agastya. "Maharishi! I am sorry for having been so rude to you when you asked me for a passage to go. Kindly forgive me and show mercy on me", he said.

Agastya told Vindhya to stay put there. "I have a passage to go now. Let me go and you stay as you are, till I return. You can resume your original form after I come back." He said. He normalised his hand and started to move on his mission. Devas honoured him with flowers and praised him for his timely help. Agastya continued his journey to Podhigai Mountains as directed by Lord Siva.

## 37. Vâtâpi gets digested

When Agastya was going Southwards he approached the Ashram of Vilvalan. Even at a distance Vilvalan identified Agastya, as the sage who drank the ocean as a drop of water to show the asuras' hiding there to Vishnu, so that he could kill them to save Devas. Vilvalan now wanted to take revenge for that. He took the form of a sage and bowed before him. As he had adorned himself with the sacred ash and Rudraksha garland, Agastya took him for a sage only.

**Vilvalan went round Agastya three times in great respect and invited him to his hermitage saying that he would feel honoured to have him as his guest. Agastya did not suspect him and so went to his**

**Ashram. Vilvalan gave him a respectful welcome again and requested him to stay there and eat with him. Agastya liked his hospitality and agreed to take**

**a humble meal from his hands. Vilvalan promised to make a good meal very soon and give him.**

When Agastya was seated there, Vilvalan cleaned the kitchen with cow dung and water, as was the traditional custom in the olden days. He went to a pond nearby and returned after a bath. He wore clean clothes and made rice with all care. He made vegetables and all delicious dishes. When Agastya was busy with his routine pujas, Vilvalan killed his brother Vâtâpi in a secret place and cooked his flesh to be mixed with the food for Agastya. When it was time for Agastya to eat, he gave him a good meal and Agastya took it with sincere love for the host. After meals, when he came out and rested there, Vilvalan called out for his brother as usual.

Vâtâpi took the form of a goat and shouted from the stomach of Agastya that he would come out soon killing the sage. At that moment, Agastya understood the magic of the Asuras to finish him. He just touched his stomach by which Vâtâpi got digested!

When his brother did not appear, Vilvalan called him again. Agastya smiled and showed him his stomach. When once he knew that Vâtâpi was dead, Vilvalan took his original form of an asura and attacked Agastya in rage. Agastya just took a Darbha grass and directed it on him as Sivâstram. Vilvalan was burnt down in jiffy! Agastya then continued his journey.

## 38.The crow spills the water in Kamandalam

Though Vilvalan and Vâtâpi were asuras, they were the sons of sage Durvasa. As Agastya had killed them both, he was a sinner for having killed two Brahmins. Their two dark shadows were troubling Agastya by going round him making great noises. He had to install a Sivalinga and worship Lord Siva to get rid of the Brahmahathi dosha, the sin of killing Brahmins.

Indra who was hiding near Seerkazhi saw Narada who passed by. When he bowed before him, Narada was happy to see him. "Maharishi! For fear of the asuras, I am hiding in the garden, which I made myself so that I can get flowers to pray to Lord Siva. As the asura has ordered the clouds to stop giving us the rains, there is acute water scarcity now. There are no flowers now in the garden and I am distressed for my inability even to offer worship as I desired", he told sage Narada. Narada consoled him, "Indra, Don't grieve. You will get back all that you have lost. Good period is ahead of you. God almighty has sent sage Agastya to come and stay at Podhigai. He has also brought Ponni river in his Kamandalam. On the way, he has put down the arrogant Vindhya, who rose as high as the sky, to compete with Meru. Agastya has also killed Vilvalan and Vâtâpi, the two Asuras who were devouring the sages who passed that side. As soon as Ponni river flows out of Agastya's kamandalam, your garden will get sufficient water."

"Maharishi! How will Ponni river flow out of the sage's kamandalam? How can I do it? Will I not incur the wrath of the sage?" Indra asked in distress.

"I am afraid you cannot do that. Please pray to Lord Ganesa. He alone can get it done by showering his grace," Narada said.

After Narada left, Indra worshipped Lord Ganesa with great devotion. Lord Ganesa was quite pleased with him and appeared with his group of men there. When Indra presented his problem to him and requested him to save the flower plants somehow, Lord Ganesa replied, "Indra! I shall help you right away. Shall I get you the Ganges from Heaven? Name any one of the holy rivers of Himalayas and you can get her here."

"My Lord! Once I do as you say, asuras will find my whereabouts. So far Soorapadhman does not know that I am here. My request to you is to see that Ponni river flows through this region. I believe that sage Agastya is coming to Podhigai along with Ponni river in his Kamandalam."

Lord Ganesa promised to fulfill his desire and disappeared.

Agastya was installing the form of Lord Siva wherever he wanted to pray to Him and was happily coming down South. When he reached Kongudesa, he was quite impressed with its natural beauty. He wanted to establish Sivalinga there and worship Him with devotion.

**At that time, a crow came flying there. It came and sat on the handle of his kamandalam. Fearing that it may make the water dirty, he tried to drive it away, waving his hand. The crow tilted the kamandalam and flew out in fear. Kamandalam turned flat on the floor and water started flowing on the ground. Ponni was happy to get released from the sage's hand and so took her course as a river.**

Looking at what happened in a second, the sage was very angry. He saw a brahmin boy going at a distance and

thought he was the one who came as the crow to play
with him. For a moment, he also thought that it could be a

magic brought by asuras. He got wild with the boy and shouted "Oh Little boy! Who do you think I am? Are you trying to be mischievous? You will now see, what I am going to do with you." Agastya ran after the boy who was also running hither and thither. Lord Ganesha made him tired and so, he stopped at a point when he could not run anymore. Lord Ganesa showed Agastya his true self in all glory.

Once he saw Lord Ganesa, Agastya was stunned. Tears poured down his cheeks and he felt very sorry. "My Lord! You have come to liberate me from my ignorance. I did not identify you. Foolishly I ran after you to hit you on your head, thinking that you were unduly playful with me. What a great mistake I did! Please forgive me." Agastya was hitting his forehead with both his hands in remorse.

Lord Vinayaka said, "O sage! Don't be sad! I did not mistake you at all."

Agastya could not rest in peace. He asked Lord Ganesa to spell out a penance for him so that he can atone for his mistake.

Ganesa laughed and said, "Indra had made a garden near Seerkazhi to worship my father. As clouds have stopped to give rain in obedience to Soorapadhman, the flower plants are withering away without water. In order to continue his worship, Indra wanted my help. I came to make Ponni river flow there, so that he can benefit. You are my father's great devotee. So I do not take you amiss at all. Please ask me for any boon that you want."

Agastya bowed before Vinayaka and said, "Gananatha! Let me always live with unlimited devotion for you and Lord Siva. Please grant any prayer of anyone who knuckles his forehead while worshipping you. I have no water now for my puja. Please let me have water in my kamandalam for my daily worship."

Vinayaka took a little water from Ponni River and filled his kamandalam. Agastya was all praise for Lord Vinayaka and with his blessings, continued his journey.

## 39. Lord Siva at Kutralam

Once upon a time, when Devas desired to get the nectar from the ocean, they started churning it without offering worship to Lord Siva. This resulted in the outpour of the deadly poison called "Âlakâlam" from the ocean. As it was unbearable to stand its strong odour Devas ran to Lord Siva for help. He also graciously took the poison and kept it in his throat.

Vishnu appreciated this kind act of Lord Siva which also saved the world from total destruction. His abode in Thirukkutralam reminds us of his appreciation.

The Brahmins who lived in that city were extremely devoted to Lord Vishnu only and hence would not care for what Vedas taught them. They will not allow devotees of Siva to come anywhere near them. Agastya, a great devotee of Lord Siva, was wearing the sacred ash all over his body. As he was walking along the streets of Kutralam, he saw the temple of Lord Vishnu and naturally wanted to have a darshan of the Lord there.

Sighting a saivite sage approaching their temple, the vaishnavaite Brahmins got angry. They stopped him and said, "Who are you wearing the ash and the Rudraksham?

Are you devoted to that Siva who is a beggar? What business have you here? Please go back or else you will face problems. Do not stand before us any longer."

Agastya was sad at their blind devotion to Vishnu, which had made them inhuman, intolerant and foolish. He did not get angry with them. Instead, he wanted them to know the truth behind these forms of God. So he pretended to be afraid of them and said that he was coming from a distant country and was ignorant of the local practice.

"Had I known about your views, I would not have come here. I shall go now", he said. They still ridiculed him and drove him away.

Earlier, when Daksha performed the yâga where Siva was insulted, the brahmins participated in it due to their greed. Sage Brughu cursed them that they should suffer for their folly. On certain other occasions, Nandikeswara, Brahma, Durvasa, Goutama, Kanwa, Dadeechi and others had also condemned brahmins for their greed. That is why they drifted from the vedic rules and saw Vishnu and Siva as two different entities. So Agastya wanted the brahmins of Kutralam to come to senses. He left that place and came back wearing  symbols of Vaishnavite sect. When he walked along the streets now, none could recognise him as a devotee of Lord Siva, who had come there a short while ago. All of them prostrated at his feet and welcomed him heartily. They praised him saying that Vishnu himself had come in his guise to bless them all. Though Agastya was laughing within himself for their ignorance to judge people by their outward appearance and symbols, he requested them to usher him in to see Lord Vishnu in the temple as he has been a tourist and had heard a lot about him.  Accordingly, all the brahmins took him inside the sanctum sanctorum. Agastya looked very much moved by

Vishnu's darshan and told them that he wanted to do
Tirumanjanam (Holy bath) to the Lord and worship him

with flowers. He wanted them to get him all the things required for the Puja. When things were ready for the worship, Agastya told them that he was used to a special mode of worship and all of them can witness it. He meditated on Lord Siva for a moment and did the abhishekam as per saivite rituals. Soon after, he put his hand on the head of the Lord and said, "Please shrink, Please shrink." The tall form of Lord Vishnu shrank gradually and became so short as a Sivalinga. He changed his form by his Yogasakti and conducted the Puja. Then only the brahmins realised the fact that he was none else then the saivite devotee who was driven away by them earlier. **The thought that he had cheated them made them quite angry. They surrounded Agastya, but he returned their anger manifold. None could stand near him, as his anger was scorching them like fire. Everyone ran for their lives and left the city finally.** Agastya worshipped the Lord in peace and then left for Podigai. He sat in meditation there.   After Agastya worshipped at Kutralam, it has become a celebrated saivite centre of worship.

## 40. Hariharan's birth

Ponni who came out from the kamandalam of Agastya got off the mountains and started flowing in the plains. Her route touched the surrounding area of the garden of Indra, before joining the sea. Having come to the South by the grace of God, both the banks of the river were green with trees, plants, herbs and gardens. Indra's garden was so beautiful now with lots of flowers and he was happily doing his pujas.

Devas were suffering a hell at Soorapadhman's palace. They were looking for Indra to get consolation and redressal of their grievances. Finally they located him near Seerkazhi.

One day they secretly met him there and asked him for a solution to their sufferings. Indra was in tears when he told them thus, "My dear Devas! I know everything about your miseries. As we had displeased Lord Siva earlier, we are put to this state of affairs. Because of Lord Siva's blessings, Soorapadman is all-powerful. I am unable to fight him and hence I am hiding here and praying to the Lord for a way out. You can also do likewise and I am sure our miseries will end soon."

Devas bowed before him and requested him to accompany them to Mount Kailas, as he was their leader. Indra asked them to wait and came to see his wife Indrani.

"Devi! Soorapadhman's tortures are far too many and we are forced to go Mount Kailas to meet Siva. I have to lead Devas and so, let me go now", he said and Indrani fainted at once. Indra brought her back to normalcy and she said, "O my dear! How can I live without you? They are searching for us. As you are by my side, I am pulling on somehow. If you go away, how can I survive? The cloud

,

takes care of Chakravaka bird and Chandra, the moon, takes care of Sahodara bird. You were caring for me all along. I don't know where our son Jayanta is. All Devas are going with you. Airavatham is with the Asuras. I have practically none with me. Asuras are too tricky. They do not bother about good or bad. If something happens to me, I would not live, please take me also with you".

Indra hugged her and consoled her, "My dear, I am not leaving you alone. Maha Sastha was born out of love, which blossomed between Siva and Vishnu. He will be your bodyguard from now on." Indrani was still in tears. She said, " I do not know about Maha Sastha's greatness. Kindly tell me all about him." Indra started narrating the story of Maha Sastha.

"Once upon a time, when Devas and Asuras churned the milk ocean, they forgot to invoke the blessings of Lord Siva at the start. So there came out the deadly poison, 'Âlakâlam', which spread its spell all over the world, making all creatures get choked.

Finally Devas surrendered to God and he was kind enough to devour the poison and retain it at his neck. He also advised them to churn the ocean further and get the nectar, which will give them immortality. Again they started on their work, but forgot to worship Lord Ganesa who is to be worshipped at the beginning of all deeds. They were so much in a hurry to get the nectar. Mandra mountain, with which they were churning, fell into the ocean and reached the bottom most layer of Nagalokam. Devas realised the mistake they did and prayed to Lord Ganesa with devotion. By his grace, Mandra mountain regained its position.

Devas and asuras resumed their work with renewed vigour and their efforts bore fruits. Nectar was out now, but both the groups started fighting, claiming that the success was due to their efforts. When it was about to break out into a big war, Vishnu adopted a trick to distract them. He came as a beautiful maiden amidst them. Everyone was attracted towards the young girl. Vishnu, who came as Mohini, pacified them by saying that they can choose either her or the nectar. Asuras who were mad after the beauty of Mohini surrounded her and Devas drank the nectar.

Mohini asked the Asuras as to who was a great warrior among them to win her hand. Again, asuras were fighting among themselves. Two asuras alone felt that this was Devas' trick to get the nectar, so they did not join the fight, but took the form of Devas and mingled with them.

When asuras were busy fighting, Vishnu came to Devas, took the nectar and started distributing it amongst all of them. The two asuras in the disguise of Devas were sitting along with them and they also got the Amirtam (nectar). When it was said that they can consume the nectar, only after the distribution was over fully, the two asuras were in a hurry to take it. Sun and the moon detected the two impersonators and took them to Vishnu. The asuras were caught red-handed in the act and came back to their real form. Vishnu chopped off their heads by the ladle in his hand. Their bodies perished, but the heads, which had taken the nectar survived. He made them two Châyâgrahas (shadow planets), Râhu and Ketu, and joined them to the galaxy of Navagrahas (Nine Planets) and thus made them Devas. Râhu and Ketu meditated on Lord Siva and got the blessings to become a red snake and a black snake respectively and to create solar and lunar eclipses from time to time.

Lord Siva has four forms of Sakthi. Devi Pârvathi herself manifests into four forms at different times to suit different needs. When she is with Lord Siva to bless the souls she is Pârvathi. When she takes a male form to protect the work, she is Vishnu. When she gets angry and controls the wicked, she is Durga and when she is in the battlefield, she is Kâli. Lord Siva wanted to show to the world that Vishnu is none other than his own Sakthi or power.

After distributing nectar among Devas, Vishnu returned to Vaikuntam. Lord Siva came there and said, "Parandhama, I believe you had taken the form of a beautiful maiden, Mohini, to attract Asuras. I want to see you in that form. "Vishnu agreed to his request and took the bewitching form of Mohini. Lord Siva fell in love with Mohini and Vishnu started to move away, realising the situation. But Lord Siva followed him.

"Maheswara! I do not approve of your desire for me. I do not think you are right in doing so", Vishnu alias Mohini said.

"Parandhama! You are a replica of my Sakthi. When I went to Dârukâ forest as a beggar to check the proud sages, did you not come there as a pretty maiden? When Brahma was dead, did you not come to me to get him back to life again? Brahma was then born again through your navel. Why do you hesitate now?" Lord Siva asked.

**He then took Mohini to the shade of a Kadamba tree in the Naaval Island in the North. By their happy union, was born a son with dark skin, red locks of hair and a bouquet in his hand.** He named him Hariharaputran and made him the chief of his army. He made a separate world for him and blessed him that he would have a big following of devotees. He became a Rudra, fit enough to be worshipped by the sages. He was also known as Iyyanaar and Sastha.

In the Nâval island, under the Kadamba tree shade
when Siva and Vishnu had their holy union, they spit their

saliva, which became the Gandagi river. Worms called Vajradanti were breeding in that water. They had chakra symbols in and out of their body and were golden in colour. They made small shells from the mud in the river water and lived there. After their death, these shells with chakra symbols used to be washed ashore. People used to remove the mud from these shells and from the chakra symbols, classify them as Vishnu's forms for worship. These are called Saalagramam.

After narrating Sastha's story to Indrani, Indra told her that he will be her guard and she need not fear anybody as he was a great warrior. He meditated on Sastha at once. He appeared there on his white elephant with his two consorts, Poorna and Pushkala and also his army. Indra fell at his feet and worshipped him. "For fear of Soorapadhman, myself and Indrani are hiding here. Devas want to go to Lord Siva to complain about Sooran's unlimited atrocities. I have got to lead them to Mount Kailas. Indrani is afraid that Asuras may whisk her away in my absence. Till my return, you have to take care of her. Only if she is in your safe custody, I can go in peace to meet the Lord. Kindly accept my prayer and take charge of her."

Ayyanar told Indra, "Leader of Devas! You can go without any worry. I shall take care of Indrani safely. Indra confidently set out to Mount Kailas with Devas. After Indra left, Sastha called one of his trustworthy generals, Kâla and ordered, "Indra has gone to Mount Kailas with Devas. In his absence, you have to protect his wife Indrani from any possible danger." Ayyanar left the place soon after.

,

# 41. The demon's hand gets chopped off

Indra and Devas reached Mount Kailas. Nandideva was guarding the main entrance. Indra bowed before him and Nandideva asked for the purpose of his visit. When Indra explained his motive, Nandideva said that Lord Siva was busy teaching sage Sanaka and others and it was not the appropriate time to meet him. Indra elaborated on the situation by which they were hard pressed to meet the Lord.

"Nandideva! Our sufferings are on the increase day after day. Soorapadhman who has received enormous blessings from the Lord is ill treating Devas so much that they have to carry fish baskets for him everyday. Lord Siva who gave him so many boons to become so conceited has to put an end to this situation very soon. His brother Târaka has defeated even Vishnu who has lost his wheel. Chakrayudham to him. How can we face him with our meagre strength? If God does not come to our rescue, we are sure to be nowhere very soon. Where is Dharma then? If this is not the time to see him we will wait for the convenient time to see him but we shall not go from here. We have already come this far, against Sooran's orders. If we go back, he will certainly put us all in jail and take severe steps to punish all of us. Kindly allow us to stay here till God is pleased to see us."

Nandideva did have a soft corner for them and but he could still not allow them inside. So, he allowed them to stay there. Devas and Indra were meditating on Him and waited for the opportune moment to have audience with the Lord.

Indrani also was meditating on Lord Siva for Indra's safe and successful return. But he was away for a long time.

Soorapadhman's sister Ajamukhi was going round the world, spoiling many young men and enjoying herself.

She happened to stray near Seerkazhi and entered the beautiful garden of Indra where Indrani was immersed in meditation. Mahakâla, who was watching the asura girl coming there hid himself to find out what she was up to.

Indrani got up with fear and confusion on seeing Ajamukhi, who desired to make Indrani, the queen of her brother Soorapadhman. So she giggled at her and said – "O My dear lady! Whom are you praying to and why? Your husband is afraid of us and lives in hiding. He is not going to be of any use to you. Come along with me. My brother will protect you and once you belong to him, all the three worlds will be at your service."

Indrani felt so pained as if pierced by Velayudham. "You wretch! What did you dare to say? Do you think of me as helpless a woman as you are? For your harsh words, you will meet with limitless punishments. Having been born to sage Kashyapa, can you indulge in such mean thinking? Those who want happiness for themselves, have to make others also happy. Those who invite trouble for themselves will harm others wantonly. What atrocious suggestions have you given? I shall not think of anyone else than Indra. Only those who are in fear of losing their wealth and longevity, think of such evil designs! I am sure your end is nearing. Better leave me and go away. Do not interfere with my life any more. I am not alone here, as you imagine. I am protected all around. Please leave me at once", Indrani said.

Ajamukhi laughed at her refusal to come with her. She was getting wild with anger. "Indrani! I wanted to help you and gave you good suggestions. I thought women should help each other. Please listen again. I am not going to leave you. If you try to oppose me, I shall eat you up. Even the Trimurthis cannot do anything with me". So saying Ajamukhi tried to catch Indrani's hand.

Indrani looked around for help. Ajamukhi's clutches were so tight that she was not able to wriggle out. Her husband had kept Mahâkâla to take care of her in distress. But where is he?

Indrani started crying aloud – "O Kailâsapati! Please save me from this wretched woman. Maha Sastha! Where are you now?" Mahâkâla heard her and came out wielding his sword. "You demon! How dare you touch Indrani when I am here? Leave her alone and run away," he shouted like thunder.

Ajamukhi laughed in ridicule. "Who are you? Even Trimurthis run away from me. You dare to oppose me?"

"You wretch! I am here on behalf of Maha Sastha who is well known in all the three worlds. My name is Mahâkâla. My master is like the dark cloud and rides on his white elephant. I have been put in charge of Indrani's safety. If at all you want to save yourself, better run away at once", said Mahâkâla.

Ajamukhi did not take him seriously. She thought he was one of Indra's guards. She threw her Soolâyudham at him and said angrily, "Wait and see, I am going to eat you up at once".

**Mahâkâla broke her Soolâyudham into two with his sword. Ajamukhi asked her friend Dunmukhi to hold Indrani's hand and sent her Soolam again aiming at the chest of Mahâkâla.** This was also broken by his sword. Ajamukhi plucked a mountain and threw it at him. Mahâkâla used his sword again and reduced it to dust. Ajamukhi was extremely angry and shouted "Don't think that I am a weakling. I can devour you in a second. After all, you are so small for me that I do not eat you up. I am the sister of the great Soorapadhman. All the worlds will bow before him. If you try to play with me, his soldiers will finish you in no time. Beware!"

She dragged Indrani forcibly and started moving. Mahâkâla stood before her and said, "Look! I kept watching your atrocity because you are a woman. If you do not leave Indrani's hand now, I shall chop off your hand." Ajamukhi just did not care for his warnings.

When she pulled Indrani with force, Mahâkâla caught Ajamukhi by her hair and chopped off her hand. When she fell on the ground, he kicked her. Dunmukhi who was nearby also met the same fate. Ajamukhi roared in pain, bleeding profusely. She was thumping the ground with her other hand.

"You crank! You dare to cut off my hand! Even Devas never dared to touch me. Wait and see. My brother will catch hold of you, wherever you may go and hide."

Dunmukhi who was nearby joined her and said, "We will not gain anything by merely lamenting here. We must teach this wicked fellow a lesson. Let us go and complain to your brother right away."

Ajamukhi told Indrani "Don't you think that you have been spared. Wherever you may go, we are not going to leave you. My brother will certainly take revenge on you. I'll go now but surely send our soldiers soon." Taking the chopped hand in the other hand, Ajamukhi was crying bitterly and left to see his brother, with Dunmukhi.

Mahakâla consoled Indrani asking her not to fear anyone. As long as he was there none can harm her and so, she can continue with her routine. Reassured and fearless now, Indrani started her meditations again.

## 42. Bhanugopan on the move

Narada happened to know about the incidents at Seerkazhi. He informed Indra at Devalokam. Though he got angry, he felt helpless. He told Nandideva and wanted his permission to get back to Bhoolokam to resume his meditation.

Indra returned to Seerkazhi with Devas. He hugged Mahâkâla for the timely help he gave his wife in his absence. "How am I going to repay my debt of gratitude to you? Only because of Hariharaputra's grace, Indrani escaped a great disaster", he said. Mahâkâla took leave of him and Indra went to a secret place to hide with his wife.

Ajamukhi and Dunmukhi went to Veeramahendrapuri with their chopped hands. Soorapadhman was in his court. Both his brothers were sitting on either side. Asuras were fanning him. Dancers of Devalokam were giving a performance. Guards of the eight directions were greeting him with flowers. Brahma was in waiting to read the panchangam which informs about the five aspects of stars, moon's position or thithi, the season, the yogam and the karanam."

Ajamukhi entered the court and fell at her brother's feet crying in misery. "O my brother! You used to boast that all the habitants of the universe were singing your praise and valour. Now, all that great honour of yours, suffers by a great blemish. You promised to my mother that you would take care of me at all times. Look at me! I have lost my hand! I have none to help me. After all, one of your slaves has done this to me. His name is Mahâkâla. He was ridiculing your valour and status. If you allow him to survive even after this insult to me, you will be the next target to suffer", she cried with tears.

Soorapadhman looked at the pathetic plight of his sister, with a hand chopped off and holding it in the other and crying in great agony. He was mad with rage and got up from his throne.

"O my sister! Who is that who harmed you so badly? Where does he stay? Please tell me now", he said.

"My brother! Indrani was hiding in a garden near Seerkazhi. I wanted her to become your queen and so I dragged her along. Then Mahâkâla stopped me and also chopped off my hand as well as Dunmukhi's"

Ajamukhi then addressed Târaka, "My brother, you could get Vishnu's chakra as an ornament for you. Look at my plight now. Does this speak good for you?"

Then, she turned to Singamukhan and showed him her chopped arm. "Look! Do you know who did this to me? Once you threw away that Indra who rides on Airavatam. It is one of his slaves who meted out this treatment to me. When I am blessed with three brothers who are equal to Meru mountain itself, I meet with such a crude fate". She cried.

Soorapadhman went crazy with anger. He raised his eyebrows. His eyes emitted fire. His breath was so hot. His voice was harsh, when he called out to his sister. The court was stunned at the extent of his anger. All the eight guards of the directions ran away. Devas went hiding. Asuras fell at his feet in fear. The sages were upset. Both the brothers got off their seats. Soorapadman addressed the audience in immense rage, looking greatly agitated.

"After all, our slaves, the Devas, have the cheeks to do this. The coward Indra who is hiding from us has sent one of his men to harm our sister! Above all, he is not Brahma, Vishnu or our God Siva, who wronged our sister! One mean creature – a down trodden slave – has chosen to do this. I left Indra to go scot free, without arresting him and putting him in prison, as he was hiding from us in fear. It was my sheer carelessness that has led to this assault. It is a great insult for my honour and me, a world-renowned emperor. We were here alive like mountains. Our soldiers are countless all around guarding every nook and corner but none could prevent this. Our sister's hand is cut off! Tomorrow we will face a worse situation. Let us not leave Indra go unpunished. Let the whole world be damned. On your march, let's go!"

Bhanugopan, his son, heard his father's war cry and got up. "Father, kindly listen to me! When you are very much alive, your sister's hand has been cut off. Is this an ordinary event? Can a coward catch the moon shining in the sky? It is incredible and ridiculous. Indra who was your slave has become tired and run away. I do not believe that Indra or his men would have dared to do this. Allow me to go first. Let me catch hold of the real culprit, Indra, Indrani and all other Devas and bring them here. If they are not traceable, I will burn the entire Devalokam and return. Please be patient till then."

When Soorapadhman heard his son's words of bravery, he calmed down and permitted him to go with the army. Bhanugopan took the blessings of his father and his brothers and started.

After Bhanugopan left, Soorapadhman summoned Brahma. He came out of his hiding place and started reading out the Panchangam. Sooran asked him to see that his sister's hand grew as before. Brahma saw to it that both Ajamukhi and Dunmukhi had their hands joined as before. Sooran asked Dunmukhi to go and help Bhanugopan and show him the place where Indrani was hiding. Though Ajamukhi's hand was normalized, Sooran was still angry. He sent for the Sun, the other planets and the stars. As soon as they came, he asked, "When my sister was hurt so badly, all of you were mute witnesses from the sky! You should have killed that miscreant and informed me. Have you become so bold as to keep quiet, even when someone insults my sister?"

Sun and the others replied, while they were shivering in fear, "Asurendra! Please do not get angry with us! We did not wrong you or slight you in any way. As usual, we were busy in carrying out your orders and so we were not aware of what happened to your sister. This was the fact", they said.

Sooran did not accept their explanation. He was convinced that they had ditched him. So he put them all in prison in utter distrust. Then Sooran summoned Vayu and all other Gods. "You are everywhere. You are fully aware as to what happens anywhere in the world. Nothing can escape your notice. You did not stop the atrocity done to my sister and none of you reported it to me either. So, you were all a party to Indra and his men." Thus, he found fault with them also and got them imprisoned, as accomplices in the crime.

Sooran had still not calmed down fully. All the kings of Bhoolokam were dragged to his court, on his orders. Everyone was shivering even to look at him. Sooran addressed them. "Indra was hiding in Bhoolokam. When my asuras came in search of him what were you all doing? You did not want to help them. Are you afraid of Indra as to join hands with him against me? My sister has been insulted because you were indifferent in your attitude. I cannot allow you to go scot free after your having done this." Saying such unkind words he punished them all in various ways. They begged of his mercy quoting various reasons but Sooran did not hear their pleas.

After the court session was over, Brahma came before the asura and told him, "Soorapadman! I want to tell you something. You have unjustly imprisoned the sun, moon and other planets for no fault of theirs. They were not guilty as you know and they were only busy obeying your orders. They could not have been aware as to what happened to your sister. If you do not release them, the whole world will suffer in several ways. So, you may please order their acquittal at once."

Soorapadhman conceded to his request and released them all with a warning that they should never form a party to Indra, at any cost.

## 43. The son of Indra lodged in prison

Bhanugopan started on his mission to capture Indra, with a huge army. He crossed the sea and reached Bhoolokam. He asked Dunmukhi, who came with him in his chariot, to show him the place where her hand was cut off. Dunmukhi took him to Seerkazhi and showed him the garden nearby. Asuras searched all over the place but could not find anyone. Bhanugopan went round the entire area of Bhoolokam but still could not locate Indra and Devas anywhere. He wanted to find them out even if they were hiding somewhere in Devalokam. As soon as he reached there, Devas were damn afraid and informed Jayanta, Indra's son. What will he do? His Guru was not available. His parents' whereabouts were not known. They had run away from Devalokam fearing Sooran. Many Devas had also accompanied them. What to do at this difficult juncture? He had no place to take refuge. Victory or end – one was certain. He gathered all the Devas available in heaven and thought of Airavatam, the elephant. He went to fight the asuras, come what may.

Both armies clashed. Asuras were surprised that, Devas have made bold to face them in the battle field, so they fought them with great vengeance. All weapons and astras were fully deployed. Blood was flowing from the broken limbs of the wounded soldiers. Devas were unable to withstand asuras' onslaught. There was no unity among them. They ran for their lives on all sides. The asuras caught them captive and Bhanugopan kept them as war prisoners.

When his army was losing in strength Jayanta fought all by himself with all his weapons. Asuras were killed in great numbers. Still another contingent attacked Jayanta on all sides. Airavatam stamped on them and forcefully attacked them with its heavy trunk, killing all of them.

Bhanugopan now sent one of his generals – Neelakesa to attack Jayanta. Neelakesa sent several astras at Jayanta who could stop them all midway in the air. He sent a hundred arrows together and Neelakesa's shield got broken. In return, Neelakesa used his Ardhachandra astram to cut the string of the bow of Jayanta. Left with no weapons to fight with, Jayanta now fought with his magical powers. Neelakesa was unable to return his attacks and got killed. Asuras were on the run, Somasooran, Mayabali, Soorakesari, Padman, Marutabali, Dandakan, Vaman, Varunan, Maakadan and the other leaders of the asura army deployed their magic spells, but yet were no match for Jayanta's hectic speed.

When Bhanugopan saw the destruction of his warriors, he chanted the gnanamantra given to him by asuraguru. Jayanta's magical skills were set to nought by that. He was there all alone on Airavatam. They fought with each other directly with thousand arrows each. Bhanugopan lost his horses and Jayanta's bow got broken.

He was very badly hit all over the body with a plethora of arrows and he was profusely bleeding. Airavatam killed the driver of Bhanugopan's chariot and attacked him with his tusk. As they got broken by the steel strong chest of Bhanugopan, he caught its trunk and slapped it. Airavatam fell on the ground roaring and Bhanugopan also was thrown away.

When Jayanta got back to his senses he saw the Asuras surrounding him and shouting to kill him. Bhanugopan intercepted them and said, "He is too tired after he fought with me. It is not proper to kill him at this stage. Put him in prison along with the other Devas in captivity. Set the Devalokam on fire".

Asuras caught hold of the rest of the Devas and put them all in prison along with Jayantan. They then entered Devalokam and looted it thoroughly. All the mansions and palaces were set on fire.

**Bhanugopan returned with his soldiers to Veeramahendrapuri. He presented Jayanta and Devas to his father, as captives. "Father! Indra and Indrani could not be traced anywhere. Indra's son and Devas have been held captive by me. Devalokam has been totally burnt down", he said. Sooran was very happy.**

"These Devas made bold to cut off my sister's hand. Do cut their limbs now, so that they feel the same pain". Sooran said.

When asuras chopped the legs and hands of Devas, they grew again and again because of their immortality and divine power. Sooran was surprised and so ordered them to be imprisoned, as he would not be able to kill them.

The Devas were suffering a hell there. Airavatam, which had fainted in the battlefield with broken tusks, regained its consciousness and came to know of what all happened. The elephant reached Tiruvenkadu and prayed to Lord Siva as per Sastras and got back its tusks. It continued to stay there itself and prayed to the Lord.

When Indra knew that heaven was burnt down and his son and Devas were taken captive by Asuras, he was extremely distressed. He prayed to Lord Siva, who promised to help him, by sending his son to kill Sooran.

Days passed by. But, the Lord's son was yet to be born. Indra appealed to Lord. Siva again, meeting him with Brahma. They decided to send Manmatha to wake him up from his yoganishta, as he was teaching the Gnanamarga to the four sages. Manmatha did distract Lord Siva, but became a victim of His anger. Lord Siva married Pârvathi and got a son Kumaran.

After narrating all these events that led to his birth, Bruhaspati worshipped Lord Muruga and said, "I have told you the past, which you already know. You are fully aware of the present. Devas do not even sleep well, fearing Asuras. Vishnu has lost in the war with Târaka. Brahma is reading Panchangam for Sooran daily. No body else can really kill Soorapadhman and save the Devas from prison."

Muruga smiled and consoled them, "Devas! Give up your fears now. I have come only to annihilate asuras. Very soon Sooran will be killed with his kith and kin and all of you will get back your coveted positions and fortunes".

Just as a child is comforted by the mother in her loving hug, Devas derived renewed hope and solace by Lord Muruga's soothing words and assurances.

## 44. Lanka faces destruction

As the day dawned the Devas woke up with new energy. Velavan called them and said, "My dear friends! I am fully aware of your woes. For God Almighty, Devas as well as Asuras are His children. He cannot show them any difference in treatment. However, when someone resorts to evil ways only, we must try to correct them. Otherwise we have to punish them suitably. That is the only righteous way or Dharma. Asuras are giving you problems, as they are so ordered by their leader, Sooran. I do agree that Soorapadhman is a cruel king. But still we will give him a final chance to retrace his steps to the virtuous path. So we will send a messenger to him asking for the release of the Devas from prison. In case he does not heed to our request, we will attack him as the last course of action open before us. So, let us first try the non-violent method."

Devas too felt that his decision was right. Lord Muruga wanted to know if there was any volunteer ready to go and meet Sooran on his behalf. All Devas looked at Brahma who in turn addressed Muruga. "Muruga! All Devas are his slaves. If one of them goes there, he will be re-arrested and put in prison. It would be better if you send your trusted friend Veerabhahu Devar as your messenger."

Arumukhan was happy about this suggestion and called Veerabhahu. "You shall now go to Sooran's capital Veeramahendrapuram. You request him on my behalf, to release Jayanta and other Devas from the prison immediately. If he refuses to set them free, tell him that he and his men will face dire consequences, including death", he said. Veerabhahu took Muruga's blessings and started.

Indra requested him to meet Jayantan and Devas, console them first and then meet Sooran. Veerabhahu agreed and met his soldiers. "As per orders of our Lord, I am proceeding to meet Sooran. If he does not pay heed to our request, I shall burn down his city and return". Leaders hugged him and gave him leave. There was a mountain called Kandamadana near the Southern Sea and it was even higher than Meru. Veerabhahu went to its peak and because of his weight, the mountain got crushed. Târaka's men who were hiding in its caves after the war, got killed by the pressure.

Veerabhahu meditated on Muruga for the successful completion of his mission. Then he grew in size and took Viswaroopam – a gigantic form by which he could clearly see the entire world. Veeramahendrapuram looked a beautiful city. For a moment, he thought of just stretching his hand and squeezing it to a paste like mud. The next moment he remembered that Jayanta and Devas were still there, and they may die, if he destroyed the city.

Looking at his size, the sun, the moon, planets and stars were terrified. He told them not to fear him. The sages and the Devas blessed him. Asuras sighted the huge figure and wondered if Krounchagiri had grown again due its magical power.

Veerabhahu folded his hands thinking of Muruga and started on his air route. By the release of his weight, Kandamâdana parvatam rose like a ball in the sky and came back to its original height. By the terrific speed of his flight, Vayu blew off all the peaks of the mountains. Water from the sea rose high in air. The Earth shook and the whole world went topsy-turvy. Just as Lord Siva sent fierce sparks of fire to burn down the three forts of the three Asuras, Veerabhahu flew with red eyes glowing in anger. Within a second, he reached Lankapuri situated north of Veeramahendrapuri.

At that particular time when Veerabhahu set foot in Lankapuri, Yaalimukhan who was guarding the city had gone to Veeramahendrapuri. His son Ativeeran was in charge with his thousand vellam strong army. His army chief Veerasingan was at the northern border.

When Veerabhahu flew in from above with greater speed than the wind, Veerasingan got angry. When he saw an intruder despite his heavy security arrangements he left for the shores at once, with five hundred vellam soldiers. He shouted at Veerabhahu. "Who are you? How dare you come here? Tell me the truth or else, I shall kill you straight away"

Veerabhahu did not care for his threats. "I am on my way to Veeramahendrapuri to see Soorapadman. If you think of stopping me, you will die. Let me proceed ", he said. Veerasingan laughed aloud and ordered his army to kill the intruder who was unaware of his might.

**When the asuras surrounded Veerabhahu and fought with him, his sword gave them a fitting reply and all of them fell dead like a bunch of fruits.** More than hundred vellam soldiers were lost, even before they could realise what was happening. The rest ran away from the scene. Veerasingan threw his Vajrayudham at him, but it was nullified by his sword. Veerabhahu then cut off both his hands and stood up on the central peak in the city of three peaks.

By this very speedy action, Ativeeran and his men tumbled and fell down. Lankapuri was shaken and it was sinking under the sea. The people in the city also were drowned in the sea and those who were running for their survival were eaten away by the sharks in the sea. There was nothing but chaos there.

Ativeeran slowly came out of water. He was very angry at the total destruction of the city. It cannot certainly be an

act of the Devas. They dare not do such things as they were mere slaves of Sooran and they knew the consequences. Brahma or Vishnu also could not have done this. "Then who else is this fighter? I must kill him somehow or the other", he thought and appeared before Veerabhahu with his men.

"So, you are the person who did all this? You are not going alive from here". He asked his soldiers to fight him. Veerabhahu was brushing them all aside as if he was dusting his body. All asuras lay dead there. Ativeeran threw his Vel, Dandayudham and finally Soolayudham, one after the other. But alas! Each one of them was broken by Veerabhahu's sword. Stunned for a moment, Ativeeran resumed his attack with the sword given to him by Brahma, with the hope that he will win now. As he was a great warrior, there was severe fight between the two. Finally when he became tired, Veerabhahu cut his limbs and head with his sword. Ativeeran met his end. Veerabhahu stopped fighting and flew in the air again. Lankapuri came out of the sea by his speeding force, but most of the city had been ruined totally.

## 45. Veerabhahu at Veeramahendrapuri

Leaving Lankapuri Veerabhahu Devar reached the northern side of Veeramahendrapuri. Two leaders Ghoran and Athighoran were guarding the frontier with thousand Vellam soldiers. Chariots, Elephants and Horses were also there in thousands of Vellam units. Without fighting and winning them over, he realised that he would not be able to proceed further.

He was not afraid of facing or fighting with the asuras' army. But he hesitated for other reasons. Even if he were to fight many more armies, he was certain to emerge victorious by Lord Muruga's grace. But if he had to fight with them, half the day would be wasted. Sooran's army guards must be pretty strong and any war with them will be made known to Sooran who will send more contingents. Even after destroying them, he may have to face Bhanugopan and his army. By the grace of Lord Muruga, he will no doubt, win the war. In case the son is killed in the war, Soorapadhman himself may come. As he is immensely blessed by Lord Siva, Veerabhahu may get defeated at his hands and return without any result. Lord Muruga will not be happy to welcome him back in that stage. Above all, he was sent for a different purpose. He was instructed to meet Sooran and give him, the Lord's message to free Jayanta and Devas from the prison.

On recalling the main purpose of his mission, Veerabhahu gave up the idea of fighting the asuras. As entry through the northern gate seemed difficult and would invite an encounter, he went to the Eastern gate. There again, two other leaders, Mahishakshan and Veerabhanu with four wings of the army were on guard. Seeing the size of the big army, he moved now to the Southern gate. Gajamukhan, a mighty asura with thousand elephant heads, thousand trunks and two thousand hands, was on duty there. His appearance itself was so frightful to look at. As Gajamukhan was quite fond of fighting he had sighted Veerabhahu arriving by air. He jumped with joy and stood before Veerabhahu. "Who are you? How dare you choose to come here? Are you Indra's soldier? Did you imagine that Devas would be here to help you? It is just like a deer entering the cave of an angry lion! Unless you go back, you will meet your end here." Veerabhahu returned his war cry and said, "O Elephant headed! You do not know who I am. If you are sure of yourself, come along to fight me!"

Waiting for somebody to fight with, Gajamukhan pounced at Veerabhahu and attacked him with all his two thousand hands and thousand trunks. He threw big rocks and trees at him. But everything went to pieces as soon as they hit Veerabhahu. When he used Dandayudham, Veerabhahu cut his hands and trunks with his sword. Gajamukhan wanted to attack him like a mountain and crush him, but Veerabhahu kicked him at his chest with great anger and force. As he could not stand it, he fell down bleeding and died on the spot. By this time, asuras who had come to know about the fight between the two, came running. As Veerabhahu did not want a big battle to break out, he took a small form and sat on the eastern tower. Asuras could not see him, but only saw Gajamukhan dead and fallen on the ground.

**Sitting on the eastern tower, Veerabhahu looked at the city, which was amazing. Great mansions and palaces, had been built in a splendid style. Asura women were happily chatting in their terraces. There were signs of prosperity everywhere and people looked very rich and gorgeous in silks and gold. All the wealth of the heaven was there. Chintamani, Kamadhenu and Karpagam tree gave them whatever they desired. In short Veera mahendrapuri looked like Devalokam itself. One cannot enjoy the riches heaped there just in one birth alone. That is why perhaps the Asuras were having more than one head, say ten hundred or thousand!**

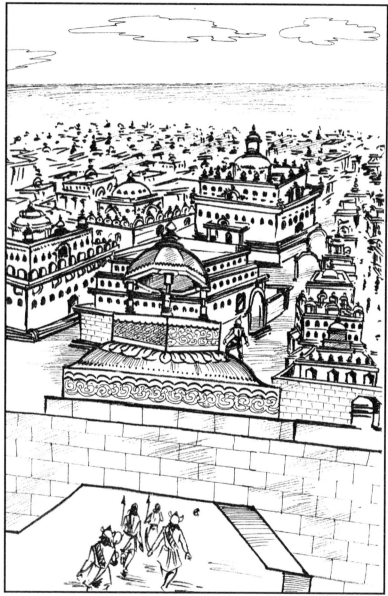

Veerabhahu wanted to enjoy the glorious scenes of the city fully, but he had no time. He had to fulfill the task assigned to him. He went past the palaces of Bhanugopan,

Agnimukhan, Iranyan, Vajravahu and others. Finally he reached the palace of the chief minister Dharmagopan and sat on the top of it.

## 46. Velan appears in dream

Devas imprisoned by asuras were not free even inside the prison. Their hands and legs were chained and everyday Jayanta and Devas were beaten up for information regarding Indra's whereabouts. As they did not have the information, they had to put up with the cruel treatment meted out to them day in and day out. Only when the asuras became tired of beating them continuously, they stopped.

. The asura jailers viz. Kandagan, Uthavakan, Karaalan, Maapalan, Nisalgan, Sangan and others were also troubling the Devas from their own side. When they lay chained and helpless there, the asuras will poke them with sticks and beat them up, asking the same questions regarding Indra. As Devas had taken nectar, they did not die despite all cruelties heaped on them. Asuras never left them until they fainted and became unconscious.

Jayanta was praying to Lord Siva incessantly. "Maheswara ! You are well known for your kindness but still you are indifferent to us. We are suffering a hell for no fault of ours. Even if we had sinned, would it not suffice to have suffered so far? You had saved Antakâsura, but you do not take pity on us. You had been good to an elephant, sparrow, crane, snake and spider but you turn a deaf ear to our prayers. Is it because we are even lesser than them? Are we not devoted to you always? Why this endless suffering for us?" He went on and on crying bitterly.

One day Jayanta nearly reached the height of his suffering and fainted at the end of the prayers. Lord Muruga wanted to assure him that he will take care of all of them. So he appeared in his dream.

On the right side were the hands with flag, Vajram Angusam, Vel and arrow, on the left side were the hands with lotus, bell, mazhu, staff and bow. One hand was pointing to his feet indicating that the devotees should surrender there (Abhaya Hastam). The other hand was showing a blessing sign indicating that he was ready to give him any boon asked for (Varada Hastam). Kandhan, with his twelve hands and six faces, gave darshan to Jayanta in his dreams. Jayanta was thrilled and said, "O Lord! You are not Brahma, Vishnu or Siva as I happen to know them. You have come to save me on hearing my prayers. May I know who you are?"

Shanmukha smiled at him and said – "Jayanta, I am the son of Lord Siva whom you worship daily with devotion. Your father Indra and Devas have already apprised me of your sufferings at the hands of Sooran and surrendered at my feet for a quick redressal. I shall kill the asura and relieve you of your ills. Krounchagiri and Târaka have already perished at my hands. I am staying now at Senthil city, expecting Sooran's arrival. In order to give a last chance for survival, before inviting his end, I have sent Veerabhahu to meet Sooran, as my messenger. Veerabhahu will meet Sooran today. You will be free from your sorrows within the next ten days." Muruga disappeared after giving him word to do the needful shortly. When Jayanta woke up, he was happy to think of Lord's grace again and again. At last, there will be an end to asuras' atrocities. He called Devas who were with him and described the divine darshan of Muruga in his dreams.

He gave a full account of His kind words. Devas also became happy and praised the Lord immensely.

Asuras who were guarding the prison gates saw them in a happy mood and were perplexed. They had always seen them in pain most of the time and so their sudden happiness triggered suspicion.

At the same time, Veerabhahu reached the prison. He saw the guards with weapons outside the prison. He was wondering how to enter without their knowledge. He thought of Lord Muruga for a moment. By His grace, the asuras suddenly fell asleep. Veerabhau praised the Lord and entered the prison.

## 47. The kind-hearted messenger at Soora's court

When Veerabhahu entered the prison, Devas were shocked for a moment thinking that he had been sent by asuras there for punishing them. But his handsome personality was baffling. Jayanta alone thought that he was perhaps the messenger from Lord Muruga. So he approached him and asked.

"O handsome soldier! Who are you? You have managed to enter, despite the high security here. You seem to be one of the Devas. Let us know who you are."

"O son of Indra! You may not know me, but I know you. I am the messenger from Muruga, the son of Lord Siva, whom you worship daily and I am also his brother. My name is Veerabhahu. I have been sent to request Sooran to release all of you from prison."

His words sounded like nectar for Devas. They greeted him with tears of joy. "Oh Our saviour! We feel so much relieved even at your sight", they said.

Veerabhahu reassured them saying that their sorrows will soon come to an end. Lord Muruga was keen to shower his grace on them and they will regain their heavenly abode very soon.

Jayanta saluted him and said, "Your words are so much soothing. But I do not know where my parents are hiding now, fearing Sooran. Perhaps, they may also be suffering somewhere else, as captives of the asura"

"Jayanta! Do not worry. Your parents are safe with Lord Muruga now. Your father specially wanted me to meet you here. Only to fulfil his request, Muruga has made these arrangements", Veerabhahu said. Jayanta was happy and took Veerabhahu's hands in his and said, "We are fully in the dark ever since we were brought here as captives. Please tell us what all happened after we left."

Veerabhahu gave them the full details from the time Indra left Seerkazhi till the time Muruga was born to help the Devas. "All this malady was due to the reason that you took part in the yâga conducted by Daksha, when Lord Siva did not go. Though Veerabhadra had punished you, the consequences of that sin still continue. Muruga's grace will wipe that out and you will regain your glory as before.

"If Soorapadhman does not heed to the advice of Muruga and release you, he is sure to meet his end on the tenth day from today. Shanmukha's Vel is so powerful that none can win him over. So, forget all your worries from now," so saying he left.

The prison guards woke up from their mid day slumber and resumed their duties with more vigilance than before.

Veerabhahu reached the palace of Soorapadhman. The main gate was guarded by two asuras named Ugran and Mayuran with a host of soldiers. Veerabhahu gained entry in the form of an atom size figure and came to the court hall.

Soorapadhman was seated in his throne. His royal splendour was amazing. The hall was studded with precious gems and Sooran was seated on a beautiful throne. His majestic personality itself was proof enough for his great valour. His sons Bhanugopan and others were seated on either side. Menaka, Tilotthama and others were entertaining him with their splendid dance performances. The Sun and the Moon were carrying umbrellas on either side. Vidyadharas and Kinnaras were providing pleasant music.

A dazzling crown studded with gems was adorning the head of Sooran. Pearl garlands on his chest were so wonderful to look at. Ear studs were also dazzling. He was wearing sacred ash on his forehead, which spoke of his devotion to Lord Siva. They were ornaments on his shoulders and arms, which indicated his warriorship. The yellow silk dress spoke volumes of his royalty and magnetic personality.

When Veerabhahu saw Soorapadman, he felt sorry for him. Even the Devas did not have such a superb stature as he had. All riches were heaped at his feet. But he did not seem to perpetuate all the blessings that he had. His thoughtless actions were inviting trouble to his happy and comfortable life.

A sparrow mistakes a particle of fire as a glow worm and takes it to its nest. It results in the entire nest getting burnt down by the fire. Like that, Sooran had unnecessarily earned the wrath of the Devas and thereby was summoning his early end. He drove Devas away from their abode,

looted their wealth and also imprisoned them. What more! He treated them so cruelly that his end was nearing and also that of his whole community!

Having thought about the ill conceived actions of Sooran, Veerabhahu entered the court in his real form. Everyone was wonder-struck at his entry and got up from their seats. Veerabhahu walked like a lion to the throne of Soorapadhman and introduced himself. "Soorapadhma! I am a messenger from Lord Muruga!"

"Why the hell did you come here?" shouted Sooran in anger. Veerabhahu also got angry at the disrespect shown to him by Sooran, who addressed him in singular without even greeting him or offering a seat.

**When he thought of Muruga, there appeared another beautiful throne, higher than that of Sooran. Its brightness was so great that everyone in the court blinked. Veerabhahu sat on the throne. There were several comments in the court. Some thought he knew magic. Others thought he is from the enemy side. A few were suspicious that he was Lord Siva Himself. He could be a sage or one of the Ashtadigpâlakas (Guards of the eight cardinal directions), some said.**

Soorapadhman's anger was on the increase. "Are you showing some magic or playing a trick here? Devas also know a lot of magic but none dares to exhibit anything before me! Do you know why? They have no guts. They know who I am. You are playing with me like a child! I could have killed you in a jiffy for having insulted me. Well, let me allow you to live for some more time. Who are you? Why did you come here? Tell me the truth", he said.

Veerabhahu, who got equally angry controlled himself and laughed. "Soorapadhma! You perhaps did not listen to me! I had already introduced myself. Let me repeat. I am an ambassador of Lord Muruga in order to mitigate the sufferings of the Devas. The Lord has come down to Senthil City. He is accompanied by a lakh and nine soldiers. I am one of them. My name is Veerabhahu. After crushing Krouncham and killing Târaka, our Lord still has a soft corner for you. So he has been kind enough to send me as his messenger to you."

Soorapadhman laughed aloud and taunted him "Oh! I had heard that a small boy killed my brother Târaka. Why did he send you here? What was the idea of Muruga in sending you as a messenger to me? Come on? Tell me Quick!"

Veerabhahu addressed him in detail- "Soorapadhma! Your behaviour with Devas was not proper. You drove them away from heavens and looted their treasures. You have imprisoned Indra's son Jayanta with Devas and are treating them cruelly. Muruga wants you to release them all and return their treasures to them. If you do not agree to do this, you will meet your end.

You are already aware that Muruga had crushed Krounchagiri and also killed Târaka. Devas always follow the path of Dharma. If you choose to wrong them, you are sure to perish. Asuras like Jalantan and Antakan ill treated Devas and so met their sad end. You are a great devotee of Lord Siva and he has given you a lot of blessings, your glorious life and everything you enjoy. You owe it to Him. So if you do not release Devas, this great life of royal comforts will come to an end. What do you say?" He asked.

Soorapadhman was furious. He tapped his shoulder and shouted, "Look! What do you think I am? Are you threatening me as if I am a child? What is wrong in ill treating Devas? They were enjoying our wealth. When we were in utter poverty, they killed many of us cunningly. They suffer for what they did earlier. Just because a small boy is blabbering I shall not release Devas. If Krouncham and Târakan have fallen, do you think I will fall at his feet and beg for my life? I have greater soldiers with me. I could have killed that small boy as soon as he killed my brother but my people prevented me saying that it was improper on my part to kill a small boy.

You listen to that child and come to advise me! As you are only a messenger I spare you. Please go and tell that child not to play with me."

Veerabhahu was feeling sorry that Soorapadhman casually took Lord Muruga only as a small child. So, he chose to enlighten him.

"Oh! You are so foolish as not to understand the greatness of Lord Muruga. You pooh-pooh him as a child. Please do not think so. He was born as the great striking light from the third eye of your beloved Lord Siva. God Almighty has been born as a child. He may still look small but he is omnipresent. Who has known him fully? All worlds are within him. The whole universe, which you think you govern is seen in a hair's breath on his holy self. If you know this you won't slight him as a child. He has come to establish Dharma. His Velayudham will kill you and your people in a jiffy. Do not invite your end unnecessarily. Release the Devas and get the immense grace of Lord Muruga", he said in order to make him come to grips with the facts.

Soorapadhman who was so conceited got furious at his words. He called his guards and said, "As he has come as a messenger I spare him though he decried my valour so badly. Take him away and put him in prison".

Asuras drew near him. Veerabhahu grew big in size, caught them by their hair and killed them. Again he told Sooran, "Asura! your end is near! That is why you chose not to take my advice. Very soon our Lord's army will kill you. Let me leave now". He moved to the gate and the throne on which he sat also vanished magically as it had appeared.

## 48. Soorapadhman and Veerabhahu

Soorapadhman's anger knew no bounds. One thousand asuras were killed by Veerabhahu in a short time and so Sooran wanted to stop him from going away, so as to catch him. He called out to Sadhamukhan in his court and told him, "This is the messenger from Muruga who killed my brother Târaka. He comes here and kills our asuras, but still goes scot free! No, he should not go! Catch him and put him in prison. Don't kill him as he is only a messenger".

Sadhamukhan went with a lakh of soldiers and stopped Veerabhahu. "You insulted our king and killed our soldiers. After all this, you try to run away! No, we will not allow you to leave", he shouted.

Veerabhahu replied without fear, "Your king talked ill of my Lord. He also made his soldiers attack me ! So I am not at fault. If you can, try to stop me".

Sadhamukhan and his soldiers pounced upon him with a variety of weapons. Veerabhahu took a mountain peak from one side and threw it at them. Many asuras got crushed underneath. Sadhamukhan felt puzzled, but still used many weapons. He sent a thousand arrows together aiming at his chest. Veerabhahu brushed them all aside and took the opponent's bow and broke it. Sadhamukhan attacked with his hundred hands. Veerabhahu kicked him with one foot and rolled his head with the other foot. Sadhamukhan fell on the ground shrieking and died.

Veerabhahu was still angry with the asuras and hence took a gigantic form by meditating on Muruga. Looking at his huge figure, people ran away. He pounced upon the central tower of the city. Fifty vellam soldiers, who were guarding Sooran's palace in the centre opposed him with Tomaram, Pindipalam, Dandam, etc. Veerabhahu gave a big shout like thunder and on hearing that, Asuran's army got thoroughly shaken. Veerabhahu ran in their midst and killed all of them with his hands and legs. He treated them as mere rubbish and threw them in all directions. The fifty vellam soldiers perished entirely.

**Veerabhahu's fighting spirit did not decrease. He could not digest Sooran's decrying Lord Muruga as a kid. He wanted to destroy his central tower. He saw an artificial mountain in front, took it from the ground and threw it at the building. Many parts of the tower got damaged and crumbled and several Asuras were killed. Many others lost their limbs.**

Watching Veerabhahu mounting more and more attacks, Sooran sent his soldiers with five hundred faces and thousand shoulders. They also ran towards him with all kinds of weapons. But Veerabhahu was going hither and thither destroying many buildings and indiscriminately killing the Asuras either directly or indirectly. Veeramahendrapuri was reduced to nothing. When the soldiers sent by Sooran surrounded him with sharp weapons, he uprooted a tree with his hands and finished them all without exception.

When soldiers with thousand shoulders were also killed, Soorapadhman was mad with rage. After all, a messenger of a small boy was causing such havoc and everyone there looked a coward for him. Then his second son Vajrabhahu approached him and wanted his permission to fight the enemy.

Vajrabahu with his ten heads, rode on his chariot of thousand horses. All the sons of the army commanders and his minister also joined him. Devas, Elephants, Horses and soldiers – all numbering in hundreds and thousands accompanied them. There were bad omens then. A bird called 'Koohai' (owl) gave a shriek. The flag from the chariot broke. Vajrabahu's bow was slipping. His left eye and shoulders were twitching. But he did not mind all these warnings and started off.

When Veerabhahu sighted Vajrabahu in his majestic ride, he first mistook him for Sooran. But when he saw his ten heads, he knew it was not Sooran.

When he looked at the large army marching ahead, he was only bothered that the war will prolong and he may take more time to return to his Lord. He first made a big roaring noise, hearing which Vajrabhahu's chariot driver, Vijayan warned him. "O Prince! The noise that we heard is from that great warrior. We have to be extra cautious." Vajrabahu laughed at him and said that he was too powerful for such a small fry and he will take him captive to his father.

Veerabhahu sprang into action very quickly. He uprooted a tall tree from the vicinity and attacked the army, catching them unawares. The soliders were caught in utter confusion and before they could get organized and gather themselves, he killed most of them and wounded others seriously. When Vajrabhahu attacked him with countless weapons, Veerabhahu caught hold of him with his chariot and threw him at a distance. When he got up to fight, he cut off his head and hands and that was his end. As it was already the sunset time, he left Veeramahendrapuri and flew in the air.

When he was near Lankapuri, Yaalimukhan stopped him. With thousand faces, two thousand hands and large mouth, he was looking ugly and uncouth and was as huge as Meru mountain. He was furious with anger and said, "Who are you? How did you go past us into our King's city and also mange to return now?"

A soldier standing nearby said, "O king! When you were away this morning at Mahendrapuri, this was the one who killed your sons Ativeeran and Veerasingan and also destroyed most parts of our city."

Yaalimukhan immediately sprang upon him with his sword and Veerabhahu cut it away. When he came to attack him with his two thousand hands, Veerabhahu cut off thousand hands. With the rest of the hands, he continued to hurl mountains and rocks at Veerabhahu. But they became pieces on hitting his sturdy chest. Veerabhahu cut off Yâlimukhan's heads now and killed him. Without further delay, he crossed the sea and reached Kandhamâdana mountain.

On seeing Veerabhahu the army cheered him. The leaders ran forward and hugged him. All of them reached the place of Lord Muruga. He smiled at him and asked for the details of his journey. Veerabhahu respectfully gave the full report.

"My lord! I met Sooran as per your orders. As his end is very near, he did not pay heed to my words. He has refused to release the Devas from prison. I warned him of the immediate disaster waiting for him and returned".

Shanmukha smiled and asked, "You have not told me what all you did there!"

Veerabhahu was touched by the Lord's kindness. "Yes, My lord. With your grace I have killed an army of asuras there". After he gave a detailed account of all the wars he fought there, Lord Muruga felt furious at the arrogance of Sooran in not taking the final chance to mend his evil ways. "Well, Sooran is destined to meet his inevitable end. We start tomorrow to wage a war against him", Lord said. Devas were immensely happy at these words. Veerabhahu also met Indra and apprised him of all that happened at Mahendrapuri. Indra hugged and thanked him for consoling his son and Devas, as requested by him.

## 49. Sooran's Sorrow

While Veerabhahu was narrating his experience of his trip to Veeramahendrapuri to Lord Muruga, Soorapadhman was mourning the death of his son Vajrabhahu. The whole city of Mahendrapuri was in great sorrow. Padumakomalai was extremely affected by the loss of her son. Soorapadhman was greatly shaken up by the unforeseen turn of events.

Then, one of his ministers, Dharmagopan tried to console him – " O King! You are the ruler of 1008 worlds. If you lose your heart and start mourning so badly, your enemies will laugh at you. Your physical prowess and mental strength are so great that any force can never defeat you. I can understand your state of mind on the loss of Vajrabhahu. But the loss of the father, mother, children or subjects does not unnerve great rulers. Even a girl can win over a losing solider nearing his end. By Vajrabhahu's death you cannot be cowed down. His destiny was over and he got killed by a messenger. If you slump down, who will be the source of strength for us? Please gather yourself and think of the next step for concrete action."

Sooran became slightly clear in his thoughts. He called his soldiers and asked, "Where is that messenger who killed my son and destroyed my city? Right now I want to see him."

The soldiers reported that they saw him going toward Lankapuri. "Then get me Brahma right away", Sooran said. The guards said, "Please do not get angry with us. Brahma has gone away from here to join Lord Muruga at Sendil City".

Sooran shouted at them, "So Brahma of this world has ditched me. Get me the other one from another world."

They rushed and got the Brahma from the next world. Sooran asked him to see that his city was rebuilt as before. Brahma assured him of renovation of all destroyed buildings. All the mansions regained their grandeur better than before. All gardens and parks blossomed with new flowers and looked more beautiful. After reconstruction of the city, Brahma took leave of Sooran and left. It was time now to plan the next move to fight the enemy.

Soorapadhman called his assembly again. The ministers and commanders were present. The two spies – Bhakan and Mayuran – who were sent to Senthil City, had returned to report to the king, about Lord Muruga's strength of armaments and Devas' preparedness for the war.

"Asurendra! Lord Muruga has a big army of two thousand demons. There are 108 leaders and a lakh and nine soldiers including Veerabhahu. Every one talks very highly of their intrinsic strength. On his way back, Veerabhahu has killed Yâlimukhan and his soldiers in Lankapuri. Lord Muruga has planned to set out tomorrow to wage a war on you."

Soorapadhman now addressed his assembly with his characteristic majesty.

**"My dear people! To take revenge on Devas, I put them in prison and tortured them. I made them our slaves and asked them to do errands for us. So, they have complained to Lord Siva and he has got a son now to help Devas. He is camping now at Senthil, after crushing Krounchagiri and killing my brother Târakan. He did not stop there. He sent a messenger to me and wanted me to release the Devas from prison. If I do not agree, he said he would kill me. That messenger insulted me and has killed thousands of our soldiers and also my son Vajrabahu. I could have killed him in no time, but I spared him because he was only a messenger and I am not supposed to harm him as per the code of conduct for kings. After all these threats, they think I will be cowed down. They are coming here tomorrow to fight with me. I can go single-handed and finish them all. There is none among Devas who can win over me. But according to rules of governance, I want to know how I should proceed in the matter. That is why I have called all of you here for your valuable advice."**

One of the ministers – Mahishan – stood up, saluted him and said – "O King! To destroy Krouncham and your son is not an easy task. We cannot be complacent, thinking that the enemy is after all a small boy. We have to act smart. To travel across the sea, destroy Lankapuri and Mahendrapuri and finally kill Vajrabahu also cannot be taken lightly, as an ordinary messenger is not capable of doing such things. Vishnu, Brahma and Indra, these three great men must have united and come in one single form as a messenger. Whether our enemy is a small boy or youngster, it is immaterial. When Krouncha's magic spells

and Târaka's powers went futile before him, we should have retaliated and waged a war on him. If we had done that, would a messenger come now and spoil our city life like this? Well, let us not delay our action any longer. It is better not to wait for their attack on us and so let us start right away".

Durgunan, another minister addressed the assembly next. "Asurendra! Kindly listen to me intently. You are a brave warrior. But you had not directly fought even Brahma, Vishnu or Indra so far. We have been trained by you so that we go to fight these men and drive them away. It is not proper for you with such a high stature and reputation, to go for war against a small boy who is still perhaps living on mother's milk. Are we not there to help you? Are we less brave? Our commanders will easily drive away Devas and demons from the battle field. In my opinion, they are to move first and not you."

Next, the chief minister, Dharmagopan, stood up and spoke on the same lines as Durgunan. "Asurendra! Durgunan said it right. What can be taken out by a nail does not deserve a sickle. Who is that boy? He is not Brahma or Vishnu. Is he a right opponent to you who has won all the Devas? Just looking at you, he may run to his mother's lap to hide himself. Your son Agnikumara is such a mighty warrior that all of them unitedly cannot oppose him. That boy was not responsible for Krouncham's fall. It was due to sage Agastya's curse. Just because Târaka failed to use the correct astra or weapon to fight the opponent he got killed. Vajrabahu was no less talented either. But you had not given him the indestructible chariot or stone to protect him when he went to war. Therefore that messenger easily killed him. It would suffice if one of your commanders goes to the war. He will return victorious".

The other ministers, Kalajit and Chandan and the army commanders – Anali and Singan – also seconded the chief minister's proposal. Before the enemy cracks down on them, it was decided to send the army choosing to be offensive and return victorious. Each one was ready to go with his own group of men. Then Soorapadhman's son Bhanugopan got up and said thus:-

"Father! You have unnecessarily called a big assembly for such a trivial matter. You should have sent word to me as soon as your brother was killed. I would have brought that boy to you. When the messenger came, you did not send for me. You sent Vajrabahu who was not experienced in war. One should not unduly make a big mountain out of a mole. The right course of action is a must than wasting time on useless things. You are quite well informed. Give me permission. Let me go with our forces to bring that boy and the Devas who are dependant on him."

Bhanugopan's younger brother Iranian also wanted to go to the war, the same night. His younger brother, Agnimukhan, also offered to go.

"Father! Are you not a great warrior? Is your brother Veerasingan lesser than you? Our army generals are great and you have your brave sons. There is a chariot with you, which can take you anywhere. You have a Chakrayudham, which executes your orders in no time. Why should you go personally? Let me go. I have Brahma's bow, Vajra shield and lots of other weapons to face the enemy. I shall win over them in a jiffy", Agnimukhan said.

After everyone expressed opinion after opinion, Singamukhan, Sooran's brother got up finally. "My dear brother! No body seems to realize the ground realities. Each one is trying to please you. Even then, it is not befitting our status. One should give sound advice to suit the context. If you listen to true and faithful advisers only, you will win.

You review your actions one by one. Just to take revenge, you were cruel to Devas. I do not think that they did anything wrong to you. Because some Devas insulted someone of our forefathers were you justified in taking revenge on this present generation? You brought them here and made them our errand boys. You put them in prison and tortured them. The whole heaven was looted. Just because you punished them without valid reason or rhyme, Lord Siva chose to send his son to do what was necessary".

Soorapadhman became red with anger. He shouted disapprovingly at his brother – "Singamukha! What are you talking? I had thought so highly of your valour. When did you become a coward?"

Though Sooran's words provoked his anger, Singamukhan controlled himself. "Brother! What fault have you found in my valour? I do not fear anyone. I tell you the truth. Even now, it is not late, release the Devas and send them to Muruga. They will get back with him to Mount Kailas. Our dynasty will be saved from disaster."

Soorapadhman drew his sword form its sheath and got up. Next moment he controlled himself and sat down. He poured out his anger in hot words:

"Brother! I am ashamed to think of your words. You are crest fallen by the fall of Krouncham and Târaka. 'But for my own power, nothing else can kill you', said Lord Siva when He blessed me. Have you forgotten it? Târakan had no such boon granted to him and so he died. I am surprised to hear you say that a small boy can bring about our end. It is just like saying that a blind man showed the Sun as a fruit and a lame man went to take it. I am tolerating your words of insult to me, as you are my brother."

Singamukhan did not mind Sooran's anger. He continued with his advice to him.

"Brother! It is but natural that you get angry with me. Everyone was talking things, which are nice and pleasant, to hear. Lord Siva gave you boons for your good long life of name and fame. He did not expect you to become vicious and do wrong things and kill Dharma. He does not tolerate your atrocities on Devas and that is why he has created a son to kill you. Do not ever think that the son born from his eye is just a small child. It is Lord Himself or His supreme Divine Power coming to fight with you. Just as a big tree comes out of a small Banyan seed, that boy has, within him, the entire universe. If you become the target of his displeasure, our whole dynasty will perish along with you. Do not get conceited that you are immortal by a boon. Your physical power is associated with this Earth. It has to perish one day. You make up your mind to release the Devas, which alone will guarantee your safety and security for ages".

Soorapadhman's laughter shook the mansion. "O my brother, you are imagining that the small child is none but Lord Siva himself. You are therefore, afraid of him and also want me to believe you. Blown about by the wind, heated up by Agni, rolled over by Ganges, tossed about here and there by Saravana lake and taking breast milk from some girls other than his mother, this little child has grown! Is he equal to Lord Siva? You are pleading for Devas and their Code of Manu says that it is not wrong to punish the guilty; but it is wrong to leave the guilty to go scot free. Devas committed many crimes against our forefathers. So they are being punished. I am not at all wrong in doing so. Muruga is too young a boy. He can do nothing to me. Can a small mouse harm the Meru mountain? I am sorry to think of your madness to equate him with God. You were so brave when you were young. You brought Varuna and elephant to prison. Now you have lost your senses due to age and so you are confused. You shudder like women. When an enemy attacks, the lion flares up and kills it. It will not try to run away and escape. You have lion's heads. They are of no use. You better not be here in your state of fear. You can go back to your kingdom. I can manage the situation alone and everyone of the Devas who oppose me will be put in prison", he said.

Sooran's insulting words made Singamukhan very sad. He was only feeling bad for his foolishness. "He does not analyse the real situation properly. He has no patience or intelligence to weigh the pros and cons of this mad hasty decision. Vanity and conceit are blinding him from seeing the truth. His ministers also trigger his anger. So whatever be my advice, he may not pay heed. His longevity granted by God is coming to an end. That is why he behaves like this, pushed by his fate. Ârumukha's Vel is going to kill him and all the rest present here. Let me not be a mute witness to his end. I should pass away before him". So thinking, Singamukhan came to a decision.

"Brother! Please forgive me. I was foolish in tendering unwanted and irrelevant advice to you. Kindly excuse me and allow me to go to the war first. I shall certainly destroy the enemy and return victorious".

Soorapadhman was happy to hear his words. "Brother I am very happy to hear your brave words. Perhaps you were trying to test my strength and will power. You must have thought that I will be unnerved by all that has happened today. To rejuvenate and cheer me up, you have spoken as if you differ from me. When all of you, my dear brothers, sons, ministers and generals are there, why should I fear? I have no doubt that we will win over the enemy when he declares a war on us." He said.

Everyone was asked to keep himself in readiness for the enemy's attack. As soon as they strike, they will go on the defensive. The assembly came to an end. The generals saluted Sooran and went back to their camps. Singamukhan told his brother, " Please send word to me brother, as soon as you get the news about the enemy's arrival. I shall meet him first. You need not worry."

Singamukhan returned to his capital Asurapuri, while Sooran was awaiting the break of war with Muruga and his men.

## 50. Muruga's Hemakootam

The day dawned. Darkness was dispelled by the rising sun. Devas woke up with new hope and enthusiasm. The Demons were ready to march. Everybody awaited Muruga's orders.

Velavan called Veerabhahu and said, "Soorapadhman has committed many blunders and finally rejected our suggestion for peaceful settlement of issues. Let us get going to his city, Veeramahendrapuram in order to kill him and his men, so that Devas' sufferings can come to an end."

Devas cheered him. Veerabhahu Devar brought the excellent chariot called Manovegam (As fast as you wish) before Muruga. Vayu was its driver and when Muruga got on there, musical instruments played so loud as to reach the eight directions. Devas prayed to Lord Siva with Vedic verses.

"Let us march", Muruga said and everyone began to move in their vehicles. Vishnu was on his mount Garuda, Brahma was on Annapakshi (Swan), and Indra was on his white elephant, Airavatam.

Veerabhahu and his brothers were on their chariots. Subran, Megamali, Subedhaseeridan, Kapali, Aprachithu, Chitrangan, Suvalan, Tâlan, Vajran, Veeman, Ugran, Ugresan, Pippalan, Nandisenan, Bramasan, Bramasenan, Paduman, Karâlan, Dandan, Bhadran, Pariganemi, Udavakan, Pushpadattan, Rudracharan, Veeran, Adisayan, Kethumali, Vakran, Bramakesan, Adipathi, Kalingan, Goran, Achuthan, Achalan, Santhan, Chitrasenan, Poori, Suseelan, Mâsayan, Singson, Utharan, Adangapaeron, Upadittan, Jayan, Easan, Mathagan, Madhangan, Chandi, Mahabalan, Suvetan, Neelabhadran, Suvaku, Vandabaranan, Kâkapâdan, Pingalan, Samânan, Mâyan, Nikumban, Kumban, Sangabalan, Visakan, Sadanavan, Ayakreevan, Angaiyayirathan, Sengannan, Vadanan, Nandan, Vâman, Mangalakesan, Soman, Vajramali, Chandan, Ajamukhan, Sarabhan, Kundana dakan, Kabhandan, Meghan, Vijayan, Vidruman, Dandi, Vyaghiran, Kala Pasan, Dasamukhan, Kumudan, Bhanu, Dhananjayan, Rishabharoopan, Kasiumukhan, Analakesan, Pathu Thooradiagal petron, Bhanukampan, Padangan, Suddhan, Anikhan, Seetan, Sunâdan, Sumâli, Mâli, Atri, Avunarkootran, Arikesan, Jwalâkesan - These 108 generals commanded the army to order and marched on. Flags were carried in the first row.

Instrumentalists walked in front of the army and made the war music sound aloud. The roads were filled with dust. The Earth shook with their march past. Aadiseshan was feeling the pressure. Veerabhahu Devar and his brothers were followed by lakh soldiers carrying various weapons. They were already expecting a great war with asuras. As brave warriors, they were eager to reach Mahendrapuri at the earliest and fight the asuras.

All the dust mingled with the sea water. The water level was only up to their ankles and when they walked along, it became muddy. Fish were moving away to save themselves. When the demons walked along the sea route, Muruga and the Devas went by air. Very soon, they crossed Lankapuri and reached Mahendrapuri.

Vishnu, Brahma and Indra saluted Muruga and reported, "We have approached the asura's capital city. It is not proper to launch the attack straight away. Let us camp here beyond the city limits. We shall plan the next move soon after".

Vadivelan took their suggestions and called Deva thachan (the architect of Devas) to build the camping site there. Viswakarma bowed at his feet and erected a well-equipped war camp, greater than Mahendrapuri with His Blessings. It was named Hemakootam.

Muruga got off his chariot and entered the newly built city with his army of demons. He proceeded straight to his special abode there.

## 51. Muruga and Narada meet

When Narada came to know that Muruga and his army of demons are camping at Hemakootam ready to declare war against Soorapadhman he went straight to Soorapadhman and greeted him.

Sooran could not recognize who he was. So he asked him, "Who are you? Where do you live? Why did you come here?"

"O Soorapadhma! I am one of the sages living in Mount Kailas. I do pray everyday for your fame and safety of your clan. I do not like Devas, so I give them lot of troubles and make them suffer. I am a close friend of your guru, Sukracharya. I am known as Narada. I have come to give you an important news. In order to kill you Lord Siva has created a son from his third eye on his forehead and sent him with the Devas. The Devas have surrendered to him and have complained that you are ill treating all of them beyond limits. So he has promised to save them from you. He was the one who destroyed Krouncham and killed your brother Târaka. He has taken a vow to annihilate you with your kith and kin. Now he is camping with the Devas in the northern border of your city. Take immediate action against him. I came to warn you in advance.

Soorapadman laughed, but his mad rage was invisible in his eyes. "O Narada! I have already heard about this child. He has no idea about my city. Can he wage a war here? It is just like an elephant calf entering the cave of a lion. I had spared him so far only because I thought he was a child. Since he is bold enough to cross the sea and reach my city limits, I shall not be kind to him any longer. Just because Târaka and Krounchan have been destroyed he is under the impression that he can easily win over me also. What is he, compared to my soldiers? I shall send my son Bhanugopan now and you can wait and see what happens to him."

"Soorapadma! I am unable to explain as to how happy I will be to witness that fighting scene. I did not want you to be indifferent. Now, I know that you have realized the seriousness. I have no fears now. I shall leave", Narada said and left the place.

Soorapadman's face became red with anger. He called Ghoran and Utghoran who were there and asked them to bring Varuna. When they brought Varuna there, he was shivering, not knowing what is to happen next. "O Varuna! What are my orders to you? None of my enemies ought to have crossed the sea. What were you doing when they came? Why did you not prevent them? How did Muruga and his army cross the sea? Have you decided to flout my orders?" Sooran shouted. Varuna fell at his feet and he could not get up. He was so terrified to reply.

"Asurendra! Please listen to me. Muruga and the Devas have reached here by air. The army of demons walked along the sea. When I tried to stop them, they pushed me aside and walked over me. The dust is all over my body and I am so ugly now. When a snake hears the noise of thunder, it gives up its life. Please believe my words", he said.

Right then the spies came in and reported that Muruga and Devas are camping in the north. Sooran rose violently. He wanted to see the enemies' heads roll on the grounds at once.

"So, they have come to our entrance itself to meet their ends. Get Bhanugopan at once." He ordered. Bhanu gopan arrived there within a short time with his ministers and generals.

"Father! You sent word for me! I am here! Give me orders. I shall execute them." He said.

"Oh! My son! This is the time for you to prove your mettle. The son of the Lord has reached the northern frontiers of our city with Devas and demons. March with your army and come back victorious". Sooran ordered. Bhanugopan saluted his father once again and took his blessings.

"I start moving right now, as per your orders. I shall defeat Muruga and make him take to his heels. I shall also hold captive Brahma, Indra and other Devas who defied you and bring them before you", he said.

He went back to his palace and ordered his army to get ready. He then went to his Ayudhasala and prayed to Veeralakshmi, took his astra and started. The garland of Tumba flowers was adorning his chest. Vijayan, Nemiyan, Mayan, Masali, Kandakan, Muran, Karan, Mongan, Dasamukhan, Kanali, Chandan, Vicchandan, Chomukan, Madhu, Sasijit, Susimukan, Asani, Soorniakethu, Asurasenan and other commanders also started with their weapons. Ten thousand vellam soldiers, ten thousand vellam chariot, horses and elephants formed the huge army. The noise of their departure to the war field was heard in the heavens.

Seeing Bhanugopan on the move, Narada met Muruga and greeted him. "My lord! Soorapadman's son Bhanugopan is on the march with his ten thousand-vellam army to fight you. Sooran has sent his son to wage war on you. We should not under estimate the asura's son. Even as a child in the cradle, he caught hold of the sun and kept him under check. Either you or Lord Siva alone can fight him and win him over. None else can handle him. He has captured Varuna Pâsam and Yama's soolam also. So, you have to personally go to the war", he said.

Karthikeyan smiled and called Veerabhahu. "O Brother! Sooran has sent his son Bhanugopan with his army to fight us. You shall go with thousand vellam army and come back with victory", Muruga said.

Veerabhahu took the Lord's blessings and started on his chariot. A thousand vellam army followed him. When asuras saw Veerabhahu approaching, they informed Bhanugopan that the messenger who had come the previous day was out there to fight again. Bhanugopan felt happy to meet him.

"Very Good. He ought to have met his end yesterday. He will fall a prey to my astras today. Let me handle him and the boy who sent him to me will also take to his heels very soon," he said.

He came out from the northern gate and had a look at the army forces. There was no Deva there. He thought the demon army must be stronger than Devas. So he was planning to use his war tactics suitably.

Both sides, had a fierce battle. Asuras pounced upon the demons and attacked them with a lot of weapons. Javelins were thrown. The elephants wielded iron rods and punished the enemies. The soldiers on the horses used sharp Vels and Javelins; some others hurled mountains, rocks and trees at the enemy's army. Those affected lost their limbs and died.

The demons were also highly mighty. They returned Asura's war tactics with double force. Blood flowed everywhere. Attacked by demons and their armours, Asuras ran hither and thither for their life.

Looking at the bad shape of the army, one of the commanders named Anali just pulled his bowstring. The noise was so great that demons were shaken and the Devas in the camp shuddered. Anali fought with firearms while one of the demons' generals – Singan returned the attack. He killed the horses drawing the chariots with the staff in his hand. While Anali sent in simultaneously a multitude of astras, Singan got on his chariot and broke Anali's bow.

Anali angrily hit Singan with his staff. Singan prevented the astra touching his body with one hand and slapped him on his chest. Immediately, he took him in his hand above his head, swerved him around several times and threw him on the ground. He went to pieces!

Chandan, another general, saw the fate of Anali and stopped Singan with his attacks. Both of them indulged in fierce fighting with the staffs, with the result both fell down exhausted.

In order to help Chandan, another general Mâyan ran to him. Neelan from the demons' side attacked him. Mâyan pierced Neelan's chest with his Soolayudham. Blood was flowing out profusely. Neelan got wild and hit Mâyan on his chest. When he stood there in a weak state, Neelan held Mâyan tightly and drank blood from his neck making a slit there. Mâyan lost his life suffering from severe pain.

In the meanwhile Singan and Chandan got up. Singan broke Chandan's staff to pieces. Though he had no weapon, Chandan pounced upon Singan with all his might. Singan chopped one of his hands with his staff. Chandan used the broken hand itself as a weapon and attacked Singan with courage. Singan managed to escape and finally slapped him on his face. That made him die instantly.

After Chandan, it was now Ajamukhan's turn to fight Singan. A demon general named Madhu stopped him mid way. Ajamukhan pulled his bowstring and made a big noise. Madhu did not care but up-rooted a tree and hurled it at him. Ajamukhan lost his balance and his bow and arrows fell from his hand. When Madhu saw him without weapons, he pitied him and allowed him to get away alive. Ajamukhan was put to shame so badly, but he gathered himself after a while. His target was again Madhu whom he attacked with full force. When Madhu was still able to withstand all astras, Ajamukhan stole Vishnu Chakra by a magic and threw it at Madhu. As he was without weapons, Vishnu Chakra did not touch him, but went back to Ajamukhan who had sent it and cut off his head. The chakra then returned to his master – Vishnu.

As asura forces were losing ground, Bhanugopan entered the scene and sent in a shower of weapons on demons. When they returned them with big mountains and trees, Bhanugopan made them all useless. Because of his indiscriminate fighting the front row of demons army got shattered. They retreated and reached Veerbhahu's line behind.

At that time, Ugran from the demons' side attacked Bhanugopan, who tried to pierce his body with his arrows. As his body was so hard and strong, all the arrows got broken and fell on the ground. Ugran destroyed all those arrows with an iron rod. Then he killed the horses of the chariot, which was also crushed to pieces. Within a second, Bhanugopan got another chariot and attacked Ugran. In return, Ugran lifted him with his chariot and threw him into the sky. Though Bhanugopan fell down, he managed to get up and throw Ugran with his two hands up in the air. When Ugran was falling, he hit him with his Soolayudham by which Ugran fainted on the ground.

Dandi interfered now and hit Bhanugopan with the peak of a mountain. His horses were also killed. But Bhanugopan sent ten thousand Soolayudhams at a time and made Dandi faint.

When another demon leader Pinaki rushed to help Dandi, Bhanugopan hit him also with thousand arrows. Many other leaders also attacked Bhanugopan one after the other, but everyone retreated after a while unable to withstand his weapons.

Next came, Veerabhahu's lakh soldiers. There was a heavy exchange of arrows from both sides. Bhanugopan's horses were killed. The driver was no more. Flag was cut. The top of the chariot crumbled, but Bhanugopan again fought with another chariot and made them all run away.

Veerakesari, one of Veerabhahu's brothers now opposed Bhanugopan. He shocked him by his Ardhachandra astras (Crescent moon shaped weapons). His skill and strength were amazing. Both were equally good match for each other. Bhanugopan finally sent the Narayanastra. Veerakesari could not prevent it in anyway. The astra pierced Veerakesari's chest and he fainted on the chariot itself. By Muruga's grace, he still survived.

Veeramarthandar entered the field next. Bhanugopan waged a fierce battle with him also with countless weapons and broke his bow and the chariot. Veeramarthanda tried to cut him with his sword. But Bhanugopan's shield was pretty strong. Bhanugopan struck on his chest and forehead, by his sword with the result that he also fainted.

Next to come was Veerarakadar. He thought of Lord Muruga before launching his attack. Bhanugopan's crown was smashed to pieces. His arrows were very well aimed at Bhanugopan who in turn destroyed his chariot by thousand arrows. He took another chariot and resumed fighting while his bow got broken. He jumped in the air and caught hold of Bhanugopan's chariot to be hurled aloft. While falling, Bhanugopan hit the enemy with his Soolayudham and Veerarakadar fell to the ground unconscious. Bhanugopan got up on his feet again, when Veerandakar, Veeramaheswarar, Veeradheerar, Veeramahendrar and Veerapurandarar – all the five surrounded him from all sides. Bhanugopan was absolutely unruffled and he went round and round in his chariot, attacking all of them simultaneously. All the five were stunned at his extraordinary skills. They only had time to prevent his attacks but not retaliate any. Having defeated everyone who confronted him, Bhanugopan drove his chariot in front of Veerabhahu, who on seeing him merely pulled the string of his bow and its noise was deafening and terrifying the asuras.

Bhanugopan laughed and said, "Oh! You are not the son of Siva, whom I wanted to fight with. Don't you imagine that you can destroy all of us, just because you have killed my father's brother. He has sent you again because that boy was afraid. Yesterday you escaped. I should have met you yesterday. My father did not send me. So, you killed my younger brother and destroyed our city also. Today, you are caught. You cannot escape now. I will kill you and also take that Siva's son captive."

Veerabhahu smiled and said, "A true soldier never boasts about himself. Instead, show yourself in action". There was heavy exchange of weapons between the two. It was so fearful a fight that was being witnessed and cheered by one and all. Sometime they were not to be seen because of the rain of weapons. Suddenly they would come out of those clouds as if the sun was rising. Their chariots were spinning incessantly. Bhanugopan broke Veerabhahu's bow. Veerabhahu angrily made

Bhanugopan's crown fall off his head and broke his chest shield. He was soaked in blood and looked like the setting sun.

Veerabhahu's astras played havoc for the asura army. Those wounded and killed were countless. Bhanugopan pounced upon Veerabhahu and hit him with seven hundred arrows. Veerabhahu's chariot broke and his driver and horses were killed. Again he got on another chariot but Bhanugopan did not give up this time also. Any number of times, they attacked each other. The fight continued on and on and without any interval or lull.

Finally Bhanugopan realized that Veerabhahu will not fall for any astra. He used his magical skill and rose to the sky. He sent the Mohanastram, given to him by Brahma. The demons came under its spell and fainted. Bhanugopan attacked them from the air.

Veerabhahu was free from the magic and still could not decide on its antidote quickly. Muruga was monitoring the events in the battlefield from a distance. He sent His astra to counter the Mohanastram. Before it could exactly reach the field, the demons were already on their feet again, by its effect.

**Veerabhahu's patience was failing. He decided to kill Bhanugopan and used Sivastra. Bhanugopan did not have his own Sivastra to counter the on-coming one. He had kept his astra in his puja room, as he usually does not take it out unless it was necessary. So, for fear of being killed by Veerabhahu's Sivastra, he slipped away from the field and reached his palace.**

When Bhanugopan went away, the asuras could not oppose the demons and so, they also retreated. Demons wanted to take Bhanugopan captive, as he was weak now.

,

But Veerabhahu prevented them, as it was not proper to chase a warrior who was retreating from the field. The demons sounded their victory, as the Sun was setting in the West.

The war stopped, as it was dusk. Devas showered flowers on Veerabhahu in their happiness. Everyone returned to the camp and Muruga was apprised of the day's events. He was all praise for Veerabhahu.

Soorapadhman had his own reporter at the battlefield. They described Bhanugopan's consistent effort to fight the enemy in the field and his final return in fear of Sivastra. Soorapadman was quite angry at the end result and took a vow to go to the warfront himself the next day.

## 52. The splendid war by Asura's sons

Soorapadhman did not sleep the whole night. It looked as though the night was too long. He very much wanted to defeat the demons and the son of Lord Siva. Bhanugopan's returning after the day's war, without achieving a decisive end, was infuriating him.

He did not wait till the day dawned. He woke up in the early hours itself. He ordered all the soldiers in the 1008 countries to assemble at Mahendrapuri ready to go to war. All the four wings of the army rushed with a greater speed than the wind. Soorapadhman took his bath and offered Puja to Veeralakshmi, the Goddess of valour. He wore his shields and took his armours. With a garland of tumba flowers in his chest, he started. He went up the highest peak of a mountain and inspected the army. Asuras greeted him loudly. Singamukhan's son Athisooran and Târaka's son Asurendran joined him. He blessed them both and asked them to take charge of the army units and lead them to battle.

Tondakam, Tudi, Ambai, Tooriyam, Murudu, Kombu, Pataham and other musical instruments were played. The elephant trumpeted and the horses neighed. The chariot wheels started rolling. A thick cloud of dust arose. When the armies marched on, the Sun rose in the East.

When Indra saw Soorapadhman leading the army to the war, he reported it to Lord Muruga in great fear. "My Lord! Sooran has come to fight the battle. You should defeat him", he said. Vayu brought the chariot for Muruga. Velan started on his march to defeat Sooran. Brahma and Vishnu showered flowers and saluted him. Devas recited vedic verses. Takkai, Udukkai, Sallari, Tadari and other instruments played as the demon forces marched on.

At the battle field, there was hectic clash between the two equal forces. Asuras threw rocks and trees. Demons used weapons like Dandam, Kazhumal, Chakram, Vel, Soolam, etc., Arrows were flying in the air.

A commander of the demon army, Ugran opposed Athisooran. Weapons flew on either side, Ugran wielded the Dandam on Athisooran. It broke his chest shield. In return, Athirsooran pierced Ugran's body with a series of arrows. Ugran destroyed Athisooran's chariot and horses. Athisooran got on another chariot and hastened to send Âgneyâstram. Looking at the weapon emitting fire, Ugran prayed to Muruga and devoured it. Lord's grace saved him. Next came Varunapâsam, Yamadandam and Vayvâstram and Ugran devoured them also. Athisooran was surprised and angrily sent Sivastram now. Asura thought that Ugran will now be dead. Devas were worried as to how Ugran will face it. Sighting Sivastram, Ugran threw his staff away and closed his eyes in prayer to Lord Siva, chanting His panchakshara – the five-letter mantra. When he stood there in prayer and also without any defense or weapon, Sivastram came round him and returned. As per Siva's condition while he gave the astram to Athisooran, if it is aimed at an armless person, it will return to Himself. Hence, the Sivastram did not harm the defenseless Ugran but returned to Lord Siva.

Devas showered flowers and danced in joy. Athisooran was pained at his jubilation. He jumped off his chariot and pounced upon him with his Dandayudham. Ugran stopped him with one hand and smashed his Dandayudham by the other hand. While he hit him hard with that, Athisooran's chest was ripped open into two pieces and he fell down dead on the ground.

When Asurendran knew this, he attacked demon ranks with great force. Kanakan a demon leader, jumped on to

Asurendra's chariot and killed its driver in a single blow. When Asurendran stood shocked for a while, Kanakan broke his bowstring. Asurendran used another bow and sent a thousand arrows together aiming at Kanakan's shoulders. When he was bleeding profusely from his shoulders, he stood motionless due to extreme pain.

Unmathan, another demon leader saw Kanakan's condition and rushed to oppose Asurendran. But he also could not contain him. Asurendran fought very well and made Unmattan retreat. At that time another leader Mathan threw the peak of a mountain at him.

Asurendran took it on his chest without fear. It bounced back as a ball without harming Asurendran. Mathan also succumbed to Asurendra's arrows and lost his balance. Next followed Singan, but he also could not gain an upper hand over Asurendran.

When the demon leaders were losing the fight with Asurendra one after the other, one of Veerabhahu's soldiers Dandakan sent in number of arrows together aiming at Asurendran's face. Though he found it quite hard to withstand this forceful attack, he gathered himself and sent eight astras well aimed at Dandakan's forehead. Bleeding heavily Dandakan had to retreat.

After Dandakan, Somukhan and Vijayan tried to show their might to Asurendran. But whoever fought with him, became tired and withdrew, because Asurendran was incessantly keeping them engaged with his arrows. If his bow was broken, he got it replaced by another in quick succession.

Veerabhahu realised that all the demon leaders were struggling hard to face Asurendran and so, he decided to destroy him. Both of them faced each other in a stiff fight as they were equally talented and trained in war fare.

Veerabhahu literally pierced Asurendra's body fully with his rain of arrows. Though bleeding, Asurendran also returned the attack by a thousand crescent-moon shaped astras on Veerabhahu. He was also fully drenched with blood, but the war continued vigorously. If one chariot was broken, both could get another chariot almost instantaneously.

Veerabhahu angrily rose in the sky and landed on Asurendran's chariot. By his sudden jump, the chariot broke into two. He drew his sword and cut off the asuran's hand. The asuran took his Dandam in the other hand and pounced on Veerabhahu. He stopped him and cut off his head in a jiffy.

Devas rejoiced at the death of Asurendra. The rest of asura army retreated, as their leader was no more.

## 53. Sooran's fury

Soorapadhman was watching the fight, sitting on his chariot from one side of the battlefield. He was greatly distressed at the demise of both the sons and also for the retreating army. He made a big noise from his bowstring and asked his driver to take him to the front row.

Devas were shivering at the very sight of Sooran himself getting ready to fight. They merely wanted to escape from his anger, but not to oppose him. Veerabhahu signalled to his army to attack. All the 108 commanders pounced upon Sooran in one go, with their huge armies.

Sooran was least worried, even when the enemy was attacking him from all sides. He swerved round and prevented all the arrows. When mountain peaks and rocks were hurled at him, he could still make them go to pieces by his arrows. Even before the demons could think of the next weapon, Sooran's weapon put them down. Veerabhahu's lakh soldiers also came to help the demons, but all of them got too tired in no time and retreated.

Veeramarthanda came to the front and opposed Sooran. But none of his weapons could even approach him; Sooran had already sent his arrows to pierce Veeramarthanda's chest. He fell down like a tall tree and died.

Veerarakshatar came forward now and Sooran aimed his arrows at him, very casually. Veerarakshatha sent thousand arrows and tried to block Sooran's field of vision completely. But Sooran's arrows could easily get through that cover, just as a boat steers clear through water.

Veerarakshatha got wild and jumped on Sooran's chariot. He tried to cut the Sooran's bow with his sword. But alas! The bow remained intact and the sword got broken. Sooran laughed and drew him near so as to kill him with his sword. But on second thoughts he spared him, as the enemy had no weapon to defend himself. He kicked him like a ball and he fell at a distance and fainted. Veeramahendran who was watching Sooran's acts wanted to take revenge on him. He went round and round his chariot and continuously attacked him from all sides. But Sooran also met him on all sides circling along with him. After a stiff fight, Veeramahendrar jumped into Sooran's chariot but Sooran hit his knees and shoulders and made him unconscious.

Veeradheeran came next and Sooran made him faint near his chariot attacking him with arrows. Veeramahes waran now threw a Vel at his chest. Sooran's thousand arrows to counter the Vel went in vain. Sooran's shield saved him from the Vel, which went to pieces as if made of glass. Sooran mocked at him and made him also faint by his seven arrows.

Veerakesari attacked Sooran with great noise. Sooran again sent another seven arrows to break his bow and the chariot. Veerakesari now threw a mountain peak at him but Sooran could stall it with just one arrow. Then he sent arrows in succession to make Veerakesari bleed heavily. Then he came near him and slapped him on his chest. His bow got broken and Sooran made him go round and round and finally threw him far away into the Ocean of Milk.

Veerapurandara and Veerantaka also faced Sooran next, but met the same fate as others. No weapon could deter Sooran even for a moment and he was quite energetic, steady and strong in the field. Veerabhahu came forward now as all his brothers had already failed.

Soorapadhman was fretting and fuming at him like a volcano. "Just because you came as a messenger you could get back alive. Today, the position is different. I shall certainly overpower you and kill you also", he said.

"Soorapadhma, I act according to my Lord's orders. The other day I fulfilled my assignment as a true messenger. Now I am your enemy in this battle field. Let us not waste time talking. You fight me now", Veerabhahu said.

Soorapadhman was furious. His eyes were red with anger. He speedily sent a plethora of arrows in order to hide Veerabhahu's field of vision. But Veerabhahu easily came out of the smoke screen of arrows, just as the Sun comes out from behind the clouds. When he shot him with arrows, they fell as flowers on Sooran who laughed at him in ridicule. Veerabhahu got wild and sent the Yamastra. Soorapadman again laughed and did nothing to stop the upcoming Yamastra. When it came near him, it fell down as dust! Then Veerabhahu sent Âgneyâstra, Nirutyastra and Indrastra one after the other. None of them worked and as Sooran was laughing at them, all of them either failed or touched him as a flower.

Veerabhahu was stunned at the mighty pose and cool attitude of Sooran. He had been gifted and blessed by the Lord so much that the Brahmastram and Narayanastram also had no sway over him.

"Oh Veerabhahu! Do you now realize as to who I am? You and your men are relying upon all these astras which can do no harm to me. Even Brahma and Vishnu have failed in fighting with me. If at all you want to save your life, better run away", he said.

Veerabhahu was feeling very much jolted. He prayed to Lord Siva and sent Sivastram on Sooran. It was such a fierceful one that the whole world felt its intensity and strength. Soorapadhman also prayed to God and sent his Sivastram to counter it. Both astras dashed against each other. Finally as they could not destroy each other, they returned to the respective senders. Thus, practically, no astra could be used to fight Sooran.

Now Veerabhahu thought of Lord Muruga and sent a Vel on Sooran, which went straight to his chest. But broke into two. Next went Veerabhahu's Dandam. Sooran sent his Dandam, which nullified it and also attacked Veerabhahu's chest. Veerabhahu felt as if a mountain dashed on his chest and lost his balance. As he fell down unconscious in his chariot, his driver Vishali took the chariot away within a second.

"Veerabhahu has fallen", shouted Sooran and the asuras rejoiced and attacked the demons with renewed vigour. There was utter damage and disaster everywhere.

Lord Muruga who was watching everything from the rear side got up angrily and told the driver of his chariot to take him immediately near Soorapadhman. Soorapadhman saw the son of Lord Siva sitting in his chariot shining with the brightness of a crore Suns. Six faces beaming like red lotuses, twelve eyes, ornament adorned the ears, a golden crown, broad chest with beautiful garlands, twelve hands with different weapons, anklets on the feet, Soorapadman had a vivid darshan of every aspect of the Lord's son with great surprise.

"Is this small boy going to kill me?" He had all love and also indifference for him. Muruga smiled at him. When Devas, right from Indra, shiver before him, he was surprised to see the small boy making bold to smile at him. Though shaken for a minute, Sooran laughed.

"O my child! You are so young when one does not know what fear is. Have you not seen that your army had been destroyed? Your demon leaders are not to be seen anywhere? Veerabhahu, who came as a messenger and gave me stories is no more. Even your father Lord Siva, Vishnu, Brahma do not dare to oppose me! Devas have misled you to the battle field. Please do not be carried away by their word and face your end. Just because Krounchan and Târaka could be defeated do not take me also for granted. Please go away", Sooran said.

Vadivelan looked at Soorapadhman and smiled again. "Soorapadhma! You have not realised the inherent ego in your words. You could win my father's love and have been blessed with many privileges. You have acquired a status in life, which even Indra can never aspire for. Countless treasures are at your feet. You are the ruler of 1008 countries. So you are belittling me as a boy and doubt my power and prowess. The moment you started boasting about yourself, you have not realized that you are on your way to be doomed to total disaster. When we wage a war we should never underestimate the enemy. Whether he is young or old, it is but only proper to face them. It is better to understand me in action than by mere words", the Lord said.

"After all a small boy is making fun of me" thought Sooran and sent thousands of arrows at him. Muruga stopped them all mid-way in the air. He sent fourteen astras to pierce his shoulders. But they went in vain. Sooran's body was like a huge rock. The Lord broke his bow with a thousand arrows but he got another bow to continue the attack.

Muruga sent seven arrows and cut the umbrella above Sooran's chariot. His one arrow was sufficient to break his crown. Thousands of arrows destroyed all his armaments. Devas were aghast at the ease with which Muruga was fighting the mighty asura.

Soorapadhman stood without any weapon to defend himself. He did not even know that his bow had been broken. Asuras immediately surrounded him to give him protection. Muruga now started attacking the asuras. His Chakrayudham went into their army. When they were being destroyed by the Chakra, all their efforts to counter its attack went futile. Within a period of a short time, the hundred thousand vellam Asuras were reduced to dust after which the Chakrayudham returned to Muruga.

Soorapadhman felt sorry that his whole army was destroyed completely by a small boy within a short span and he was at a loss to know as to what weapon was used by him. He sent his Brahmastram with anger. Muruga's Vel came and devoured it. Sooran's Narayanastram also met the same fate. Sooran sent Sivastram next. It was so fierce that the whole Earth shook. Demons ran hither and thither. Devas were terribly afraid and prayed to Lord Siva. Muruga saw the Sivastram approaching him and realized that it was his father's weapon. He politely stretched his hand and it landed in his hands with filial affection.

Soorapadhman got the first jolt only now. At last, he realized that his opponent was not a small child. For once he thought he was equal to him and tried to change his strategy.

Now Muruga stood up in his chariot with the bow in his hand and addressed Sooran. "Soorapadhma! You have been torturing Devas without limits. For a long time, you have imprisoned them and the son of Indra. I sent you a message and requested you to release them, but you did not agree. That is why I have come to wage a war with you. Even now it is not late. It would not take a long time for me to finish you when you stand defenseless now. But it is not a right course in war. I am not boasting that I am capable of doing this or that, just as you were bragging a short while ago. You would have, by now, known that I cannot be taken for a ride as a small boy. Your hundred thousand vellam army has been reduced to nil. You have witnessed it happen right under your nose. Let me give you another chance. If you release the Devas from prison, I can still allow you to live."

What can Soorapadhman answer? He was boiling like a volcano. What if the army of hundred thousand vellam gets wiped out? He has been blessed with a boon by Lord Siva that nothing other then his own power can win him. Should he fear someone said to be Lord Siva's son?

His army may be destroyed; his weapons may be lost; What should be his next move? He can try again with new forces. With these thoughts, Sooran created a magical spell around in the battlefield and under its cover, he reached his palace in Veeramahendrapuri. He did not speak to anyone there. He sat alone and started planning a strategy to defeat the mighty enemy, who is but a small boy!

When Soorapadman was not to be seen in the battle field, Devas and demons started rejoicing. Asuras started retreating in fear. Devas and Demon leaders got permission from Muruga to chase the asuras, enter their city and attack the compound wall.

Athighoran was guarding the compound wall. His soldiers were wielding Tomaram, Parasu, Soolam and such other weapons. A fierce war took place and there was hectic fighting from both sides.

Unable to fight with the son of the Lord, Sooran had disappeared from the war field under a magical smoke screen. This gave the Devas and the demons a new impetus to fight the Asuras. Devas tore the Asuras to pieces and there was a huge loss of lives there.

Athighoran, true to his name, fought bravely. He attacked Devas and demons with great might and Devas had a tough time. A demon leader Meghan threw a mountain at him, but he could push it aside. Meghan next caught hold of him and slapped him in his cheek, which proved fatal to him.

Devas and demons now pounded the compound wall and the surrounding moat was filled up with its debris. Whichever asura was sighted, he was thrown into the moat. The fish and sharks in the sea took away the dead bodies of the asuras. As the sun set at that time, the army returned to Muruga's camp.

When Bhanugopan heard that his father had returned from the battle field, tired and dejected, he went to see him. He had never seen him sitting all alone, in a thoughtful depressed mood. He felt sad at his sorrowful state. He went near him and said:

"Father! I came to see you as I heard that you had returned from the war field. Yesterday Devas and others just could not stand against me and fight me down. Had you been there, you would have been proud of me. Veerabhahu who came as a messenger and killed my brother, was totally baffled. I deployed Mohanastra and everything came to a standstill there. At that time Siva's son used another antidote and cleansed the air. I wanted to fight with him today, face to face with new replenished forces. By that time, you had started and I stayed away. I was hoping that you would take me along, but you did not. You need not go to fight the small boy. Why should you go when we are all here? Well the past is past. Let us not talk about it. Tomorrow please allow me to go. You will feel happy when the spies report about what is going to happen there. I will not return unless I take Muruga captive with me. That is definite."

Soorapadhman silently heard him and laughed.

"My son! I am encouraged very much by your soothing words. But he is not a small child as you imagine. I am the only one who can face him. I do not discourage you from going to war tomorrow. You deal with Veerabhahu separately and I will win over that Muruga myself."

"Father, if that is your view I shall abide by it", Bhanugopan said. When he returned to his palace, reports reached him that Athighoran was dead and the moat had been drained. The compound walls have been smashed and the main gate had been destroyed. He was very angry and called asurathachan to repair everything immediately. Over night everything was restored to its place and the moat was made further deep. He then called Mâkâyan, another mighty asuras leader to take charge of the new compound wall. He left with his army at once.

The night was slowly wading away.

## 54. The prince fights again

Bhanugopan did not sleep that night. He was waiting for the dawn. He finished his morning chores quickly and got ready to start. The previous day's defeat was worrying him. He was planning to employ new strategies and weapons for the war on that day. So, he thought of his father's mother, Mâyai.

Mâyai appeared before him and asked, "Bhanugopan! Why did you want to see me?"

"Grandma! I am going today to fight with Veerabhahu. Day before yesterday I was tossed about too much by him. With all my hectic fighting, I could not conquer him. Today, I must win over him and his men positively. Give me a suitable weapon to fight him", he said.

"My dear child! Your drifting from the path of virtues was the basic reason for your defeat. You joined hands with your father and tortured the Devas. You harmed many sages. Just because you were bent upon doing evils only, your weapons failed you. Anyway, let the past be forgotten. Who can win over destiny? I will give you a magical astra. You can use it chanting this mantra and it will enable you to conquer any kind of enemy".

Mâyai gave him the astra with the mantra. Bhanugopan was happy. He wore his shields and started off to the battlefield with a huge army. There were ten thousand vellam horses, ten thousand vellam elephants, ten thousand chariots and twenty thousand vellam soldiers.

As soon as he reached the main gate, he called an asura with a thousand horse heads and sent word to Veerabhahu. As Bhanugopan had taken a vow to finish Veerabhahu that day, the messenger was to invite him to the field.

Accordingly, when the asura conveyed the message to Veerabhahu, he laughed. "Do you know what is to happen today? I am determined to take the life of your Bhanugopan. Go and tell him that", he said.

The news of Bhanugopan calling Veerabhahu to fight reached Muruga. He called him and said, "My dear brother! You have a call from Bhanugopan. He is a wicked asura, as you are aware. You go and face him. In case, he deploys any magic, my Vel will take care of you". Veerabhahu took his blessings and left with the demon army and his lakh soldiers.

The battlefield witnessed a fierce fight between the two forces. The casualities on both sides were heavy and many lay there wounded or dead. Even horses and elephants were used as weapons. Bhanugopan and Veerabhahu fought terribly. It was an amazing sight that both could stop each other's weapons mid air. When their chariots were moving, the earth quaked. They were on the ground sometime or in the air, attacking each other with no break at all.

Veerabhahu destroyed the asura army with his weapons and also cut open Bhanugopan's chest into two.

The Devas were laughing merrily and this enraged Bhanugopan more and more. He sent his Varunastram, making a big noise and the whole world shivered. It rose high like a sea, which was countered by Veerabhahu's Âgneyastram emitting fire. Along with Varunastram, it swallowed water even from the sea.

Asuras were shivering with fear. Bhanugopan consoled them and sent Vayvastram now. It rose like a tornado and devoured the demon army. Veerabhahu saw his forces being caught in the gale. He chose Nagâstram to oppose it. When thousands of snakes marched on emitting fire, Vayvastram was of little avail. When the snakes started attacking the asuras, they were shattered to pieces. Bhanugopan sent Garudastram now, which scared away the snakes. Veerabhahu opposed it with an astra with the power of Nandideva, which swallowed Garudastra.

Bhanugopan angrily sent Yamastram, which was also swallowed by Nandideva. Finally, mad with fury he sent Brahmastra. When it saw Nandideva, it bowed before him and returned saying that it was driven by Bhanugopan. The other course before Bhanugopan now was Narayanastram, which also fought with Nandideva briefly and then returned.

Finding that Veerabhahu was a very hard nut to crack, Bhanugopan sent Sivastram, which again was met by another Sivastram from his opponent. Both tried to put down each other vigorously, but it resulted only in Rudras and Kaalis coming out of them and fighting. By the sheer noise of their fighting, many Asuras died of shock.

The Devas and demons took shelter near Veerabhahu. There were sparks of fire all over the place. Chariots got burnt. Elephants and Horses were thrown about. There was total destruction everywhere. Bhanugopan's Sivastram lost its strength and went back to him. The whole asura army had perished and Bhanugopan stood alone.

When the two Sivastrams were fighting with each other, Soorapadhman could feel the tremor in his palace. He wondered whether it was the end of the world and sent his spies to check. When they reported what happened, he was feeling sorry that he took Veerabhahu lightly without assessing his power properly.

Bhanugopan was again jeered at by Devas and demons when they saw his helpless state. He finally decided to resort to magic now to defeat Veerabhahu. He rose up in the sky making himself invisible. As the sun had set by then Devas and demons declared themselves victorious in that day's war. They congratulated Veerabhahu and went to Muruga's camp to tell him about all the events of the day.

Bhanugopan watched the jubilant scenes from the sky. How would he return to his palace? Having promised to kill Veerabhahu, how can he tell his father that his entire army was wiped out, leaving only him all by himself? He could catch hold of Sun, even as a child, but what has happened to his prowess now? The enemy cannot be defeated by tricks. He has to face him directly, for which he had no weapons. All his weapons have already been lost!

Bhanugopan was in deep peril. He had only Mayastram left with him. He cannot use it hiding from the sky. Then he would be seen by the enemy. So, he has to save his honour and sneak away by using only his grandmother's trick .

He took Mayai's astra and prayed to it thus: "You go now and take my enemy's life out. You shall not be physically visible to anyone by your sound, sense and sight or by the mind. You go stealthily, without any one detecting your approach, take the life of Veerabhahu and his men, after mesmerizing them completely. Throw their bodies in Suddhodaka sea". With these orders, he let go Mâyai's astra.

Launched by Bhanugopan from his invisible place in the sky, the unique astra attacked Veerabhahu and his army. They became unconscious at once. As Muruga's grace was protecting them, they were still alive. Their unconscious bodies were wrapped up by the astra and thrown into the good water sea. The astra later stood guarding them there. Bhanugopan was happy and now came out to reach his palace.

He went straight to his father and fell on his lap shouting, "Veerabhahu is no more". Sooran could not believe his words and so expressed surprise.

"Yes father! The blemish to our valour has been wiped off. Veerabhahu and his army were put to such a lot of troubles in the war today. You would have been happy, if you were there to witness how they suffered at my hands."

"My son! The spies told me that your Sivastram also could not help you and you lost your whole army", asked Soorapadman.

"That was true, father. Sivastram could not even go near Veerabhahu who nullified all my weapons and astras one after the other. He ruined my entire army. But he could not do anything before my grandmother's Mayastram. All their bodies are now in Suddhodaka Sea for us to see", said Bhanugopan with a victorious pride.

Sooran was immensely delighted and he hugged his son. "I knew, my son, about your valour and I trusted you. You have restored our superior position now."

"Father, you can rest in peace now. I shall go again tomorrow and bring Siva's son captive before you". Sooran's joy knew no bounds. He nodded his head approving the next step proposed by his son.

When the father and son were rejoicing here, there was another miracle happening at the other end, which they did not know. When Bhanugopan's Mâyâstram had bundled up Veerabhahu and his men and thrown them into the sea in an unconscious state, Devas were startled and so, rushed to Muruga. Before they could reach, Narada had already apprised Muruga of what all had happened. Muruga got wild and took his Vel. "Please go at once and wake up Veerabhahu and his men lying unconscious in Suddhodaka sea", he directed his Vel.

The Vel went with unlimited fury. Sparks of fire were emitting from its sharp edges. Many poisonous snakes and multifarious weapons accompanied Vel. Hearing its great noise, Mâyâstram could no longer stay there and so it vanished into thin air. Veerabhahu and his men regained their consciousness. The king of the seas bowed low before Velayudham and saluted it.

"O Velayudham! You are here from the hands of Lord Siva's son. I salute you. Please have pity on me! I was not guilty in any way. Bhanugopan is a mighty asura, before whom I was helpless. So, I had to lie low fearing his revenge and punishments, without doing anything. Please forgive me". Veerabhahu and his men thanked Muruga for his abundant grace towards them.

## 55. The son's advice

Veerabhahu and his army men, who regained their consciousness through Muruga's grace, were returning by air to see him. On the way, when they saw Veeramahen drapuri, he recalled the cowardice of Bhanugopan who employed a cheap tactic, instead of fighting with him face to face. He not only made them lose their consciousness but also pushed them into a far-off sea. To return to the camp without taking revenge on him was not agreeable for him and his men.

They suddenly appeared at the western gate of Mahendrapuri and made a big noise. The soldiers there were perplexed at the sight of Veerabhahu and his demon army speeding towards their city. They could not imagine that they could return alive so soon, when the whole city was celebrating the victory of Bhanugopan despite the fact that the night had already fallen.

Western gate was being guarded by an asura leader, Vyagramukhan, who gave immediate orders to fight Veerabhahu and his men. At the entrance to the city, there was fierce fight. As the demon army had already met with a debacle during the day and also faced a lot of suffering, they were very ferocious and asuras could not meet their challenge. So, there was heavy loss for the asuras.

Vyagramukhan was confronted by Singan, a demon general. Both of them fought with Soolayudham and blood was flowing like a river. Still they went on and on until Singan defeated Vyagramukhan and kicked his dead body to a distance. The demons were jumping with joy.

The western gate was broken. The compound wall was smashed to the ground. They chased the asuras into the city. Anyone sighted on the way was done to death. Big mansions and towers were set on fire. Veerabhahu deployed very many fire arms which resulted in a big fire. Asuras were in great panic. Beautiful mansions went to ruins. Women and children were running out of their houses.

The spies carried the report to Soorapadhman. "Asurendra, Veerabhahu and his men who were pushed into the good water sea by your son Bhanugopan, have been saved by the Vel of Muruga. They have entered our city through the western gate with an aim to take revenge. Our guards have been killed and our mansions have been destroyed. They have set fire to the city and it is burning like hell".

Soorapadhman's anger was at the peak. He called the clouds, which were in waiting to destroy the worlds at the end of all ages. All those seven clouds were there at once and Sooran asked them to put out the fire. As per his orders, the clouds spread all over and started pouring. heavily with thunder and lightening. The great fire got quenched.

Veerabhahu was wondering as to what magic was done by Sooran to put down the wide spread fire in no time. Narada enlightened him that they were the clouds reserved for the end of all ages and suggested that he counters them with Vadamukhagniastra. Veerabhahu did likewise. Vadamukhagni sucked in all the water in the clouds and they dispersed without any trace immediately. Soorapadhman got a rude shock by this new development. He wanted to kill Veerabhahu straight away and Kumaran also without delay. His son Iraniyan, who happened to be nearby, tried to contain him.

"Father! How can you go, when I am still here? I have been thinking very seriously on all these events. We are such great giants that we rule over 1008 countries. Why should we equipped with such super natural powers, suffer? We were blessed by God Almighty and given a wonderful life. Still we are suffering now. Why are we facing disasters only, one after the other? It is all because we treat Devas with enmity. We are ill-treating them. We have imprisoned the son of Indra and Devas. We have compelled Varunan, Vayu and Agni to be our errand boys and do mean things for us. That is why God is angry with us. Should we incur His wrath, after having been the beneficiaries of His grace all along?"

"Father! Please think for a while. None survives God's anger. Manmatha was burnt. The three forts, the asura in disguise, were burnt. Antaka was pierced by Soolam and put to a lot of suffering. Kâla was kicked to death. Ganges, who boasted of her fast flow, was changed into a drop in Lord Siva's locks of hair. When the worst poison came out of the milk sea to ruin the whole world, Lord Siva took it and retained it in his neck to save the world. You are well aware of all these details".

"Let us take the examples of Devas also. When Vishnu took Narasimhavatara to destroy Hiranya, he sucked his blood and ran amuck causing disasters. Lord Siva had to calm him down finally. When Vishnu took Varahavatara to save Bhooma Devi, the Earth, from Hiranyakshan, he became wild again after fighting with the asura. When he was about to cause havoc all over the place, Lord Siva broke his protruding tooth and contained him. When the milk ocean was churned, the Mandra mountain was shaking badly. Vishnu had to become a tortoise and carry it on his shell. After that also he went crazy, making the sea water muddy and unsafe for the sea creatures. In order to save them, Lord Siva had to appear and control him, by removing its shell for his garland".

"When Brahma became too arrogant , Lord had to cut off one of his heads and punish him. When Daksha did a yâga, without offering the Havis (offering) to Lord Siva as required, because of his personal rivalry, Lord Siva had to undo the whole yâga and also make him get a goat's head. When sages did an inauspicious yâga in the forest to create Muyalagan and make him an agent to destroy Lord Siva, did He not drag him and stamp him under His feet?"

"Father! Please consider the lesson that we should get from all these episodes. Anyone who had incurred His wrath has not been spared alive or left unpunished. Because of Lord's anger with us only, he has created Muruga from his third eye in the forehead and sent him to punish us. Even now, it is not late. We have suffered enough. Let us release the Devas from the prison and send them back to Him. We will ask Him to pardon us. Once we repent for our mistakes whole-heartedly, we will be forgiven. If one does something wrong to a person who has been good, the evil that he did itself would bring about his end. No separate killer, Yama, is necessary to execute the job".

"We cannot still think of Muruga, our Lord's son, as a small boy. If we surrender ourselves now, it will not be a humiliation for us. If we avail ourselves of this last opportunity to mend our ways and stand corrected, it will be honourable for us. This alone is the proper benevolent route for us."

Soorapadhman listened to the long sermon from Iraniyan from the beginning without interrupting him. Every word  uttered increased his anger manifold. He laughed aloud like a thunder.

"Iranya! You have talked very well about the enemy's strength. Who taught you all this? They are to be punished first. You are blabbering some non-sense, without knowing who I am and what I am capable of. You have become terribly scared of the enemy. If you talk like this once again, you will lose your life. You coward! Get away from here", he shouted.

Iranyan realised that Sooran's mind cannot be changed by any amount of advice. He unnecessarily did not want to magnify his anger any more.

"Father, please forgive me. I am after all, a small boy. It was due to my ignorance that I blabbered. Please do not get angry with me. Give me permission. I shall leave at once to kill Veerabhahu and all other Devas right away".

Soorapadhman happily gave him permission to go to war. Iranyan took his weapons and his four thousand vellam strong army with him. He ordered his troops to encircle the enemy on all sides.

**When Iranyan with his three heads arrived majestically in his chariot, Veerabhahu was stunned. "What a magnetic personality!" he thought within himself. Narada came near and warned him. Iranyan was quite well versed in tricks and a mighty warrior too. One had to fight with him carefully. Veerabhahu asked his troops to attack the asuras and himself came to face Iranyan.**

As the two were equally strong heroes both of them fought fiercely. Iranyan simultaneously attacked Veerabhahu and also the demon forces. The demons got scattered. Neelan, a demon leader, immediately rushed to stop Iranyan.

Iranyan threw a Vel at him with anger. Neelan stopped it with a tree and also smashed his chariot. Iranyan got into another chariot and cut his chest into two parts. Neelan

threw Iranyan and his chariot together up in the air. When he fell down, Neelan kicked him again. Iranyan was suffering badly. He created an illusory figure like him. Neelan took the false image to be true and fought it. Now Iranyan attacked him from behind and made him lose his balance.

When Veerabhahu saw Neelan's unsteady condition, he grew angry and sent Gnanastram. It destroyed all the magical illusions of Iranyan. Again a great fight ensued. Weapons were flying criss-cross. The whole world was shivering. Blood flowed all over the area.

Iranyan, by now, realized that Veerabhahu could not be killed by any weapon. He also knew that it will be difficult to survive after fighting with him.

When Soorapadhman did not pay heed to his well-meant advice, Iranyan was sure of his end. He was equally sure that along with his father, Bhanugopan, Agnimukhan, Singamukhan and everybody else will die sooner or later in the war. At least somebody has to be alive to do their last rites. So, he wanted to escape from the battlefield and manage to stay alive. He used his magical skill and escaped. He went to the sea and stayed there as a fish. Veerabhahu understood that Iranyan got defeated and so he hid himself in the sea. He immediately blew his conch and announced his victory over him. The demons cheered him with joy. The sun also rose soon in the East to witness their happiness.

## 56. Agnimukhan Gets Killed

When Soorapadhman came to know that Iranyan had run away to hide himself in the sea after being defeated, he felt very much ashamed. Agnimukhan, one of his sons, came to him and asked him, "Father! Why are you looking so sad? What happened?"

"My dear son! I do not think that I have to experience more than what has already happened. Though I know my enemy's strength, I have not gone myself to put him down. Instead, I trust others foolishly. Iranyan went with all promises, but now he has been defeated and what more, he has run away and hid himself in the sea."

Agnimukhan said with all humility, "Father! Do not be worrying on that! Give me permission to go. I shall defeat Veerabhahu and make amends for Iranyan's cowardice."

Soorapadhman hugged his son blessed him and sent him to war. He started at once with all the weapons given to him by God and also the bow given by his grandmother, Mâyai.

Agnimukhan was very strong right from his birth. Even when he was in his mother's womb, his body could emit fire sparks. His grand mother Mayai had congratulated his mother Padumakomalai on his birth and blessed him that he can emit fire from his face any time he wants. That is why he was named Agnimukhan. If he gets angry he can spit fire from his face. He fought the eight mighty guards of the directions and brought all those Ashtadiggajas to the palace. When he was a child he brought the swan from Brahma and Garuda from Vishnu for his play. He had to be cajoled in several ways to get them released. The Sun and the Moon had been imprisoned by him and put to a lot of trouble.

Such a mighty Agnimukhan went to war accompanied by Somagandan, Soman, Sooryajit, Meghan, Pingalan and their armies. As soon as he reached the battle field, he sounded his bugle and invited Veerabhahu to fight. The demons ferociously dashed with the asuras. All kinds of weapons were deployed and fire sparks were seen when they dashed with each other. Both sides suffered heavy losses and there was a stream of blood flowing along.

Agnimukhan sent his commander Somagandan first to the front. Veerapurandarar opposed him with all his might and both attacked each other hard. Veerapurandarar cut off Somagundan's hand with just an arrow. At the same time, Meghan who was near Agnimukhan used his Dandam to kill Veerapurandarar's driver. This made Veerapurandarar so angry that he pierced Meghan's chest with a Vel and killed him.

When his commanders were destroyed thus, Agni mukhan got wild and blindly attacked Veerapurandarar. He used Ardhachandra arrows to chop off many heads and the trunks were dancing in the war field as if it was the end of the ages.

All the seven brothers of Veerapurandarar came to his help. Agnimukhan sent thousands of arrows at all of them. They also returned so many arrows that Agnimukhan found it difficult to cope with them. So, he used Sivastram next, which was mistaken for Âgneyastram. The seven brothers sent Varunastram. It was destroyed by Sivastram while it was racing. When they were attacked by Sivastram, they called out to their brother but died pathetically in the field. The rest of the army fled the scene and there was a big commotion and loud uproar in the front row.

Veerabhahu rushed there to see what was happening. Agnimukhan stopped him and shouted "Look here! I am waiting for you, Veerabhahu. You will very soon reach the place where you are destined to go". Hearing his challenge, Veerabhahu was fuming.

"You! son of the asura! Iraniyan ran away in great fear of facing me! So, you have come in his place, as an affectionate brother. You can do nothing to me. Except Bhanugopan, all the rest have fallen to my arrows. If you want to survive, better get lost at once", he said.

Agnimukhan sent his first arrow aiming at him. But it was stopped midway by Veerabhahu. Agnimukhan followed with several hard hit arrows. But Veerabhahu diverted all of them like a child's play. Agnimukhan felt that the enemy was ridiculing him and so sent thousands of arrows together to pierce his body. Veerabhagu also tried the same way to attack Agnimukhan. When he was bleeding very badly, he called out to his personal deity, Kaali to come to rescue him, as he had already prayed to her for help in times of need and stress. She appeared in response to Agnimukhan's prayers, with her thousand associates called Koolis. Looking at their red hair, sparkling eyes and ugly figures, demons were retreating. But Koolis were causing great havoc, attacking them as they were on the run. Kaali sent her Velayudham to take the lives of all demons. When that was on its way in high velocity and aim, Veerabhahu destroyed it with fourteen arrows. Kaali got wild and sent another Soolayudham, directing it for success at all costs. But Veerabhahu could again stop it with thousands of arrows.

**Kâli's anger was at its peak. She jumped down from her lion mount and got into Veerabhahu's chariot with her sword. Veerabhahu held all her eight hands by his single hand and punched her at her chest, with the other hand. She got hurt so**

**badly that blood flow was imminent. When she fainted, Veerabhahu kicked her out to the ground.**

Within a second, Kâli was up on her feet. She realised that Veerabhahu had the support from Muruga and none can ever harm him. She blessed Veerabhahu, "Agnimu khan offered lots of sacrifices for me and when I was pleased with them, he requested me to come and help him in warfare. When I came to help him, I could see your great valour and enjoy it too. I shall now disappear with my a team of Koolis. You shall kill Agnimukhan and come out victorious". Kâli and all her Koolis disappeared from the field.

Agnimukhan saw Kâli's exit after blessing Veerabhahu. He declared that he needs nobody's help and will fight all alone. He attacked with all force, but Veerabhahu left him greatly baffled with his counter attacks. He also broke his magical bow given by Mâyai.

Agnimukhan brought another bow and sent Brahmastram now. Veerabhahu sent Veerbhadrastram in reply which not only destroyed Brahmastram but also cut off Agnimukan's hand and returned to the sender with the enemy's life. Devas expressed their joy by showering flowers and cheering Veerabhahu. Agnimukhan's army attacked Veerabhahu. But all his twenty four thousand troops got killed except a few who ran away.

After the asuras took to their heels, Veerabhahu went to the front row to search for his seven wounded brothers. They were not to be seen alive. Ugran approached him and reported the death of all of them at the hands of Agnimukhan. Veerabhahu was in deep sorrow and wept bitterly on their dead bodies. After a while he controlled his grief and got up. "Even if Agnimukhan had sent the arrows at them, it was Kâla who took their lives away. Veerabhahu got very angry with Kâla. When Kâla came to take the life of Markendeya, Lord Siva had kicked him out with His leg. He has perhaps forgotten about it. Let me remind him", he thought.

"Carrying the divine Velayudham in his hand and protecting his devotees, Lord Muruga showers his Grace on all creatures. I am his younger brother Veerabhahu. You have taken away the lives of my seven brothers. Please bring them back to me". So wrote Veerabhahu on a palm leaf, tied it with an arrow and sent it to Yama's place.

Veerabhahu's arrow with the message crossed the seven seas and reached Yamapatnam situated South of Manasottara mountains. Dharmarajan took it in his hands and read the message. He started shivering in fear. He had not brought the lives of Veerabhahu's brothers. When he checked with his vision of wisdom and found that they were in Mount Kailas, he rushed there and saw them happily playing with some demon soldiers. Dharmarajan told them politely, "Blessed sons of Lord Siva! Veerabhahu is searching for all of you in the battlefield, please start, let us go".

All the seven sons started happily with Yama, got into their bodies, and came back to life.

Veerabhahu was very much delighted to see them again. He hugged them all and enjoyed their coming. Dharmarajan came there with his guards and said, "Veerabhahu! I did not take their lives. As they were hit by Sivastram, they had gone to Mount Kailas. I have brought them all from there". Veerabhahu praised Yama for the kind steps taken by him to restore them back. When they were all rejoicing here, Mahendrapuri was in deep mourning over the death of prince Agnimukhan. His mother Paduma komalai was in great grief and so were all others too.

## 57. Three thousand sons disappear

When Agnimukhan was killed in the war, Soorapadhman's three thousand sons came to console Sooran and took his permission to go to the war. They also took the asura army and a variety of weapons with them.

Now on the other side, the lakh soldiers and thousand warriors including Vijayan sought permission from Veerabhahu to fight the asura princes. When he consented to this proposal, Vijayan, Jayan, Rishabhan, Karaveeran, Atighoran, Achalan, Atikonan, Vamanan, Sasikandan and the rest attacked the Asuras like the tornado at the end of the ages. While they returned their attack, all the rest except Vijayan got totally perplexed, unable to do anything. Vijayan single handedly fought the entire asura troops and cut off their limbs by his arrows. But, as a big surprise the limbs started growing immediately, enabling the Asuras continue the fight. Vijayan realised that fighting the asura will be at a great risk for his life and so prayed to Muruga sincerely.

Muruga appeared in the sky and guided Vijayan. "Vijaya! Once upon a time, Brahma has given them a boon by which the limbs will grow for asuras whenever they lose them. Bhiravastram alone can kill them. Now it is for you to aim at them". He gave him Bhiravastram and disappeared.

Vijayan was very happy. He took it in his hand and again offered prayers before sending it. An asura captain, Unnarthan saw this and thought he is going to kill them all together with some mighty weapon. In order to stop it at the first stage itself, he sent Mâyâstram whose effect spread all over the place. Vijayan prayed to Muruga and soon his Bhiravastram destroyed Mâyâstram first and surrounded all the three thousand Asuras. All of them perished within a second. A few escaped and ran away. Veerabhahu blew his conch to indicate victory over the asuras. Devas showered flowers and greeted them. The Sun was happy at the destruction of asuras on that day and started setting in the West.

## 58. Diggaja gets back to its place

Soorapadhman was terribly distressed at the total loss of all his three thousand sons. His chief minister, Dharmagopan, consoled him.

When a true warrior goes to the battle field he should not be unduly rattled by the death of relatives or friends there. They ought not to retreat to mourn their death, but march forward with the sole aim of victory or death. Accordingly as a true warrior, Soorapadhman was advised not to mourn the death of his sons in the war.

He was bent upon taking revenge and will not rest until and unless Veerabhahu and Muruga were killed. As enough damage had been done to his kith and kin, he wanted to go to war himself. But Dharmagopan offered to go with his troops. He called for Pundareekam, the mighty elephant which guards the Southeast direction and rode off on it to the battle field.

When he saw Veerabhahu and his demon army, Dharmagopan was skeptical for a while about the outcome of the war. But he gathered himself, thinking of the fact that this time he was very well equipped to face the enemy with a large army and countless weapons.

The war began. Demons and Asuras dashed. Dharma gopan attacked the demons. His elephant Pundareekam threw the soldiers with his trunk, pierced them with his tusks, stamped them with his feet and thrashed them with his tail. The soldiers, on their part, attacked the elephant with deadly weapons and rocks. Bleeding profusely, the elephant still fought bravely chasing all away.

Veeramartthanda and Veerapurandara tried to stop the force and fury of Pundareekam with their arrows. But Dharmagopan made both of them helpless with his arrows. Veerabhahu now stood before him in his chariot. Dharmagopan angrily aimed his arrows at him. Veerabhahu aimed his Vel at him, which pierced him and came out through his back. He lost his senses and fainted on the elephant. Pundareekam went forward and destroyed Veerbhahu's chariot. He got another chariot and attacked the elephant with many arrows. When Pundareekam again marched forward, Veerabhahu caught its trunk by one hand and slapped on its cheek by the other, before he threw it at a distance. When Dharmagopan fell on the ground with the elephant, he regained his consciousness. He attacked Veerabhahu with Vajrayudham now. Veerabhahu stopped and snatched it, attacked him with it at once.

The heavy unexpected blow by Vajrayudham killed Dharmagopan.

After his death, Pundareekam went to Veerabhahu and saluted him. "I am one of the eight mighty elephants guarding the directions. I am assigned the South-east corner, but ever since Dharmagopan imprisoned me, I was his slave. I have suffered enough at his hands and I had to fight here also, as I cannot overrule his orders. Please understand my position and kindly allow me to go back to my place and resume my duties as the guardian of Southeast".

Veerabhahu gave permission to Pundareekam to go Southeast, as requested. Since the asura had already been defeated and it was night time, the war ended for the day. Veerabhahu and others returned to their camps happily.

## 59. Bhanugopan on the move

All the sons and the chief minister have perished in the war. Soorapadhman was quite upset by this fact and was sitting all alone brooding over the enormous losses. Nobody dared to approach him. So, the spies went in search of Bhanugopan.

"O Prince! Dharmagopan fought yesterday evening with the enemies and has gone to the world of the brave warriors. Yesterday afternoon, all your three thousand brothers have been killed in the war. Veerabhahu and his men, whom you had pushed into the good-water sea have been saved by Muruga and they are causing great havoc day after day. Your father is greatly distressed at the destruction of his dynasty. None dares to go near him. The enemies are rejoicing", they said.

Bhanugopan was furious and reached his father's place. On one side he was also distressed over the unhelpful turn of events and losses in the war, but all the same, he was fully aware of the ground realities with regard to Veerabhahu and his warriors. The great rule the 1008 continents by his father was coming to an end. Otherwise, Veerabhahu could not have come as a villain before their matchless valour and prowess. He was mistaken as an ordinary messenger, but he turned out to be their most powerful main enemy. The root cause for all this evil was the enmity towards Devas. Torturing them and ill treating them have ultimately led to this great fall of the empire.

Bhanugopan bowed before his father and apprised him of the bad state of affairs. Soorapadhman addressed his son with tears in his eyes.

"Bhanugopa! Your words do not please me. If I release the Devas now, what will be the state of my honour? If one is mocked at for his physical handicap like a hunch, blindness, deafness, lameness or dumbness, it will be wiped out when that body perishes. If one is mocked at for his incapacities, it will not get wiped out even after seven births. I have lived a royal life all along. Should I feel helpless now? Have I lost all my strengh? Beauty, youth, strength, bravery, body, relations and riches – all these are perishables. But fame alone lives after one's death also. If I am to die in the war, I do not mind it. I welcome it, because those who are born are to die one day or the other. I will not hesitate and retreat now, just fearing that I will be killed. Let anything befall me. I am not a coward. If you are afraid, you go to your palace and hide yourself. You will be safe there. I am ready to go to the war, myself, right away today", he said.

His words were painful for Bhanugopan. He felt that his father was totally blind to the facts before his eyes. But who can win over destiny? Things will happen definitely as they are ordained by God. He consoled himself and addressed his father.

"Father! Please do not be angry with me. Forget what all I said as non-sense from a fool. As long as I am alive, you need not go to the war. I will go now and defeat Veerabhahu to make you happy".

Soorapadhman praised his son and sent him to the war with his blessings. Accompanied by all the four wings of the army, Bhanugopan was on the move. At the sight of Bhanugopan, demons sounded their war drums. Asuras also raised a war cry with their instruments.

The war began. Demons were fighting left and right with big trees. Asuras deployed Mazhu, Dandam, Javelin, Soolam and such other weapons to fight. There were heavy losses on both sides. The battlefield was full of blood streams.

Bhanugopan showered a heavy string of arrows to stop the trees and rocks sent by the demons. His fiery weapons were torturing the enemy ranks. Bhanugopan's army faced total destruction at the hands of Veerabhahu. Their weapons were lost. The sight of the dead horses and elephants looked like mountains. Chariots went to pieces. Even at that stage, Bhanugopan challenged Veerabhahu. "Do you think that you can threaten me by destroying my supporters? I shall not go back until I kill you today. You are not going back alive", he shouted.

Veerabhahu was badly wounded all over the body. He also hit back Bhanugopan on his shoulders and chest. Suffering very much by the wounds, Bhanugopan continued his attacks. He broke Veerabhahu's bow. In return, Veerabhahu threw his Vel. Bhanugopan became unconscious by its piercing him in his forehead. After a while he forcefully returned his arrows. Veerabhahu sent Vâyuvâstra, which was nullified by the same astra, sent by Bhanugopan. Veerabhahu sent Âgneyâstra, which also met the similar one from the opponent. As both were equally well equipped with identical strong astras, the war was never ending. The Earth shook at the intensity of the war. The soldiers were dazed due to utter shock.

Bhanugopan used his magical skill and attacked Veerabhahu from all sides. Veerabhahu was flabbergasted by the all-round attack and bled heavily by the countless arrows all over his body. Veerabhahu undauntedly used Gnânâstra at once, which dispelled the magic. There stood Bhanugopan in the sky with his chariot.

"Now, you cannot escape me". Veerabhahu also rose to the sky with his chariot. Both were going round and round with their chariots. For a moment they would fight in the sky. Next moment, they would fight on the ground. Very soon, they will fight on the sea. Devas stood amazed at the horror of their incessant fight.

Bhanugopan destroyed Veerabhahu's chariot. Veerabhahu paid him back in the same coin by destroying his chariot. Bhanugopan sent twentyfive arrows aimed at his chest. Veerabhahu sent fourteen arrows to break his crown. Bhanugopan broke his shield with fourteen arrows, while Veerabhahu used seven ardhachandra arrows to break his bow.

Bhanugopan used Brahmastra now. Veerabhahu sent thousands of arrows to counter it. Brahmastra destroyed all the thousand arrows and was moving to its target. Veerabhahu prayed to Muruga and used his sword to cut it. By Murugan's grace, Brahmastram was destroyed. Asuras were stunned. They did not imagine that Veerabhahu will survive Brahmastra. But when it was broken, they were confused.

Veerabhahu now took his bow and arrows and attacked Bhanugopan again. Though heavily wounded, he cut his bow by his sword. Veerabhahu now went on for a sword fight in the air. Fire sparks and heavy noise marked the fierce fight. The attacks and counter attacks by the two equals made everybody awe-struck.

**Bhanugopan used a zigzag movement to cut Veera bhahu's shoulder by his sword. Devas were aghast. Veera bhahu was once again highly furious. He cut Bhanu gopan's right hand. Before Bhanugopan could overpower him, he cut off his left hand also. He roared and fell on him. But Veerabhahu cut off his head also now. Bhanugopan's body fell on the ground lifeless.**

The demons and the Devas declared their victory. They were hilarious and praised Veerabhahu as the greatest warrior.

Veerabhahu told his men that his vow to kill Bhanugopan was fulfilled and they could now return to their camps. They bowed before Muruga. He hugged Veerabhahu and asked him to spell out a boon for the extraordinary feat of killing Bhanugopan. Veerabhahu was greatly moved by his kindness and only requested for the blessing of being his servant throughout. He did not desire any other status including that of Indra. Muruga granted his desire.

Soorapadhman was informed of Bhanugopan's death. He was totally non-plussed at the tragic news. He could not control his feelings. His sorrow was quite unbearable.

"Oh my Son! Where did you go leaving me? You said you'll make me happy by killing Veerabhahu. Even when you were in your cradle, you imprisoned the Sun, as he was too hot for you. Now you have fallen dead before him! I am still living even after you. I did not ask for the boon to quit my life as soon as I have the greatest sorrow. I forgot to ask Lord Siva for that! Even when my all other sons died, I was brave enough not to grieve. I relied upon you as you were as

strong as a mountain. I was courageous to digest anything till now. Devas who were shivering at your sight will now rejoice!"

The soldiers brought Bhanugopan's dead body to the palace. Soorapadman acted mad with sorrow. He tried to unite the severed head and hands with the body. But alas! The pangs of permanent separation from his son were so unbearable. The queen mother Padumakomalai was also equally inconsolable.

"Please give up your atrocities on Devas and save the dynasty". This was my prayer to your father many times. Now I have lost you also". She wept bitterly.

"I will kill my enemies and with their blood I will conduct a yâga to resurrect my son. Please keep his body safe", Soorapadhman ordered. The soldiers did accordingly. Soorapadhman called his men and asked them to get Singamukhan from Asurapuram. They immediately left obeying his command.

Veeramahendrapuri was deep in sorrow for the irreparable loss it suffered due to the demise of Bhanugopan.

# 60. Illusory tactics

Singamukhan was shocked when he got the call from Soorapadhman. When he asked the messengers for details, they told him about all the developments in Veeramahendrapuri. He became furious and got the four wings of his army ready to go there by air without delay. As soon as he reached the palace, he jumped out from his chariot and rushed inside.

Soorapadman was in deep sorrow. Singamukhan also felt very sad for him. "Brother, I heard about everything from the messengers. If you had sent word earlier, would I have not come? I warned you then that you do not take the son of Lord Siva lightly, as he had already destroyed Krouncham and Târakan. Well, destiny blinded your eyes. There is no point now in building a dam after the floods have swept across the country. Everything happens according to pre-ordained rules. Let me go now to defeat the enemies". So, saying, he left for his palace in Mahendrapuri, took milk, curd, honey, liquor and everything that he wanted. He also ate meat to his heart's content. Then he got ready with all the deadly weapons and proceeded with his hundred sons called "Sathaveeras." Their armies also accompanied them. Singamukhan had thousand heads and two thousand hands. The asura leader, named Singan who also had thousand heads, led the troops.

Brahma and Indra became jittery at the entry of Singamukhan, as he was equally strong as Soorapadh man. So they went to Muruga immediately.

"O Lord! Singamukhan is coming to fight us. He has thousand heads and two thousand hands. He is also equally strong like Soorapadhman and when he walks, the whole Earth trembles. He threw Meru mountain itself

,

on Andakadakam. No ordinary warrior can, indeed, match him and so, we need your advice to kill him."

Shanmukha asked for his chariot to be brought. Veerabhahu approached the Lord and said that he wanted to go to fight with Singhamukhan and kill him. Shanmukha smiled and gave him permission.

Veerabhahu took his blessings and started. Demons up-rooted many trees and accompanied him. His eight younger brothers and one lakh soldiers also went along with him.

A demon leader, Singar, faced an asura leader, Dasamukhan. Both fought like elephants. Singar broke Dasamukhan's chest with his Dandam. Dasamukhan threw his Dandam at Singar, but the weapon broke into two. Dasamukhan threw his mazhu next. Singar nullified it with his Dandam. Dasamukhan sent a fire-arm, but Singar destroyed it with his chakra. Dasamukhan again hit Singar at his chest but Singar pounced on Dasamukhan and punched him. Dasamukhan fell down dead, bleeding heavily.

Anaghan now fought with the asuras. They were so badly hit that all of them took to their heels. Another asura, Dhunmukhan tried to stop them from running, "Why do you run? How can these small insects face the Sun? Be brave and fight them". But none would listen. So Dhunmukhan attacked Anaghan with great anger. His arrows made Anaghan and his soldiers lose heart. But they used trees as their asthras and fought asuras fiercely. All weapons of asuras were also destroyed by trees. Finally the asuras had to run away from the battle field.

Dhunmukhan realised that weapons are of no use before demons. So he took illusory images and fought them from various angles and directions. Demons were losing ground. Veerabhahu saw his army's plight and sent Gnanastram which killed the illusions all around. Dhunmukhan got wilder and hit Veerabhahu with many arrows. Veerabhahu ripped open his shield and broke his bow. Arrows pierced all through his body. Dhunmukhan now knew that he will be killed, if he stayed there a minute more. So he rose up in the sky, hid himself in Maya and sped away. Demons wanted to chase and kill him. But Veerabhahu stopped them, as to fight with some one who is unarmed was not a fair play.

Singamukhan who was at the rear saw asura forces leaving the field. He rushed to the front row so that they could stay and fight the enemy ranks.

Singamukhan's figure itself was fearful for demons. Still they fought him with trees and rocks. They went to pieces and Singamukhan laughed at them. He showered his arrows of many kinds. Some emitted sparks, some emitted poison, some were very sharp. Demons could not estimate the force with which they attacked them.

Singamukhan got off his chariot and walked towards the demons with his big mountain like figure. The demons threw their arrows and weapons at him. But he brushed them all aside and started attacking with all his two thousand hands, simultaneously. He beat a few, punched a few, crushed a few, threw a few, slapped a few, stamped a few, kicked a few, pierced a few; in short, he tortured all of them in several ways.

Demons started retreating. There was utter confusion. Singamukhan came back to his chariot and threw arrows at them. He made a hell of noise, which shook the whole world and the elephants and horses ran amuck in shock.

Azharkannan, another commander of the demons, now faced Singamukhan. His soolayudham hit the enemy's chest but fell down as pieces of a mud pot. Azharkannan killed his driver with his Dandam. When Singamukhan retaliated with the same Dandam, Azharkannan fell down unconscious.

Now, Sumali, another demon general, aimed a mountain peak at Singhamuhan. But he folded it and rolled it as a ball and returned it to Sumali who got hit and fell down.

Dandi got on to Singamukhan's chariot and hit him in his chest by Dandam. But Singhamukhan threw him high up into the sky. Dandi came back and fell on his shoulders and tried to twist his heads. Singhamukhan caught him by the palm and threw him away, after crushing him like a mosquito. Veerabhahu's eight brothers rained arrows on him. But he could brush them all away without much effort. Once again, he got off his chariot and started torturing the demons who had no other option except to run away.

Veerabhahu angrily fought the asura army tooth and nail. Sathaveeras, the hundred mighty sons of Singhamukhan, invited Veerabhahu for a sword fight now. He drew his sword and there followed a hectic clash of swords between him and the hundred warriors. When the swords were flashing round and round, the hundred soldiers became too tired. They wanted to bind Veerabhahu and cut off his limbs one by one. But Veerabhahu succeeded in killing all of them. When all his hundred sons were killed, Singhamukhan was mad with rage. He stood before Veerabhahu and asked him as to who he was. "You do not seem to be the son of the Lord who has come to save the Devas. They said he has six faces. Who are you?"

Veerabhahu laughed and said, "It is a surprise that you do not know who I am. I am Veerabhahu, who came as a messenger to Mahendrapuri and destroyed it. Whoever opposed me was sent to Yamapuri. Now I shall crush you and your army".

With these words, he drew the string of his bow and the noise echoed all over. Demons rejoiced, but asuras shivered.

Singamukhan replied roaring. "You have fought so far only with inexperienced warriors. I can tear all the 1008 countries to pieces. Yama wants me to get him your life. Let me fulfill his desire now."

Veerabhahu sent eighteen arrows aiming at his chest, which simply fell through. Singamukhan attacked with his Dandam, which was destroyed, by four mere arrows. Then he sent thousands of arrows aiming at his faces and foreheads. Singamukhan threw his Velayudham at him. Veerabhahu could not stop it with his arrows. So, he prayed to Lord Siva and used the sword given by Him to cut the Soolayudham. It broke into two, sending waves of joy among demons. Veerabhahu and Singamukhan sent Sivastrams on each other. Both asthras clashed in the air only to return to the senders at the end.

Having realised the fact that Singamukhan can be done away with, only by Arumukhan, Veerabhahu concentrated on destroying his army now. His driver and horses got killed. Asuras died in great numbers.

Singamukhan also fought fiercely. His two thousand hands were fully busy sending countless arrows at demons from the ground and the air. When attacked from all directions, the demons were thoroughly shattered.

Veerabhahu hit him with thousand arrows, which were destroyed by his two thousand arrows. The battlefield was fully engrossed in their fight, when Veerabhahu broke all his thousand bows in one shot. Singamukhan could not stand this big blow, as Devas were also cheering Veerabhahu at every one of his feats. He had to resort to another strategy to overpower him. So, he deployed his mother Mâyai's magic and bound Veerabhahu and his men together. He bundled them all and threw them near Udayagiri, where the Sun rises and asked the magic to remain there as a check.

When the magical spell was approaching as a dark cloud, Veerabhahu could not exactly foresee its nature or identify it rightly. So, before he could act, the magic enveloped them and took them to Udayagiri and kept watch on them. Devas went back to the camps, without realising as to what had happened.

Singamukhan had none to face him now. He giggled and shouted, "Where is that son of the Lord? I would kill him and the Devas now." The spies told him that Muruga was at his own camp, Hemakootam.

"Oh! Is he hiding in his camp? I shall do well to go there myself and finish him". So saying, he proceeded further on his great task.

## 61. The heads grew again

When Veerabhahu and his troops lost consciousness, Vayu rushed to Hemakootam to inform Muruga.

"My Lord! Singamukhan had deployed his Maya Paasam, magical net, on Veerabhahu and his men. They are unconscious and pushed to Udayagiri. They will not be able to come out of it as the magic power is still patrolling there". Muruga angrily asked, "Where is Singamukhan now?"

"My Lord! He is heading towards our camp now", said Vayu.

Shanmukhan left his camp and got on his chariot Manovegam. Thousand vellam soldiers, who were in readiness, followed him. Drums were sounded; conches were blown; Bugles were sounded;

"Lord Muruga, who is greater than all the three Gods – Brahma, Vishnu and Siva has come. He is the dear son of the three eyed Lord Siva. He is a lion for the enemies. He has the most powerful Velayudham. The one who is beyond all our comprehension, Shanmukha, the God supreme, has come". So sounded the Symbals.

As soon as they reached the battle field, asuras were attacked by demons. Soolam, javelin, Vel and other mighty weapons killed the asuras. Trees and rocks were hurled at them. asuras perished in large numbers along with their elephants, horses and chariots.

Singamukhan was furious to see his army in shambles. He grew to a giant size and stood there between the sky and the Earth. His thousand mouths were as wide as thousand lakes. He stretched his hands, caught hold of the demons and devoured them. When he breathed in, many were drawn into his mouths. When he breathed out, many were jettisoned out. Singamukhan did not leave them there. He grabbed and swallowed them. If they chose to run away, Singamukhan could stretch his hand and catch them from any corner. Though some demons tried to attack with weapons, not a single scratch was on his body, but all the weapons got broken. Very soon, all the thousand vellam demons were inside his stomach, unable to come out.

Shanmukhan was the only one now in the field without even a single soldier.

Soorapadhman was continuously getting reports from the battlefield. He was happy that Singamukhan could control Veerabhahu and his men with Mâyapâsam and send them to Udayagiri. He was doubly happy when he learnt that Singamukhan had swallowed all the demon army men and Shanmukha was the only one spared so far. "My dear brother, I am proud of your capabilities. You shall win over the son of the Lord also and return", he praised him. He called his guards and ordered, "Singamukhan could have lost a portion of his army. Let the others who are in waiting here, leave immediately to support him in the field."

Accordingly, new regiments also marched on. When Singamukhan received additional men to help him, he was in great spirits. Kumaran raised a noise from his bow to draw his attention. Singamukhan came to him and said, "O son of the Lord, let me clarify my stand point. Asuras are duty bound to punish their enemies. They shall not derelict from their duty. Devas are their enemies, so they have been punished. You are not one among them. We have no malice against you. Why don't you go back?'.

Shanmukhan smiled and said, "Asura, as you are the king of asuras, you have certain responsibilities. We also have similar duties. If strong men punish the weaklings, it is our obligation to protect them. You treat Devas with enmity and they have done no harm to your people. I have come to get them released from the prison. Your brother did not care for my advice. Even now there is good time. You may release the Devas and live happily."

Singamukhan laughed contemptuously. "O my little child, have you come to get Devas out of prison? Even Lord Siva cannot get it done. As Târaka had not known about your strength, he got killed. I am different and I know you in and out. Veerabhahu and his men lay dead at Udayagiri. Your thousand vellam army is getting digested in my stomach. Still you make bold to fight with me? You listen to my words and get back. You are a small boy. I feel so sorry that you have come to die at this age."

Muruga did not reply, but sent an arrow aimed at his chest. It pierced through and Singamukhan was shocked. As the arrow went through, there was a big opening in the chest and the back.

The demon soldiers who were inside his stomach came through this passage and reached Shanmukhan. Singamukhan's efforts to stop them proved futile. So, he hurled his Dandam at Shanmukhan, which went to pieces by four arrows of Shanmukhan. They also attacked Singamukhan in his fore head and made him unconscious for a while. During this time, Muruga sent an arrow to Udayagiri to destroy the Mâyapâsam and get Veerabhahu and his company to senses. Very soon, by Murugan's grace, the arrow became an air borne vehicle and carried Veerabhahu and his men to the battlefield.

Veerabhahu arrived there, safe with his people. On seeing them Devas cheered. The Asuras became disturbed. They surrounded Muruga and threw their fire arms at Him. Muruga destroyed all of them with his countless arrows. Some emitted fire; some poured out poison; some took the shape of venomous snakes. Some others pierced them like Yama himself. Many asuras met their end at Muruga's weapons. They lost their limbs and ran all over the place with blood flowing out of their bodies, reeling in pain. Finally the entire army of all the four wings were totally annihilated by Muruga.

Singamukhan stood there alone. In his utter dismay for the loss of his army, he threw many weapons with his thousand hands. All of them were successfully destroyed by Muruga and there was a multiplied retaliation of them also. Singamukhan now attacked Murugan's driver, Vayudeva who sat rudely shocked for sometime when he was attacked in his chest.

Singamukhan sent Soolayudham, Dandam and Yamapasam, one after the other but Shanmukhan could easily blow them all up.

Muruga was wild with anger. He started cutting off Singhamukhan's hands and heads one after the other. But what a wonder, all of them grew again and again! Devas were perplexed and wondered if Singamukhan could ever be killed at all. Singamukhan asked Muruga with contempt. "Why do you still bother? Don't you know by now, that it is beyond you to defeat me?" Muruga replied, "Asura! you are blabbering because your end is very near". He ripped the asura's chest open again with thousand arrows.

The asura threw heavy rocks and trees at him. But everything got crumbled to pieces. Muruga cut his head and hands more than 1008 times. They were strewn all over the battle filed and the vultures gathered to eat them. Devas got worried at this endless game of chopping off limbs and their appearing again and again.

At one point of time, Muruga wanted to bring about the last stroke. Singamukhan was standing with one head and two hands. All other hands and heads were on the ground. When they started growing again Muruga made a big sound, which stopped the growth.

Singamukhan got shocked. He threw a big mountain at him. Muruga powdered it with his Vajrayutham and reversed it back on the asura. It killed him at last and his lifeless body fell on the ground like a big mountain. Devas cheered him and praised him for this grand finale of the war. All of them returned to their camps.

Soorapadman did not believe that his brother was dead. When he knew it was true, he cried loudly and the noise made Devas rejoice more and more.

## 62. A miracle at the battlefield

Soorapadhman himself, got ready to fight with Kumaran. All armies stationed at the 1008 countries were called to Mahendrapuri. Accordingly, they arrived and a big ocean of asura army was in readiness.

Soorapadhman took his bath and had his food of five kinds with six tastes. He prayed to Lord Siva and smeared the sacred ash on this forehead and chest. He then took sacred weapons from the Puja viz. Saswatam, Veerabhadram and Sarvasankâram.

**He had done a yâga and obtained a golden chariot. It was equal in splendour to the Indragnala chariot given to him by Lord Siva. It can fly faster than the wind with its lion flag. A number of lions, horses and demons drew that chariot. It was capable of carrying thousand crore worlds and was non-perishable even at the end of the ages. That chariot was decorated and kept ready for him. Soorapadhman got on his chariot and started, as the avunas cheered him with flowers and greetings.**

The drums were sounded. Nichalam, Sallikai, Bheri, Kombu, Tannumai, Kahalam, Tudi and such musical instruments were played. The big sound was heard by Devas in Hemakootam.

Along with them, Indra was also afraid of the outcome. On learning about Soorapadhman's coming to fight, Shanmukhan's chariot also was brought. Mazhu, Vajram, Soolam, Vel, Sword, Parisai, chakram, Dandu, Ezhu, Bow, Arrows, Kaivel and such weapons adorned his hands when the son of Lord Siva started in his chariot. Veerabhahu, his lakh and eight soldiers and two thousand vellam strong army followed him. Indra and the Devas were singing the praise of their Lord, as they walked behind.

# Sri Kandha Puranam

At the battlefield, demons saw the ocean of asura army and hesitated for a while. Next moment they made bold to attack the enemy as their Lord was their guide and commander.

Indra was worried at the extent of asura forces. He told Vishnu by his side, "O Lord! Their army is as vast as the ocean. It may take ages for us to win over them. When will be our victory? When will our suffering end?"

Madhava laughed at him, "Indra, we have Lord Siva of Mount Kailas with us in the guise of his son. His power is insurmountable. When he showed his Viswaroopam (Universal Form) before Meru mountain, did we not see the thousands of continents on his body? When Kumaran is a replica of Lord's power, Soorapadhman or his army will not be a match for him. He can burn all of them with his smile or he can destroy all of them by a mere sound."

"Who knows his tremendous strength? His coming to the war with Veerabhahu, lakh and eight soldiers and two thousand vellam strong army is all a mere play for him. You do not worry. Muruga will very soon destroy the entire asura crowd and get Jayanta and Devas freed from the prison". He consoled him in so many words.

Both the huge armies clashed with each other. Trees, sharp weapons and countless arrows were deployed. Asuras faced demons very well. All the weapons of the demons were totally destroyed. Veerabhahu and his men became tired as all their war tactics were of no avail.

Muruga saw the declining spirit of demons and gave a big sound in his bow. Demons got encouraged. The Asuras, and their horses and elephants were terrified. Muruga aimed his arrows in quick succession at the asuras and the enemies lost their lives immediately. Elephants fell like a pack of cards. Chariots were reduced to dust.

Vayudeva took Kumaran's chariot all over the battlefield. Many got crushed under the speeding wheels. Many were killed by the horses. Asuras lay dead and scattered everywhere with broken limbs surrounded by dead horses and elephants. As time passed by, there were heaps of dead bodies. Blood ponds were filled with trunks of asuras. Demons were finding it difficult to cross them to advance further and fight. Muruga solved their problem by emitting fire from his twelve eyes, which was equal to Vadamukhagni. It burnt down the entire leap of bodies, within a second. Devas wondered at this miracle and praised Muruga.

## 63. Padumakomalai's husband turns a bird

Soorapadhman was extremely angry at the total destruction of the asura army by Shanmukhan. With the blessings he had from Lord Siva, he was fully confident that none would defeat him. So, he hastened to the front row, "This boy has come to fight me, instigated by Devas and he does not know my strength. I will kill him and the Devas". He thought and took his bow and rained arrows at them. Demons were very badly wounded and started running away. Some fell down like uprooted trees.

Veerabhahu attacked him with his one lakh and eight men. Although his arrows could completely cover Sooran's body, none could pierce through. Demons were unable to withstand arrows from the asura. Veerabhahu got on to his chariot and cut his bow into two with his sword. Soorapadhman caught him by one hand and slapped him by the other. When he fell down unconscious, he raised his feet to crush him. Suddenly he remembered that it was wrong to kill a motionless person and so lifted his body and threw it in the sky.

Veerabhahu fell at the feet of Muruga. Soorapadhman aimed his arrows directly at Kumaran. They raced through the air emitting fire, but fell like faded flowers on the ground. Velavan stopped most of the weapons mid way with his arrows. Sooran destroyed the flag flying high on Murugan's chariot and sounded his bugle as a sign of victory.

Shanmukha got angry and pulled down Sooran's flag by his arrows. Just as he sounded his bugle, Bhanu kumbhan sounded thousand bugles with his thousand mouths to indicate Kumaran's victory. Devas cheered loudly.

On seeing Devas' happiness Soorapadhman turned his anger on them. Those who used to shiver on hearing his name, were dancing with joy now. This was not tolerated by Sooran who rose in the sky with his chariot. When Devas were on the run from the field, Muruga came to their rescue by countering Sooran's arrows midair by his arrows. Then he also rose to the sky in his chariot.

Both of them fought face to face fiercely. The arrows were destroyed by each other. They fought in the air and on the ground alternately. Each one tried to hide the line of vision of the other. Sooran hurled two thousand arrows at Muruga and Kumaran destroyed them all and also broke his bow.

Soorapadhman fought with another bow. Kumaran's arrows were continuous in their flow. Sooran went into the sea, where Muruga followed him. Sooran next got on to Meru mountain. There again Muruga encountered him. He went to the underground world – pâtâlalokam – where also Muruga chased him and made him totally nonplussed by his continuous attacks. There was not a single place, where he was left unattacked.

Sooran saw that all the gates had been sealed off on all directions so that fresh troops could not enter. Immediately he broke the fencing and made it possible for more forces to come into the field. Asura armies were pouring in like flies. But Murugan's one angry look burnt them all down. Sooran was puzzled and so attacked Murugan again. The Lord returned his attack and ordered his fire weapons like Mazhu, Soolam, Dandam, Chakram, and Ezhu to go to the other countries to destroy the asura forces then and there. All the troops in the 1008 continents were destroyed totally. Sooran wielded his chakra at Muruga and it was welcomed and taken in his hand by Muruga.

Sooran was boiling with anger when all his channels of support got shut completely. So he used his magical powers and took various forms to fight Muruga. Kandha used his Gnanastram and dispelled the magical illusions. Sooran was all alone in his chariot, riding away through one of the gates. Muruga chased him wherever he went, continent after continent. Both fought incessantly without a break. The continuous encounter was so tedious and quite long.

When Muruga did not return even after a long time, the Devas got worried. Was their Lord safe? Has the asura harmed him? Vishnu consoled them and told them that the asura was merely chased by Muruga. At last Sooran returned to his capital Mahendrapuri and Muruga followed him there. Devas felt relieved.

As the whole army was lost, Sooran thought of his mother, Mayai, who appeared before him. He asked her to spell out the correct tactic to resurrect all those dead in the war.

"O my Child! You wronged the Devas badly and that sin is taking its toll of revenge on you now. When your own destiny beckons you, are you going to listen to my words? You do not still feel like releasing the Devas. Well, if you decide to continue fighting, there is only one way. Do it if you please. There is a mountain called Amudaseeta Mantrakootam, near the seas at the frontiers. That should be brought in if you want the dead to come back alive". she said and disappeared.

Sooran got off his Indragnalam chariot and took his lion mount. He then gave orders to his chariot to go and fetch him the great Amudaseetha Mandrakootam. As it can travel through all the continents, it did the job precisely as per his command.

As soon as the breeze from this mountain blew, all those dead, including the elephants and horses came back to life. All those who were killed right from the first day of the war till that moment, Singamukhan, Bhanugopan, Agnimukhan, Vajrabhahu, Dharmagopan, all got back to life. Asura princes like Athisooran, Asurendra, three thousand soldiers, and the hundred warriors, all of them got revived. The city was again full of Asuras and Sooran was extremely happy on seeing them.

When the Devas saw that all the great asura leaders who were killed after the hectic war were back to life, they were totally shocked. They were so much disturbed that they took the forms of crows, cuckoos and parrots and left the city for fear of being caught and imprisoned by Sooran again.

Shanmukha saw Soorapadhman's tactics with the help of his mother, Mâyai and the wonderful Amudaseeta Mantra mountain's strange feat and was struck with awe.

He took the help of Rudra Pasupatastram and ordered it to destroy the asuras. Emitting fire, the unique astra went into the city and destroyed the entire crowd of asuras. Amudaseeta Mantrakootam also went to pieces.

All those who were restored to life were once again dead. Sooran was all alone again and he was boiling with anger. He commanded his Indragnala chariot to take all the troops around Muruga to the roof of the world. Accordingly the chariot mesmerized the two thousand vellam demons and the lakh and nine soldiers including Veerabhahu and took them to the roof of the world as commanded.

Muruga was now left alone, but he knew how to counter the Asura's trick again. He sent a weapon to bring back the chariot and the army back to Earth. The chariot's power was put down and it was brought back to Muruga who retained it with him, without sending it to Sooran.

Sooran now took the Velayudham obtained from Lord Siva and went to attack Muruga, taking his lion mount. He slapped the horses of Murugan's chariot first and made a big roaring noise. Then he aimed the Soolayudham at him.

Emitting fire on all sides and making a thunderous noise, Soolayudham was fast approaching Muruga. The thousand arrows sent by Muruga in a jiffy tried to stop it but Soolayudham fought them all down and sped towards Muruga. Muruga now sent Vajrayudham to catch hold of Soolayudham. Accordingly, Vajrayudham caught the three sharp edges of Velayudham and brought it to Muruga. Kumara now sent two thousand arrows to kill the lion on which Sooran was riding. The lion pierced by the arrows roared and died.

Having lost the Soolam and the lion, Sooran used his magic skills and took the form of a Chakravaha bird. With a huge mountain like form and flapping its large wings, the bird flew into the demon army, which started running in fear. The giant bird caused havoc all around with its wings, beak and mouth. It attacked the driver of Muruga's chariot, Vayu. The horses of the chariot received many injuries all over and the bird was posing a big threat to one and all.

Shanmukhan wondered at his magical skill and tried to attack him with his arrows. Sooran brushed them aside lightly with his wings. He was flying hither and thither and it was too difficult to trace him at one place for an attack. Muruga also felt that it was not proper to kill him when he was a bird. He looked at Indra, who understood his indication and came as a peacock before him.

"My Lord! How can I thank you and praise you for your great help and kindness to put an end to our sufferings. I am honoured to think that I can carry you now on my back. Please sit on me and I shall take you to all the places that Sooran goes to", he said.

Muruga sat smiling on the peacock, who was none other than Indra in disguise. Indra flew in the sky and took him near the Chakravaha bird.

Soorapadman was enraged at Indra helping Muruga in the form of a peacock. So, he wanted to finish Indra first and hence started fighting him.

The Chakravaha bird now wounded the peacock with its beak. It tried to break the peacock's beak and also hit its eyes and head with its wings. Indra, as the peacock, fought back. He tore chakravaha's wings with his toe nails. Sooran hit Indra's face and tore his beautiful back. Shanmukha saw to it that his arrows kept Sooran away from Indra. Sooran flew over the seas, mountains and forests and fought Muruga who also untiringly fought him back and forth at all places.

The asura became a little tired. Muruga's bow was his next target.

But before he could approach it, Muruga cut his neck with his sword. The bird fell down as two pieces on the ground. The Devas cheered and raised slogans of victory saying that Sooran is dead. They rejoiced for his end at the hands of Lord Muruga and felt greatly relieved.

# 64. Mayai's son in magical illusions

Soorapadhman who was cut into two pieces did not die. He gave up the form of the bird and took a giant form ranging from the Earth to the sky. His huge figure covered the sun and the directions. So, there was darkness everywhere. One could not see anyone standing even just opposite.

Detecting asura's magic, Muruga tore his huge figure by seven arrows. They became seven seas and destroyed his mighty form. Sooran merged with the water of the seas and flowed all over the place. Even big mountains got drowned in the floods.

Muruga now sent hundred arrows to take the form of a huge wide spread fire. They attacked the surface of the water and the entire flood was devoured by the fire.

The asura now took the form of a huge column of fire and started burning down everything. The heat was unbearable for all the creatures in the world. Muruga deployed thousand arrows to create a big gale, by which the fire got extinguished.

Soorapadhman changed his form to that of a gale and the whirlwind was going round and round to roll off the whole world. Muruga directed a lakh arrows now and produced a number of snakes. They destroyed the illusions of the magic forms of the asura.

Sooran fought incessantly with Muruga for the next four days. He took several forms by his Maya skills. He came as Devas and created confusions. He changed himself as demons and then as Yama. The seas, the mountains, the ashtadiggajas, the lion and what not. He roared as thunder and attacked their eyes as lightening. He came as poisonous snakes and spat venom all over the place. He came in disguise as the killed heroes, Bhanugopan, Târaka, Singamukhan, Agnimukhan, Dharmagopan etc. The Devas were perplexed totally without being able to identify him in any form and how to overcome his magical attacks.

Whatever form Sooran took, Muruga was able to counter him with his weapons and dispel the Maya totally. The confusion, which prevailed for Devas and demons, was thus cleared then and there.

Finally Muruga decided to deal with Sooran's magical tactics once for all. So he sent thousand arrows to destroy the magic in its entirety. These arrows became seven fold forms for each one of the magical forms and annihilated all of them finally.

## 65. The child takes the majestic form

Soorapadhman was standing all alone in the battlefield. His eyes were red with anger. Vadivelan on the peacock talked to him.

**"Soorapadhma! You have shown me many illusory forms so far. I have destroyed them all with my arrows. Let me now show you my indestructible giant form". He took his universal majestic form, Viswaroopam and stood up to the sky as the limit.**

Soorapadhman saw his exquisite image. Under the Lord's feet were the mountains. The oceans were flowing with waves and washing his feet. Thunder and stars were seen in his toes. Varuna, Kubera, Niruti and Rakshasas were in this feet. Sages, Chintamani and such precious gems were seen at the ankles. Vidyadharas were at the knees. Indra and Jayanta were on the two thighs. Yama and Kâla were at the beginning of the thighs. Asuras were in the hip. Devas were in the ribs. Nagas were in the centre. The nectar was in the midst. All creatures were seen in the navel. All scriptures were to be seen on his chest. Wisdom was his Upaveetam or the sacred thread across the chest. The countries were hanging in his hairs. All pleasures were enshrined in his palms. Vishnu and Brahma were seated on his two shoulders. Celestial women were there in his fingers. The vocal chords and the fire were in his neck. Vedas were in his mouth. Letters lived in the teeth. Sivagamas were in his tongue. The lips had the seven slogans and mahamantra. Vâyu was in his nose. The sun and the moon were his two eyes. The directions formed his ears. The Omkara or the Pranava was in his forehead and head had Urisavam.

The Lord's most delightful form left Sooran absolutely wonder struck. The great light without the beginning or

the end stood there as Shanmugan's most stunning Viswaroopam. When his eyes were fixed at the image, the Lord gave him the vision of wisdom for some time.

"The son of Lord Siva whom I considered as a small boy has destroyed the entire Asura Army. He chased me in all the continents and fought with me untiringly. He has snatched away the most powerful and indestructible chariot, Indragnalam, from me. Whatever magical form I took, he destroyed them. Now he stands as a gigantic figure from the Earth to heaven, which I shall never be able to do. He is the embodiment of everything, as I am able to see right before my eyes. I had slighted him as a small boy, all along. He is God Almighty, greater than Brahma, Vishnu and Siva. He is none else than the God whom I adore, a great spectacle on the peacock mount. My 1008 continents have been contained in one hair on his leg. None could have had this darshan. I have been fortunate to see this. What a wonder! What Beauty. Even if thousand crores of Cupids – Manmathas come together, will they get this unimaginable beauty?"

Singamukhan and Iranyan advised me rightly not to think of Lord Siva's son as a small child. They had the wisdom to know who he was. It was all a fact. What a majestic form! One wants to have this darshan for ages together. How fortunate have I been for such a mighty Lord to fight with me?"

Lord Siva's son has come to mitigate the evils done to Devas and protect them. My own sins were the root cause for the war, which caused total destruction according to Iranyan and Singamukhan. It is not true. As far as I can see, my ill treatment of Devas was justified. That has alone given me the great pleasure of this wonderful darshan of the Lord today. Only because I imprisoned Devas and tortured them, God who is unapproachable to Devas and Indra has come in search of me and has also given the rarest opportunity to see this world wide spectacle.

This is a non-satiating sight. I feel a true transformation of mind. My anger has disappeared. My eyes are shedding tears of joy now. I am thrilled beyond description. My hands come together automatically to salute him. I want to prostrate and worship this Lord. I desire to place my head on his feet and bow down in reverence. My right eye and right shoulder are twitching and my pride has vanished. I want to love all. My mind is full of good thoughts for everyone. I am the most blessed of all. I have reaped the greatest benefit of this birth. I have been the most fortunate on Earth. I want to be a servant always at the feet of this Lord. How can I get those blessings? I want to have the grace of God in the fullest measure."

Soorapadman's thoughts were filled with great joy. His mind was well set on Lord's glory and grace. The change of mind stayed for a moment only. Muruga reverted from the Viswaroopam to the simpler form seated on the peacock. At the same time, he changed the asura's mind also, as before.

# 66. Asura becomes the cock and the peacock

As soon as Muruga changed the mind of Sooran, his extreme anger and enmity came back to him. Tapping his two shoulders, as a mark of showing his strength he shouted at the Lord. "As you cannot fight with me face to face, you try to show your magic and mesmerize me? Nobody can entice me with a non- perishable body. You have a silly courage to face me still. Just wait and see what happens now". Then Sooran chanted a mantra and prayed. There was extreme darkness everywhere with the result nothing was visible. He hid himself in this cover of total darkness and made a big noise. Devas were terribly afraid of that utter pitch dark atmosphere and awaited further nightmares. In the dark, Sooran took the form with several heads and long hands and tried to devour Devas. They read his thoughts and the camouflaged image was invisible. They ran on all four sides in great panic, praying to Lord Muruga.

"You are the sweetest for those who approach you,

The purest one with the Vel,

The Lord of all wisdom,

The simplest for  poets to reach,

The God of all the sages who sing your praise,

The god with twelve strong shoulders!

The source of all brightness,

All the three moorthis are rolled into one,

The farthest for all thoughts to reach

Thou the supreme creator of the universe,

Save us from Sooran;

Oh, The son of the Lord with three eyes

We pray unto thee.

You are the God Almighty!

The Protector of all Devas;

The greatest and the mightiest Lord,

The heaviest thunder for the snakes"

Devas sang Muruga's praise in several such ways and surrendered at his feet.

Sivakumaran sent his Velayudham at Sooran with the command to break open Sooran's chest. Soolayutham went straight to its target, emitting fearful sparks and shining like a crore Suns rising together. The thick darkness got dispelled instantaneously.

**Sooran saw the angry Velayudham aimed at him. He went to the mid seas and stood there like a huge mango tree. Its branches, extended up to the world's frontiers. Its roots went right down below the Earth, touching the patalalokam. When Sooran shook his body as a tree, the earth quaked heavily and all things rolled down from their places.**

Kumaran's Velayudham with its terrific speed pierced through the mango tree. The tree was cut into two. Sooran suddenly took his original form and tried to cut the Vel into two with his sword. But Vel overpowered him, cut him into two pieces and pushed them into the sea. After achieving what was to be done as per Lord's command, the Vel returned to Muruga's hands. Devas showered flowers and danced in joy playing on divine musical instruments.

Because of Lord Siva's special blessings, Soorapa dhman did not die, even though his body was torn to two pieces. So he took the two forms of a cock and a peacock and rushed to attack Muruga. Devas were shocked by his speed. Muruga took pity on Sooran and gave him the wisdom to realise Him. By His grace, Soorapadhman lost his anger and enmity at that very moment and also all his devilish qualities were totally wiped out. Muruga asked the cock to be his flag on top of his chariot. The cock climbed up his chariot, sat on his flag and crowed. Then he got down from the peacock mount, which was Indra in disguise. He now sat on the soorat turned peacock and ordered it to carry him always.

**Sooran in the form of a peacock took Murugan on his back and went round all the continents.** Agni who was hitherto his flag and Indra who was hitherto his peacock mount were restored to their original forms by the grace of Muruga. They worshipped him now in their old forms as Agni and Indra.

Everyone rejoiced at the new delightful form of Muruga with the cock flag and the peacock mount. There were several hymns sung in his praise. With tears of joy, all the devotees were immersed in the ocean of true happiness. Their thoughts were fully concentrated on the Lord, without centering around their own selfish desires.

## 67. Mahendrapuri gets destroyed

When Soorapadman was attacked by Muruga's Velayudham, his body broke into two pieces and fell into the sea. Messengers immediately rushed to his palace and informed his wife Padumakomalai about Sooran's demise. She could not digest the news and cried aloud. Due to extreme sorrow, she passed away at once. The other wives also could not bear the sorrow of Sooran's death. They made a big fire, for Padumakomalai's funeral and followed her.

Iranyan who was hiding in the sea like a fish, heard of Sooran's death. But he was afraid to come out lest Veerabhahu and others kill him. So he hid himself there for sometime. Later, he stealthily reached his guru, Sukrachariar, Who consoled him and made him do the last rites for his parents and others. After that, he developed a hatred for all the riches which was the cause for all evils. So, he left to meditate on Lord Siva and to seek salvation.

Shanmukhan called Veerabhahu to go to the prison at Mahendrapuri and get Jayanta and all the Devas there released. Veerabhahu took his orders and left. There was absolutely none there to stop him or fight with him. All mansions and palaces were empty without a soul. Jayanta and Devas felt happy and relieved on seeing Veerabhahu. They welcomed him knowing fully well that he had come to set them free.

"Oh Devas! Your guess is right. Senthilnathan has destroyed Soorapadhman. His entire army has been wiped out in the war. Lord Muruga has sent me to set you all free and bring you there." Veerabhahu broke open the jail doors and went in. He unlocked the chains and took them to Shanmukhan. They bowed before Him and He blessed them all and said, "You have suffered enough in the prisons of Sooran. Now you can get back to your places and live happily hereafter".

Indra hugged his son Jayanta and wept. "Jayanta! For my sake you underwent countless sufferings in the jail. From the moment you were taken captive, I was quite upset about you. I cried thinking whether I will see you again at all. By Lord's grace, we have been reunited." He hugged the other Devas also one after another and consoled them for all the sufferings they had in the prison.

All the demon soldiers who were dead and wounded in the war came back to life by Murugan's grace. They thanked the Lord profusely as they were all hale and hearty as before.

Shanmukhan called Varuna and asked him to wipeout Mahendrapuri. He went as a deluge and submerged it under the high tides.

After Mahendrapuri was washed away, Murugan left Hemakootam and reached Senthil. It was the twilight time before the night spread its wings. Lord Brahma approached Muruga and said that Devas wanted to offer worship to him then and there.

Senthil Kumaran agreed and all Devas worshipped him with flowers throughout the night. As the next day dawned, Kumaran established a temple there for Lord Siva and got a Sivalingam installed there. Pujas were performed as per Vedic rules. Immensely pleased, Shanmukha left the place with the Devas.

## 68. Thirumuruga at Tirupparankunram

When Shanmukhan and the demon army left Tiruchendur, otherwise known as Senthilpati, Devas also accompanied him. Lord Brahma came on his swan and Vishnu was on his mount Garuda. Devas chanted Vedas and accompanied him. They travelled through mountains and places around mountains, which are generally classified as Kurinji or hilly terrain. They reached the city of Madurai, known as the city of four high towers at the four directions. When Muruga reached Tirupparankunram, a hillock West of the city, he thought that it was a suitable place for his residence. The sons of the sage Parasara, who were in meditation there, requested him to take his abode there to which he consented.

Devathachan, the architect of Devas, converted the place equal only to the heavenly abode of Gods. Big gardens, fountains, wide roads and big mansions were made there to make it comfortable and convenient for living. He made a beautiful temple for the Lord. Murugan stayed there, after blessing Devas for a happy life. The six sons of the sage Parasara also worshipped at his feet. The Lord, as agreed before, taught them the path of salvation. Veerabhahu and other soldiers stayed along with the Lord there, taking care of his comforts.

Tirupparankunram acquired a festive look, equal to Kandhapuri in Mount Kailas, the divine abode of Lord Muruga.

## 69. Wedding arrangements for the Princess

Indra desired to give his daughter Deivayanai in marriage to Lord Muruga, who had put an end to the atrocities of Soorapadhman and gave Devas a fresh lease of life and happiness. He consulted Lord Brahma on his desire and he readily approved. Vishnu also was all praise for his desire and Devas congratulated him.

"O King of Devas! Your daughter Deivayanai was meditating to get Saravanan as her husband. This is the opportune time to fulfill her desire. So, start making all arrangements for the auspicious occasion". They all encouraged him thus for a speedy action.

Indra called one of the Devas and asked him to go to Meru mountain and fetch Indrani and Deivayanai from there. The Deva located Indrani who was meditating on Lord Siva in a secret place in Meru mountain and saluted her.

"O my mother! I have brought you good news. By Lord Siva's immense grace, His son Kumara, who was born to protect the Devas, has since destroyed Soorapadhman and all his men. His city has been ruined and sunk into the sea. Your son Jayanta and the other Devas have been released from the prison. All of them and our king Indra are now at Tirupparankunram worshipping Lord Murugan. Your husband has sent me to fetch you and your daughter Deivayanai to that place", he informed her.

Indrani was immensely pleased to receive the good news. Without a minute's delay, they all started on Airavatam, the divine elephant. Deva ladies accompanied them. They flew by air and reached Tirupparankunram. When Indrani saw her husband and son together, tears of joy rolled down her cheeks. She hugged her son and felt very happy.

Indra narrated to her the events from the time he sent her to Meru mountains from Seerkazhi to the time of their meeting now. Though he was not fully capable of expressing his gratitude to Lord Muruga, he desired to give his daughter in marriage to him. Indrani rejoiced at the proposal.

Accompanied by Brahma, Vishnu and Devas, Indra came to Lord Muruga. He first saluted him and said,

"My Lord, you were extremely kind to us in saving all of us who were hiding in the fear of Soorapadhman and suffering a hell. You have restored our happiness in no small measure. I am just like a fly before you. I have no capacity to express my gratitude fully to you. Yet, I am keen on getting my daughter married to you. You should kindly give your consent to accept Deivayanai as your bride".

Murugan smiled at his request and said, "Indra, I shall fulfill your desire happily. She had already been in meditation at Saravana lake in order to marry me. I shall get married to her tomorrow. You may go ahead with the arrangements."

Indra's happiness knew no bounds and he looked at Viswakarma, the architect of Devas. Viswakarma understood what he meant and started elaborate preparations to make the place more beautiful for the festive occasion. Grand mansions came into being. There were festoons and welcome arches all over the place. Gardens were full of sweet smelling flowers. Their fragrance filled the pretty mansions. There were lakes with flowery arches, on its banks.

Thirty-three crore Devas, Sages, Siddhas, Yakshas and Gandharvas were to enjoy the wedding festivities in a big hall of splendid decorations. Bright garlands of beads, festoons, flags and colourful curtains beautified the whole area. At the centre of the marriage hall was a stage studded with gems. All accessories required for the performance of the marriage were heaped there as mountains.

Indra sent messengers with invitations to all emperors like Musukunda, all sages and seers for the happy occasion of the marriage of Lord Muruga with Princess Deivayanai. The messengers immediately got busy on their assignments with great joy.

## 70. Monkey does Sivapuja

Once upon a time, Lord Siva was having a good time with Umadevi in a beautiful garden at Mount Kailas. There were many Vilva trees around the place and a group of monkeys lived on those trees. One of the monkeys was playfully showering vilva leaves on the Lord and Devi. On seeing it, Umadevi got angry.

Lord looked at her and said, "Devi, do not get angry. The monkey is just not playing with the leaves. It is worshipping us with these vilva leaves which I like most".

Devi was pleased with Lord's explanation and looked at the monkey. Her kind look gave the monkey enlightenment and divine vision. The monkey came down from the tree and begged His pardon. "I am sorry, I foolishly indulged in throwing the leaves at you. Please forgive me".

Lord blessed the monkey and said, "O monkey! You did not do anything wrong. You worshipped me with Vilva leaves, which I like most. I am extremely pleased with you. You will have to get the benefit for your worship. So, you will be born as a king in the world, in the dynasty of Manu".

The Monkey replied, "O my Lord! I am now blessed to worship you daily. I am happy to see you everyday rather than have all the wealth of a kingdom, which will fade away one day. How can I get relieved from the bondage of the world and get back to you?"

"O monkey! Do not fear. Even after you become a king, you can get back to me one day", Lord said. The monkey was not satisfied with the vague answer. It fell at His feet again.

"My Lord! I am not sure whether I will be able to retrieve myself from the worldly pleasures if I am born as a man. So allow me to be born with a monkey face."

God appreciated its request and granted it. The monkey left Mount Kailas and was born on Earth with a monkey's face. His name was Musukunda, Musu meaning monkey. Musukunda ruled over Karuvoor in the Chola Kingdom. He was also afraid of Soorapadhman and lived in fear under his control. Now, that he came to know that Lord Muruga had destroyed Sooran, he was happy to rule the place with all freedom and happiness.

## 71. The wedding of Deivayanai

Indra's messenger reached the court of King Musukunda and conveyed Indra's invitation for his daughter's wedding. The king was asked to grace the happy occasion with his kith and kin.

King Musukunda was extremely happy to receive the invitation to attend the divine wedding at Tirupparan kunram. He asked the messengers, "You have brought me such a good news. What can I give you in return? Will you accept gold or gems? Please tell me what you would want?"

The messengers politely replied, "Oh King! we bow before your kindness. If you can go with us immediately, we should be happy and grateful".

King Musukunda wanted the good news to be conveyed to all the people of the city. At all road junctions, the soldiers announced the happy event through beating of the drums and asked all the people to attend. With lots of gifts, relatives and friends, King Musukunda started off to attend the marriage. People rode on elephants, horses and palanquins. The youngsters carried the old and the handicapped on their shoulders.

Among those who moved on to attend the marriage of the Lord were the hunch-backed, blind, lame and dumb also. God saw their enthusiasm and blessed them, and their disabilities disappeared as they went along dancing with joy.

Many kings gathered there from all parts of the world. They were to witness a very rare event. It is a fortune once in a life time for all. None wanted to miss the golden opportunity. So, they were moving quite fast, rather it was God's will which was driving them to go fast.

Indra and his important associates welcomed every visitors and made them occupy their respective places. Tirupparankunram was full with the huge gathering of guests, who were all eager to see the Lord's wedding.

Deva ladies congregated to decorate Deivayanai. They applied scented ghee on her head and gave her a holy bath with waters brought from all sacred rivers. Then, fragrant cool water and sandalwood paste were applied. The hair was dried with Akhil smoke and plaited with scented oils. Edir Mukhamayil, Valampuri, Makrappakuvai and such ornaments adorned her head. Flowers with good fragrance were worn by her. New silks were her dress and a variety of beautiful ornaments were dazzling on her. Her ear-ring was Pulimukhappani. Pearl garlands, bangles and thodis were the ornaments on her neck, hands and shoulders respectively. Paadagam, Silambu and Paadayalam were worn on her feet.

Indra consulted Brahma about the auspicious time for the marriage. Brahma happily declared that all timings were good for the Lord's marriage. As all the guests had arrived, he asked them to start the function straight away. Indra accompanied by Brahma and Vishnu came to the bridegroom.

"O my Lord! All arrangements are done. You should now grace us with your presence at the marriage hall to accept Deivayanai's hand."

Lord Saravanan who was dressed beautifully and adorned with all ornaments befitting a bridegroom started for the marriage hall. All the musical instruments played the auspicious notes. Devas showered flowers. The Sun and the Moon carried two white umbrellas on either side. Vâyu was carrying the big fan. Varuna carried the festoons. Yama was his body guard with the sword in his hand. The cock crowed with a big joyful voice. The peacock carried the Lord, dancing all the way. The celestial dancers were performing happily. Gandharvas gave melodious songs. The sages were reciting vedic verses.

In this grand fashion, Lord Muruga went in procession through the wide roads and reached the marriage hall. The wives of the sages welcomed him, offering all the auspicious things. People around raised happy slogans of joy, which echoed from the skies.

Indrani came with her friends and bowed before Muruga. She washed the feet of the Lord with Kamadhenu's [Divine cow] milk, worshipped with flowers and performed Ârati, a symbol of welcome. Now Lord entered the hall with his large group of friends and followers.

Right at that time, Lord Siva and Umadevi appeared in the sky on their Rishabha mount, in order to enjoy the festivities of their son's marriage. Indra was exceedingly happy to worship him with all Prayers and invite him. Brahma, Vishnu and all others respectfully received them with honours.

Lord Muruga took the blessings of his parents, Lord Siva and Umadevi. Lord Siva hugged him and blessed him. All the visitors were greatly thrilled at the sight.

The auspicious moment arrived. Vishnu called Indra and asked him to proceed with the rituals. Indra brought his wife and daughter to the hall. Lakshmi and Saraswati escorted the bride on either side. Deivayanai first worshipped Lord Siva and Umadevi and then reached the hall.

Indrani poured holy waters with fragrant roots and Indra washed the feet of Muruga and worshiped with flowers. With ritualistic dhoop and light, he worshipped at his feet. Then he placed Deivayanai's hand in Lord's hand and declared with due respect that he had given his daughter in marriage to him.

Lord Saravana took Deivayanai's hand in his hand with a smile and made her sit beside him. Brahma got a Mangala Sutra with his prayers and gave it to Muruga. Lord Siva's son took it in his hand and tied it round the neck of Deivayanai with the accompaniment of vedic verses and auspicious auguring. Music filled the air. Flowers were showered on the newly weds. The bride and the bridegroom presented a great feast for all eyes. All the visitors were thrilled. They praised and worshipped at their feet.

Brahma now made the holy fire and completed the marriage rituals by Muruga as per customs and traditions. Deivayanai was made to stand on a stone and see the star Arundathi, as per age old practices signifying stead fastness and chastity. Lord Siva and Umadevi called them near and made them sit on their laps.

The divine family's darshan was a great blessing for all the guests who enjoyed it thoroughly as the happiest moment of their lives.

The festivities came to a grand conclusion. Veerabhahu and his lakh and nine soldiers attended on the guests verywell. Everyone greeted the divine couple, worshipped them and got their blessings.

## 72. Indra's Coronation

Time rolled on. Lord Muruga felt that the Devas should go back to Devalokam and be happy there. So he came out of his mansion with his consort Deivayanai. Veerabhahu and others cheered him.

Indra and Devas also joined him at once. Vayudevan understood the Lord's mind and brought his chariot Manovegam there. Muruga told all of them to get ready to go to Devalokam.

All of them happily accompanied the Lord. Two thousand vellam demon army and the lakh and nine soldiers came along. The sages followed chanting Vedamantras.

When the Lord reached Devalokam, he saw it in a dilapidated state as left by Bhanugopan. He called Viswakarma, the architect of the Devas, and asked him to rebuild the entire city as before.

The whole place was renovated and was given a new look. Mansions and towers were rebuilt with the original beauty. Viswakarma constructed a separate palace for Lord Muruga's stay there.

Brahma and Vishnu were very happy to see the new grand look of Devalokam. Each one occupied their

respective residences. Lord Muruga praised Viswakarma for the splendid work done by him.

**Then Muruga called the Devas and asked them to arrange for the coronation of Indra, as the king of Amaralokam.**

Devas made all arrangements at once. Indra sat on the throne studded with all precious stones. He was given the holy bath by Ganges water and decorated with silks and ornaments. With the usual paraphernalia for kings viz the umbrella, fan, sword and crown, he was installed as Amarâpati (King of Devas). The sages blessed him. Devas saluted Indra. The dancers gave a delightful performance.

Indra accompanied by Devas went to Lord Muruga's palace and worshipped him. "O My Lord! You have redeemed my kingship lost to the asuras. You have also given me back all the pleasure and riches of Devalokam. We are born again with your grace", he said. Lord Muruga blessed him immensely and desired that he ruled Devalokam as before, in all pomp and glory.

After a few days of stay in Devalokam, Lord Muruga left for Kandhagiri with Deivayanai. Indra and Devas wanted to go with them, but Muruga desired that they stayed back in Devalokam. He took Veerabhahu and his lakh and nine soldiers only along with the demon army to reach Mount Kailas. They worshipped Lord Siva and Parvati and then left for Kandhagiri. Veerabhahu and others served them well and took care of all their comforts. They had the fortune of worshipping the Lord daily.

## 73. Indra changes his mind

When Indra was ruling Devalokam happily, he was nostalgic one day about the difficult days he experienced. He was pained to think of the period when he was mortally afraid of Soorapadhman and spent his time in hiding. He wanted to renounce the life of wealth and pleasures and meditate on Lord Siva to attain salvation.

**Bruhaspati came to know of his intentions but did not approve of his relinquishing charge as the king of Devas. So he went to Indrapuri to change his mind. When Indra saw his Guru Bruhaspati, he rushed to welcome him with due honours. Bruhaspati tried to talk to him to bring about a change of mind.**

"O king of Devas! I am aware that you have developed hatred for all pleasures of life, as your regained them after a hectic struggle, due to Soorapadhman's atrocities on you and Devas. So you intend to leave your kingdom and life of pleasures to follow the path of meditation by controlling all your desires and sensous pursuits. What are you going to gain?

It is but natural that those who undergo suffering for long get to enjoy life later. You cannot be an exception. Even the sages who meditate on God, do continue with their wordly pleasures. Only after they are totally satiated with mundane life, they become true ascetics towards the end of their lives. Even Brahma, Vishnu and Siva have not desisted from the natural course of life. Why should you run away from the present happiness, thinking of the past miseries? If you go for meditation now, you will face troubles only. It is just like fearing a small fire and going to fall into a big sea. Some people opine that if you control and win over your five senses and do penance the hard

way, you will attain eternal bliss and salvation by your soul's union with God Almighty. Has anyone who reached that stage ever talked about it? Aiming at something, which you do not know about, why should you give up the joys, which you already enjoy? It is the women alone who can give us immense joy. I can enlighten you further if you so desire", Bruhaspati went on and on.

Indra was tempted by guru's words. He wanted to enjoy life in the company of women.

"O my Guru! You have never told me such things so far. Let me know more about all that now", he said.

"O King! Mature people alone can aspire to learn about it. So, I was waiting for the right moment till now. They say that there are 1008 faiths or even many more. There is one faith which gives you the greatest pleasure in this birth itself and that is called – Ulogapadam. According to this faith, men and women enjoy life in this birth itself, to the extent possible. That depends upon their family, nature, attitude, character, physique, status, time, intentions, etc., and has many aspects." The teacher of Devas detailed all about it to Indra.

Indra underwent a big change of mind. His desire to meditate and attain liberation was no longer there. He wanted to enjoy life thoroughly as before. So he gave up the responsibility of governing the kingdom to his son, Jayanta and lived a life of pleasures with Indrani.

## 74. Lord Siva is Supreme

Jayanta, son of Indra, ruled Devalokam with all care and concern. One day when he was seated on his throne, he asked his teacher present there:

"Sir, I want a clarification from you. Thirty-three crore Devas, sages, Brahma and Vishnu were tortured and belittled by Soorapadhman. What was the reason for it? Is it due to his great muscle power? I am afraid that was not the only reason. Kindly enlighten me."

"Jayanta! Once upon a time, Dakshan conducted a yâga ignoring Lord Siva but Devas and sages partook in it, which was a big mistake, committed by them". When Jayanta wanted more details about that incident, Bruhaspati gave a full account.

"One day in Brahmalokam, Brahma was seated in his court in the company of sages and Devas. Out of his ten adopted sons, the eldest one Daksha was also present there. He asked his father, Brahma, "Oh Dad! Tell me who is the God Almighty. Who is the supreme Lord of Devas, the highest repository of wisdom, greatest of all creations, non perishable at all time and omni present in all creatures".

Brahma said, "My son, once upon a time myself and Madhava entered into an argument to determine as to who was the God Supreme between the two of us. Then Lord Siva appeared before us as a big column of fire and we could not trace His head or toes. So He alone is the Lord Supreme".

Daksha then asked, "You are the creator and Madhava is the protector. How is it that both of you are not supreme, but Lord Siva, who destroys is considered supreme?"

Brahma told his son, "Daksha, you do not know the gist of the Vedas. Lord Siva was the creator of me, Vishnu, all Devas, Indra and the whole universe with all creatures. At the end of all ages, he destroys us all in entirety so that we merge with him. After that he recreates the whole set up. Just as Devas, both of us, myself and Vishnu also have to perish one day. Whereas Lord Supreme stays permanent at all times. I came from His right shoulder and Vishnu came from His left shoulder. He assigns the job of creation to me and the job of protection to Vishnu but executes both the jobs Himself residing in both of us. Whenever we faulter in our assignments by some mistake, He corrects us and takes care of the situation with His grace. Just as the oil and the seed, bell and the sound, flowers and their fragrance, gem and its brightness, He is omnipresent in and out of the universe. All vedas, scriptures and arts originated from Him. He alone is our supreme teacher. Having studied the scriptures, it is a mere folly that you equate us with Lord Siva".

Daksha was still not convinced fully. "Vedas expounded by God, call the five elements of nature, all living beings and Devas as Brahmam or Lord Supreme. Why is it so? I want to know the fact", he asked. Brahma answered his query thus:

"My son, Vedas speak of Lord Siva as the whole embodiment of the ultimate goal of life. He is indestructible and this theory is called 'Vidhivaadham'. To call other Devas, creatures or the five elements as Godly or divine is mere flattery only. This is called 'Tudivaadham'. The first is the rule and the second is only the application. Whenever we want to praise something we do exaggerate. It is just like that. Whomsoever we worship, finally that prayer reaches the Lord Supreme. Just as all the rivers reach the ocean at the end of their journey, all our prayers to other Gods and Devas will reach Lord Siva only. Lord Siva creates everything, protects, destroys and also recreates. He has no beginning or the end; He showers His grace on all his creations; He is kindness personified; He is formless; He is also in all His images; He cannot be destroyed; He has no end; He is the purest and He is the great light which cannot be understood. He is the wisdom prevailing everywhere, omnipotent and omniscient. He is only one. He is the sole witness for everyone and every act. He has no difference like male or female. He gives everything to those who surrender unto Him. He is the master of all creatures. He is the supreme soul 'Paramatma' in which all other souls, 'Jeevatmas' finally unite. Even if all souls merge into Him and though he pervades in everything, he does not acquire or mingle with other's qualities. None can discern his distinct, unique characteristics. Under no circumstances, we can equate ourselves with Him. We are only executing His tasks. Without His grace, we cannot get liberated. So, it is up to you to meditate on Him, surrender at His feet and get His abundant grace and blessings."

Brahma's didactic lecture did not impress Daksha. Instead of aspiring for Mukti, the liberated state of calmness and composure, he wanted the status of the highest position and to be worshipped by one and all including Devas. So, he asked his father to permit him to go on meditation. Brahma directed him to go to Manasarovar and meditate on Lord Siva.

On reaching Manasarovar, Daksha chose a suitable place for his penance. Unmindful of rain, floods, dew, hot or cold weather, he controlled his five senses and sat in deep meditation.

**After thousand years, Lord Siva who was pleased with Daksha, appeared before him with his consort Pârvathi and Rishabhadeva. "O son of Brahma, I**

**am quite happy with your hectic prayers. Ask me for any boon that you want from me", He asked.**

Dakshan worshipped at His feet and requested, "O My God! I should become the chief ruler of the entire world. Everyone including Devas should be obedient to me and take my orders. I should not think of anyone else other than you. I may be blessed with Devi to be born as my daughter and I should get the extreme happiness of giving her in marriage to you."

"I grant you all these boons. As long as you behave yourself, they will stay with you", The Lord said.

After getting great boons, as desired, Daksha wanted to see his father and so thought of him.

Brahma knew from his inherent vision of wisdom that his son meditated on Lord Siva and obtained a boon to subjugate all the creatures including Devas, instead of asking for real salvation. He was sorry for his wrong choice, but still reached his place.

Daksha bowed before his father and informed him about God's blessings. He wanted a city to be established exclusively for him. Accordingly Dakshapuri was created on par with Amaravati, the capital of Indra. All sages praised him and with their blessings, Dakshan crowned himself as the ruler of the whole Universe.

Bruhaspati informed Indra about the boons granted to Daksha and asked him to proceed to Dakshapuri at once to acknowledge his leadership. Indra accordingly went to Dakshapuri with Devas and pledged allegiance to him.

The leader of asuras was hiding in Meru mountain fearing Indra. Sukrachariar, the Guru of Asuras also came to know that Indra was now the subordinate ruler under Dakshan. He informed the asura leader to come out of his
,

hiding and go to Dakshan. As Indra is not to be feared any longer, Sukrachariar advised the asura leader to take protection from Daksha.

The asura leader was happy to go to Daksha, subordinate himself and accept his supremacy for his protection henceforth.

All planets, right from the Sun, Ashtadiggajas, Nagas and all others visited Dakshapuri and fell at his feet and sang his praise. Daksha was now known as Prajapati (leader of the masses) and he was the emperor of all worlds.

## 75. Narada gets cursed

Brahma gave birth to a girl from his feet. She was called Vedavalli and she was endowed with great beauty and good qualities. Dakshan married her and got thousand children. He conducted Upanayanam for all of them at the right age and also gave them vedic eduation.

One day, Daksha called his sons and asked them to proceed to Manasarovar. "You shall meditate on Lord Siva there and get His blessings to have the power to create all creatures", he told them.

Obeying his orders the thousand sons of Daksha went to meditate. Narada came to know of Daksha's directive to his sons to obtain powers to create. If it so happens, Narada could foresee disaster to the world. So, he wanted to thwart it well in advance and so went in search of those sons who were in Manasarovar.

# Sri Kandha Puranam    331

When they saw a great sage approaching them, they welcomed him with due honours. "Sir, we do not know you. Are you the Lord whom we are all meditating on?", they asked.

"My name is Narada. I am the son of Brahma. I know that you are the sons of Dakshaprajapati. Why are you all here? Whom are you meditating on?", he asked.

"Sir, we are meditating on Lord Siva, the supreme Lord, who has no beginning or end. Our father has desired that we ask Him for the power to create all creatures", they said.

Narada smiled on hearing their mission. "Look, my children. Please do not mistake me that I am finding fault with you. I am sorry that this request does not suit your status. Who are you, by the way? Brahma who is the creator now is your grandfather. To desire for powers to get his assignment is surprising. Your father Dakshan has sent you on this job. Those who are born in this world have got to die one day. The scriptures say that one should strive hard to get liberation from the cycle of births and deaths. Anyone with a little wisdom will only seek such an exalted status of eternal bliss. All of you are so well educated and learned in vedic sastras. That being so, how did you agree to aspire for this job of procreation, which increases bondage? God Almightly, Lord Siva, is the supreme creator of all creatures. He has created Brahma and has assigned this task to him. When Brahma became proud of his assignment, you know, he lost one of his heads. He has faced many other problems also. It you get the power of creations, you will have more troubles than pleasures. Once you get the capacity to create, you will tend to forget God who is the very basis of the world and think no end of yourselves. With that pride, you will commit many blunders. So, I feel that you ask for salvation only and that is the best for you". Narada explained.

On hearing what he said, the sons of Daksha got worried. They were convinced that what the sage said was right. They bowed before Narada and said, "Sir we are now clear in our mind. You should teach us the path to salvation". Narada gave them the wisdom to abstain from worldly desires and seek relief from the temptations of the mundane world. They prayed to Lord Siva as directed by Narada and attained Mukthi.

When the sons did not return even after a long time. Daksha was doubtful. Through his vision of wisdom, he learnt what all happened. He got angry for Narada's intervention. He got another thousand sons again and repeated the process of educating them well and sending them to meditate. Narada intervened again and made them also take the route to Mukthi. They also received initiation from Narada and obtained their goal of Mukthi.

When the second attempt also failed, Daksha was extremely upset. All his two thousand children were waylaid by Narada from his desired goal and he was left with no son at last. So, he cursed Narada that he will not stay permanently anywhere.

He will have to go places without a permanent abode and fend for himself all over the place. He shall have no place to call his own and so travel all the time incessantly.

The curse given to Narada by Daksha started working immediately and Narada became a globe-trotter from then on, in all the three worlds.

## 76. The anger towards the Moon

Though Daksha had two thousand sons, he could not get what he desired from them. So, he tried through daughters now. Subuddhi, Buddhi, Surasai, Dhruthi, Duttai, Kriyai, Keerthi, Sraddhai, Lachai, Medha, Kathi, Santai, Vapu, Kyâti, Sambooti, Naari, Sanidhi, Mruthi, Oorchai, Anusuyai, Suva, Sumai and Suvathai; He got these twenty three daughters. From Subuddhi to Vapu, the first thirteen were married to Dharumar. Sage Brughu married Kyati. Sage Mareechi married Sambooti; Pulastyar married Naari and Sannidhi; Pulakar married Mruthi. Oorchai married Sage Vasishta and Anasuyai married Sage Atri. Agni married Suva, Krathu married Sumai and Pithara married Suvathai.

Dharmar got twenty-seven sons. Sage Bhrugu got two sons, Vidata and Data and a daughter by name Lakshmi. The Sage gave his daughter Lakshmi in marriage to Narayana.

Sage Mareechi had four daughters, who inturn, produced many children. Pulastyar also had many children Ankra got two sons called Ankidheera and Bharata. He had four daughters after them and many sages were born to them. Pulakar had a son Dathadri. Kumbar was born in the family of Dathadri. Sage Vasishta got a daughter and seven sons.

Sage Atri had three sons called Sakthi Netra, Chandra and Sani Sankhadana.

Agni begot three sons and sage Krathu also had three sons. Pitara got two daughters – Mena and Bhoomi. Himavan married Mena and Meru parvatam married Bhoomi. Meru got a son and named him Mandra parvatam. He prayed to Lord Siva and got the boon that he will reside with Him all the time. Meru got a daughter also and he named her Velai. Varuna married Velai and got a girl Saravani. Varuna gave his daughter in marriage to Prachina. The couple got ten children.

Thus, Daksha's clan began to grow. Daksha got another 27 daughters also. They are shining in the sky as the 27 stars, from Aswini to Revati. He married them all to the Moon with the condition that he will not treat anyone of them with partiality. "All my daughters are to be equally happy with you and so, you should love them all in equal measure", he said.

The moon accordingly lived with 27 wives, treating them all equally well. Every one of them was happy. But in course of time, the moon found Karttigai and Rohini more beautiful than the others did, so, he happened to love them better than others . The rest of the wives, 25 stars, felt unhappy with the Moon's preferential treatment to Krittigai and Rohini. They told their husband that what he was doing was wrong. But he would not care. So, they complained to their father, Daksha, who got wild. When it was a condition at the time of marriage itself, he felt that Chandra, the Moon, has not kept up his promise. So he cursed him to lose his beauty day after day.

Due to Daksha's curse, the moon lost his shades of beauty day after day. Within 15 days, he lost 15 shades, one after the other and he was left with the last one only. He was afraid that if this one also vanishes the next day, the brightness will be lost completely and none would care for him. Those who praised him so far will mock at him hereafter. So, he rushed to Indra and wanted his help.

Indra felt sorry for the Moon's plight "O Chandra! Why were you so foolish as to invite such a curse? Already Lord Vinayaka had cursed you once. When you laughed at Vinayaka's big stomach and the modakam in his hand, while he was in Kailasa, he cursed you by which none would like to see you, as you would totally lose your lustre. You felt ashamed and hid yourself somewhere, without moving along the sky. Then Lord Siva and all of us begged pardon of Vinayaka who graciously consented to forgive you. He revised his curse by saying that at least for one day in the year, i.e. in the month of Aavani, on the fourth day of the Poorvapaksham (First fortnight after New Moon day) the people will not look at you, but only pray to Lord Vinayaka. Now, again, you have another curse. You go to Brahma who can, perhaps, talk to his son Daksha and get that changed".

The Moon accordingly went to Brahmalokam, met Brahma and told him the whole episode.

"Chandra! Do you think Daksha will listen to my words? It is true that he is my son. But he has changed a lot. Because of his wealth, he is too conceited these days. He takes his own decisions and does not care for others. He thinks too highly of himself. I do not think he will obey me. He may not. There is no point in talking to him about you, because you have also erred. He may point it out and refuse paying heed to my advice. I suggest you go to Lord Siva in Mount Kailas. If you complain to Him, He will help you. He never says 'no' to anyone who surrenders to him. So, the only course open before you is to go to Mount Kailas and take refuge in Lord Siva. Don't delay", Brahma said.

**Chandra went to Mount Kailasa and bowed before Lord Siva. The omniscient Lord asked him for the reason of his visit, as if he knew nothing.**

"Mahadeva! Daksha's daughters, who are the 27 stars, are my wives. As I was slightly partial to Krittigai and Rohini, who are more beautiful than the rest, Daksha has cursed me to lose all my shades of beauty. During the last

fortnight, I have gradually lost all my beauty and I am left with only one shade today. I am sure to lose that also tomorrow, by which I will be reduced to nothing but a butt of ridicule for everyone. Sarveswara! You are my only saviour", he prayed.

Lord Siva took pity on him and wore the last crescent moon on his head.

"Chandra! You do not worry. This last shade will always remain in my head. From tomorrow, you will slowly regain your form, by getting one shade each day. After you are full, you will again face the same fate of losing one shade each day. This will occur in a cycle fortnight after fortnight."

Chandra felt happy and took leave of the Lord. From then on, we have the two fortnights in a month one during which moon loses his form slowly and the other when he regains it gradually.

## 77. The Advice by Pulakar

Daksha came to know that the Moon has surrendered to Lord Siva and has got his curse altered by His grace. He got very angry with Lord Siva for His interference. Forgetting that many learned Sages were present in the court, he talked very ill of Lord Supreme.

"Even my father Brahma or Vishnu never attemped to change the curse given by me to Moon. None of them even approached me, asking me to revise it. While that is so, why should Lord Siva change it? Just because He is the only one who makes or mars the world, He thought he could do it. I meditated on him and got such a high status with His grace. Is he angry with me that I have not gone to Him begging for anything after that?"

When Daksha was condemning Lord Siva like this in an open assembly of scholars, Sage Pulakar addressed him:

"Daksha Prajapati! Please do not talk lightly of the incomparable Lord Supreme. None will care for you if you do not respect Him. Moreover, if you incur His wrath, all these riches, which you enjoy now, will vanish in no time."

Daksha laughed at his words. "Maharishi, I did not get these riches overnight. I worked very hard and did a very heavy penance to get all these. Even Brahma and Vishnu are doing what I say. They are not displeased with me and so they do not complain", he said.

"O Son of Brahma! Just because nobody finds fault with you or all your riches keep growing, it is not proper for you to talk ill of Lord Almighty. Are you justified in blaming Him, when He has showered so much Grace on you?", he asked.

"Maharishi ! I have earned this coveted position and riches by my sheer hard penance and God will never stand in the way of my enjoying them", said Daksha.

"Daksha Prajapati! Your conviction is good. But those who have belittled Lord Siva have never prospered as per Vedas. Do not make unparliamentary remarks about Him. He will never punish you. That is why when Moon went to Him, he got your curse just modified. God has still retained your curse also as the moon did not keep up his word given to you. Above all, the Moon is your son-in-law. Lord Siva is also due to become your son in law in future. Do not get cross with Him". Pulakar's advice brought down his anger slightly.

## 78. Devi gets affected by blemishes

Once upon a time, Lord Siva and Pârvathi were happily conversing with each other. Pârvathi worshipped the Lord and asked, "Oh! Lord, will you be pleased to explain your true self to me?"

Lord kindly came forward to explain His true nature, as expounded in the Vedas.

Lord Siva is formless; He has no particular character; He has no blemishes; He is omnipresent; Because of his love for all creatures, He releases them from their bondage. He manifests Himself in five powers – Parasakti (Supreme Power), Adisakti (Source of all power), Ichasakti (Power of desires), Gnanasakti (Power of wisdom) and Kriyasakti (Power of action). In order to facilitate all creatures to worship Him, He has acquired from the above 5 powers, Sivasaadhakyam and such other five. His forms of supremacy are twenty-five. From Pranavam or Omkaaram, he has four different stages. From three illusions, namely, Suddhamayai (Pure Illusions), Asuddha Mayai (Tainted illusions) and Prakruti (Nature) are born 36 philosophies. Vignânakalar, Pralayakâlar, Sakalar – these three souls and combination of 36 doctrines and those who follow these, are there and have their origin and end in Him. Lord Siva explained all these aspects about Him in detail to Devi.

Devi questioned Siva for a clarification. "Lord! You said you were formless, yet you have taken so many forms. Why did you do that?"

"My dear! I have no one single form of my own. I take several forms because of many manifestations of power – Sakthi".

Devi was pleased with this answer and said, "Lord! I am known as your power. If that is so, all the forms of power taken by you are mine."

When devi boasted about herself as power incarnate, Lord was not very happy.

"My dear! You chose to talk highly of your power in my presence. Whoever gets this pride, I see to it that it is destroyed. If I do not do that, the souls will never get enlightened but get doomed because of pride. You are derived from me and I live in thee too. If I do not act, you will also lose your identity and activity. Let me illustrate it", He said.

So saying, God stopped his motivation in all living beings for sometime. Immediately, all of them perished losing all their movements. Devi was terrified and immediately fell at His feet. "Oh My Lord! I did not know that you reside in all that moves and all that is stationary also. All creatures are lifeless now, as if this is the end of all existence. Kindly excuse my ignorance. Let all the souls get back their power of life and resume their movements as before", she requested.

With due deference to Devi's request , Lord Siva first enlivened the eleven Rudras. They understood by their wisdom that Lord was playing with His creatures. So they wanted to pray to Him and ask for restoration of living senses to all creatures. As the Sun and the Moon stayed motionless, there was darkness everywhere. They reached a holy place called Tiruvidaimarudur. As it was dark everywhere, they thought it was night time and so, prayed to Lord Siva throughout the 12 hours, as per the rules prescribed in the saivite Scriptures. Lord was pleased with their prayers and gave them darshan. When he asked them what they desired, they wanted Him to make all creatures

get back to their life. God granted their prayers. All souls resumed their work, as if they got up from their sleep.

Lord Siva told the eleven Rudras to ask for more, if they so desire. "Maheswara! We were extremely happy to worship at your feet, four times during these twelve hours. If anyone prays to you meticulously with devotion four times during the night, they may be blessed just as those who worship you on Sivaratri day in Maasi (Maga) Month on Krishnapaksha Chaturdasi".

God granted their prayer and disappeared. When God stopped the activities of the universe, Devas also were motionless and their routine was disrupted. Brahma and others started worrying about the break that occurred in their duties. They went to Kailas and told Lord Siva about their fears of becoming guilty of interrupted routine.

The Lord told them with great kindness, "You do not worry. When you were motionless, your routine activities were disrupted. The consequences of this lapse of one's duties were due to Devi only. She was responsible for creation of such a state of affairs. So, She alone will be guilty for the break of the stoppage of all works". Lord Siva clarified

Devi, who was sitting next to him, got worried on hearing this. She fell at His feet and asked, "O Lord! If all the lapses which occurred due to the intermission in the movement of creatures were to revert to me, according to you, what does it mean?"

Lord clarified, "You were boasting of your power in front of me. So I wanted to point out your mistaken impression and correct your attitude. So, the movement of the entire universe was made to come to a standstill for sometime, so that you realize your folly. When you understood the truth, I made them resume their routine. So, the lapses due to the break in their schedule have to necessarily reach you only. You are the mother of all creations. You alone are capable to take the burden and atone for these sins", he said.

She prayed to Him again and asked him to suggest ways and means for her to make amends for the mistakes she committed unwittingly due to her ignorance.

"Devi! You take the form of a conch and do penance in Kalindi River. Daksha will come there and take you. You become a child and grow in his palace. After you are five years old, you start meditating on me with devotion. I shall come and marry you to bring you back to Mount Kailas", he said.

**Devi was quite distressed to get separated from her husband. She repented for her mistake, took leave of the Lord and reached Kalindi River, which flows in the name of Yamuna in Bhoolokam. She took the shape of a conch and rested on a lotus in the riverside. She was lying there chanting "Om Namasivaya ", the holy five lettered Mantra to propitiate Lord Siva.**

## 79. The child found in Kalindi River

Mâsimakham (The day on which Makham star occurs in the Tamizh month of Maasi) is said to be very auspicious for taking a holybath in sacred rivers. Those who take bath in Yamuna river on that day get a lot of fortunes. Daksha wanted to do this with his wife Vedavalli and his other relatives. Brahma and sages blessed him and gave him leave to go.

On reaching Yamuna River, Daksha took a dip there with his wife and worshipped God Almighty.

When he was returning, he was attracted towards the lotus flowers in the riverside. On a beautiful lotus in the centre, he saw a white conch. He thought that it will be suitable for worshipping the Lord and so went near it. As soon as he took the conch in his hand, the conch became a lovely girl child. His surprise knew no bounds. He understood with his vision of wisdom that Devi has come to him as a child as per the Lord's boon. He was very happy and fondled the child in great joy. He gave her to his wife with great happiness that Devi herself has come to them as their child due to his great fortune.

Vedavalli hugged the child when milk poured out of her breasts instantaneously. She fed the child and everyone praised her. Devas visited the palace of Daksha to see the divine child.

Daksha's daughter was known as Uma. When she attained the age of five, she told her parents that she wanted to meditate on Lord Siva in order to get Him as her husband. She wanted a suitable place to be earmarked for that. Daksha and his wife Vedavalli were extremely happy that she was devoted to the Lord at the tender age itself. They constructed pretty hermit outside the city for the daughter to meditate. He asked many girls also to stay with her to keep company. Umadevi took the blessings of her parents and left on her mission.

Vedavalli was greatly surprised that a five-year-old girl was eager to meditate on the Lord. She asked Daksha, "My Lord! How is that our daughter has decided to meditate on Lord Siva at this very early age itself and also to marry Him only?"

"Vedavalli, when I sat in meditation at Manasarovar and had Lord Siva's darshan, I asked Him for a boon that I should get Devi Herself as my daughter so that I can give her in marriage to Him. God granted it. In order to fulfill my desire, Devi has come as a conch on a lotus flower in the riverside of Yamuna, to attract me and become my daughter. Do not think that she is an ordinary child", Daksha said.

Umadevi stayed in the hermit with her friends and meditated on the Lord with great devotion. Her thoughts were fully fixed on Lord Supreme only.

## 80. A confusion in the marriage

In the outskirts of Dakshapuri, Umadevi prayed to Lord Siva in her exclusive hermit. Her strict adherence to the rule of meditation pleased Lord Siva very much. He decided to grace Her with his presence and so, came there in the disguise of a Brahmin.

With the sacred ash adorning the forehead, a Brahmin was sighted by Umadevi's friends who took him as a devotee of Lord Siva. They duly informed Umadevi of his arrival.

Umadevi received him with due honours and asked him for the purpose of his visit.

"My dear pretty girl! I have come here with a desire. Would you fulfill it if I tell you about that?", asked the Lord in the guise of a brahmin.

"Oh, Lord! I respect you as a devotee of Lord Siva. If it is within my capacity, I shall fulfill your desire", said Umadevi innocently.

"My dear girl, I heard a lot about your beauty. I am desirous of marrying you. So I have come here with that aim only", said the Lord.

Umadevi was shocked and closed her ears in disgust saying 'Siva, Siva'.

"Oh Lord! It is not proper for you to say such words. I have already made up my mind to marry Lord Siva, who is praised and worshipped by one and all", she said.

The Lord smiled and said, "O my dear girl! That Lord Siva in not easily accessible for even great saints. How is it possible in your case? Don't indulge in day dreams and spoil your health".

"You do not seem to know my mind. I have taken a vow not to marry anyone else except him. I shall meditate firmly until I achieve my goal. In case He does not come in response to my severe and sincere prayers, I shall sacrifice my life by continuing my penance, but not marry anyone else. This is certain. So you may please leave now. I do not want you to be here any longer", she said angrily.

The Lord was happy to know her steadfast love for him and showed his real self, only to be seen by her. Umadevi was thrilled by his darshan and fell at His feet.

"Lord, I did not realise who you are. I was harsh with you as I took you to be a Brahmin asking for my hand. You must kindly pardon me for my foolishness", she pleaded.

"Umadevi! Don't you worry. You did not commit any mistake. I am happy to know that you are firm in your mind."

Devi's friends could not make out anything from their conversation. For them, he looked like an ordinary brahmin bachelor only. So they thought he has somehow enticed Umadevi and has made her fall in love with him. If Daksha comes to know about this, he will get angry with the girls who brought the brahmin boy there. So, they wanted to inform the King themselves before the matter reached him through other sources. They met Daksha and told him that the brahmin bachelor was still in conversation with the princess Umadevi.

Daksha understood the truth with his vision of wisdom. He knew that the visitor was none else than Lord Siva himself. His joy knew no bounds. "I shall give my daughter in marriage to Lord only", he said dancing merrily.

He checked up for a good day immediately. That very day was quite auspicious. He was doubly happy. He wanted to conduct the marriage without delay. He sent out his messengers and got the Devas to make all arrangements. Viswakarma took the responsibility for all decorations.

Daksha rushed to his daughter's hermitage. He fell at the feet of the brahmin bachelor. "Oh! Lord, I know who you are. My daughter has decided to marry you and so was meditating here. You must kindly come to my palace and accept her in marriage", he requested.

Lord Siva consented and reached the royal palace with Daksha and Umadevi. The women welcomed him with all auspicious things. Vedavalli gave her daughter a holy bath and decorated her as a bride with silk and gold ornaments. Devas had thronged Dakshapuri to partake in the wedding celebrations of the Lord with Umadevi. Brahma and Vishnu were also present.

Vedavalli helped by pouring holy sacred waters on the feet of Lord Siva and Daksha washed His feet. Chanting Vedamantras, he worshipped His feet. Then he placed his daughter's hand in the Lord's hand and asked Him to accept her. All Devas and Indra praised him. Brahma came forward to help with the customary rituals. Vishnu recited Veda mantras and conducted the function in a grand manner.

**All the invitees and visitors were fortunate to see the divine couple there stand hand in hand. Suddenly the Lord hid himself from everyone and went to Kailasa. Umadevi was shocked at the disappearance of her husband. Daksha and others got perplexed. None could guess the reason.**

**Vedavalli consoled her daughter who was weeping. "My dear child! Don't get disheartened. The only way to get him back is to meditate again. Please continue to do it and he will come to take you", she said.**

Saraswati and Lakshmi also consoled her. "Devi, we are surprised that you are upset. Have your forgotten that you are the mother of the world? All things in this world are your manifestations only. You are worried that your Lord has left you. This is a mere play for him. Who knows his mind? We have all been happy to see both of you as the bride and bridegroom".

Umadevi resumed her meditation in her hermitage. Daksha was greatly upset by the Lord's mysterious behaviour. In front of the Devas who are in his attendance, he had to face a situation when they took pity on him!

"The Lord's gesture of disappearing suddenly from the marriage hall was mainly to insult me. When he had earlier so kindly agreed to his request that Devi should be born as his daughter and she would be given in marriage to Lord only, what was the idea in this disappearance from the wedding scene, all of a sudden? I had made all fine arrangements. Was there any omission? Now, I have to face a pathetic situation before the Devas. Why should I suffer

this punishment when I am not guilty?" Daksha was getting more and more angry with the Lord, thinking on all the sequences of events.

Umadevi was with her friends in her hermitage, and resumed her meditation. Lord Siva decided to bring her back to Kailas and chose an auspicious day for that. He adorned himself with sacred ash all over the body and wore Rudraksha garlands. With long locks of hair, he took his Soolayudham and came like a saint to her hermit. Umadevi mistook him again to be a devotee of the Lord and welcomed him.

He then gave her darshan, sitting alone on His Rishabha mount. Umadevi was thrilled and with tears of joy, she worshipped at His feet.

"My Lord! You left me in the midst of wedding festivities and disappeared from the hall. Please take me now with you and make me happy", she pleaded. The Lord made her sit by His side and went to Kailasa.

Daksha came to know that Lord Siva came to the hermitage as a saint and took Umadevi to Mount Kailasa. As he was already angry, this news made him burst like a volcano. He told the Devas who had come there to salute him. "Devas! Please listen. Look at what that Siva, who is a beggar in the Kailasa has done. When I gave my daughter in marriage to Him, he suddenly disappeared from the marriage hall. He insulted me before my guests. Now, he has come to the hermitage and taken my daughter to Mount Kailasa. Is it proper to behave like this, without the parents knowing about it? He has come as a thief and taken my daughter without informing anyone!" Daksha talked so low of Lord's behaviour that the Devas were feeling helpless to talk to him. None could say that he was exceeding his limits of propriety.

He was so ungrateful and hostile to Lord Supreme by whose grace he was enjoying a great status. Devas could only regret his folly within themselves and so they silently left the place.

## 81. Dakshan get insulted

Daksha's anger towards Lord Siva was growing day by day. So, he indulged in uncomplimentary talks about him as much as it pleased him.

Brahma and others were feeling bad at Daksha's attitude. Daksha was bent upon expressing his anger for Lord Siva in his own loose talks. It was feared that he will incur the wrath of Siva and die. If they continue to carry out his errands without trying to correct him, it will be misconstrued that they were in agreement with him. They had no courage to tell him that his actions were wrong and they do not want to be a party for his blaming God Almighty all the time. Daksha might get angry with them if they do so and also trouble them more and more. They were totally confused as to what to do and which was the right course for them. Sooner or later, there has to be an end for this state of affairs.

Finally Brahma made up his mind and boldly went to meet his son Daksha. He told him, "My dear son! After Umadevi went to Mount Kailas with her husband, you have not cared to visit her so far. Just because you are angry with Lord Siva, you may not like to go there very much. If you continue to nurse your anger, the relationship with your son-in-law may cease slowly. This does not become of your dignity. You have to give up your wrong thinking. It will be proper if you choose to go and see your daughter and son-in-law at Mount Kailas". If only Daksha agrees to go to Mount Kailas and a meeting takes place between him and the Lord, the anger may vanish soon, he thought.

The Father's advice appealed to Daksha as the correct thing to do and so he consented to make a trip to Kailasa to meet his daughter and son-in-law. The Devas wanted to accompany him. But he asked them to stay in Dakshapuri itself and went alone. He went to the gate where Nandideva was on guard. His demon army did not allow him to go in.

"Who are you to prevent me? I have come to see my daughter and son-in-law", he said angrily. The demons were not afraid of him.

"You have been blaming our Lord for everything. You received a number of boons from him only after doing penance the hard way. But you are very much ungrateful and so find fault with him all the time. Even looking at you who is talking ill of my master will make us sinners. If you will behave yourself when you see our Lord, we will permit you to enter, otherwise, you better get back to your place", they said.

After all the gatekeepers were pointing out that he was guilty and were so rude to him, Daksha could not tolerate this insult. He had no mind now to call on his daughter or son-in-law He was furious at the demons that confronted him. "You dogs! You are servants here and you do not know who I am! Who is that Siva whom you praise so much? He is my son-in-law. He has to respect me. Am I to go and worship at His feet? No, never. You are instigated by Him to talk to me disrespectfully. That is why I face this insult. I will see to it that He suffers for posting you here to offend me. Nobody shall praise Him or worship Him. All of them will only blame Him and disrespect Him. You will see that all this happens very soon". Daksha returned to his palace in the same angry mood.

He called all the Devas immediately to report to him. "Devas! I went to Mount Kailas and thought of meeting my daughter and son-in-law in order to bridge the gap between us. Do you know what kind of welcome awaited me there? That beggar had posted demons at the gate and I was not allowed inside. Do you know what all those demons said about me? I cannot repeat their words, which were so mean. My daughter has joined hands with Him. I should solely blame myself for having condescended to visit them without realising my status and hence I deserved it all.

Well, listen to what I say now. None of you hereafter praise or worship Lord Siva. If you disobey my orders, you will be given severe punishments".

What can poor Devas do? For simple fear of Daksha, they took his order silently.

## 82. Brahmayâga gets disrupted

Some time passed by. Devas were not worshipping Lord Siva, for fear of Daksha. At that time, Brahma decided to conduct a yâga. He made all arrangements and invited Vishnu, Indra and Devas to attend and conduct the yâga. Lord Siva is to be given the first place in the yâga. Daksha may not agree to this rule as Brahma could guess. But still he was firm to follow the custom as per rules.

Brahma went to Mount Kailas to invite Siva formally for the yâga. When the Lord asked him for the purpose of his visit, Brahma requested him to attend the yâga and take the first honours as per traditions and rules. Lord smiled and said that his representative, Nandideva would grace the yâga.

Brahma started to perform the yâga in the city of Manavati in Meru mountains. He had also invited Dakshan for the yâga. Vishnu, Indra and the Devas called on Dakshan and informed him about the invitation extended to them for the yâga arranged by Brahma. They were apprehensive of his views in the matter, because Lord Siva would be the presiding deity for the yâga. Dakshan welcomed all of them and offered to join them as he was also one of the invitees. Brahma welcomed all the guests with pleasure and gave them seats. He made Daksha sit next to him.

When the yâga was about to begin, Nandideva came with his demon companions. Brahma received them with due honours and gave them seats. Daksha was upset and so he commented that Nandideva was the messenger from the beggar in Mount Kailas. He did not stop there, but went on addressing the gathering there:

**"Vishnu, Indra, Devas, Sages, Lakshmi and all divine personalities are assembled here. Is it proper for Nandideva and his friends to join this company? He is after all a servant of Siva, who takes poison and dances in the graveyard". He then turned to his father and asked, "Father! Had you invited Nandideva, who is only a gatekeeper in Mount Kailasa? You go to invite Lord Siva and he sends His watchman. You receive him as if he is an important visitor and also make him sit on par with me in the august assembly of celestials? Is this all right? You behave exactly against my wishes only to place me in an embarrassing situation. As you happen to be my father, I have to keep quiet by**

just digesting all this. **If any other person had done
this, I would have cut off his head. Please
understand one more thing from today. Nobody
should give the first offering to that Siva who is
only mad to dance with dead bodies in the**

**graveyard, wearing garlands of bones and snakes. He is not qualified for such coveted honours. Let us hereafter accept Vishnu as supreme and give him the first offering".**

When Daksha was thus directing and misleading all the visitors there to revolt against Lord Siva, Nandideva could not tolerate it. He got very wild at the silence of Vishnu, Indra and others without any reaction merely for fear of punishment by Dakshan. So, he got up from his seat in great anger and looking at his violent reaction, the sages and Devas there began to shiver.

Nandideva addressed Daksha, "O Son of Brahma! Your words are not becoming of your status. I would have cut your tongue for having spoken ill of my Lord. God has not permitted me to do it, so you are spared today. Next time, I hear you do this, I will cut off your head itself. You said that Lord Siva has no place in a yâga. For your information, Lord Siva is the yagnapati or the presiding deity for any yâga. If you defy His supremacy and honour somebody else, who will be the Lord of the yâgna? If Vishnu is the Lord Supreme, please note that Siva created Vishnu. If there is no offering for the Lord Siva in the yâga, it is not a yâgna at all. Anyone who does such a yâga, let his head be cut off! You hate Lord Siva and decry him. Let your head with the polluted tongue fall down! Let another ugly head be there, so that people laugh at you! Let all the Devas who supported you be dead and gone. When they are reborn, let them suffer at the hands of Soorapadhman!" After pronouncing a series of curses in his anger, Nandideva left the place in a huff. His demon associates also went out with him.

Nandideva's curses and exit made Devas very upset. Brahma was afraid to continue the yâga and so abruptly stopped it mid way. In case he wanted to continue as per rules and conclude it, Dakshan may create more problems, as Lord Siva alone will have to be the presiding deity. As the yâga was thus abandoned half way through, everybody was feeling very sad when they returned to their places.

## 83. Dakshan does yâga without Lord Siva.

It was long since anybody performed yâgna in the world. If at all anyone wanted to do yâga, they had to give Lord Siva the first offering for which Daksha would get angry. If they did the yâga without propitiating Lord Siva, they may invite the curses of Nandideva. So, Sages, Brahmins and Devas totally avoided doing yâga.

Daksha came to know that everyone stayed away from doing yâga for quite a long time now. He asked Devas one day about this, when they called on him. As they were afraid of Daksha, they gave an explanation to please him. "O Prajapati! Nandideva has given a curse that anyone who does a yâga without offering Lord Siva his due place, will lose his head. For fear that this will happen, nobody does the yâgas these days", they said.

Daksha laughed at their answer. "When my father did a yâga, that lunatic who dances in the graveyard had sent Nandideva. He blabbered something in his own way and you are all afraid that it will come true. Well, you do not fear any longer. I shall do a yâga the way I want. You can follow me later."

Immediately, he called Viswakarma and asked him to choose a suitable place for a yâga and make all arrange ments. On the banks of the River Ganges, in a place called Kanakalam, Viswakarma made a big yâgasâlâ.

Indra, Devas, Brahma, Vishnu and all others were to attend the yâga and so the yâgasâlâ was done up on a grand scale. All necessary things were also brought there. To feed all the brahmins who came there, Kamadhenu, Chintamani, Karpagam tree, Sankhanidhi, Padumanidhi, etc., were readily available there. He sent messengers all over the world to invite everyone to the yâga except Lord Siva.

The Sages, Brahmins and the Devas assembled on the spot. Vishnu came with his two consorts, Bhoodevi and Sreedevi. Brahma came with his wives Saraswati, Gayatri and Savitri on his swan mount. Ashtadiggajas, Yakshas, Siddhas, Vidyadharas and all others arrived. Chandra came with his 27 wives. The Asura King also arrived there from Chonidapuram. Just before the yâga began, Dakshan called his messengers and asked them if all the invities had come or if there were any absentees. They replied that a few sages viz. Agastya, the four Sanakadiyar, Atri, Vasishta, Bhrugu, Dadeechi, Durvasa and Parasara have not come and they had also found fault with Daksha for not inviting Lord Siva for the yâga. Daksha laughed and said, "So they are all sincere devotees of Lord Siva perhaps!"

Right then, Sage Dadeechi came there with the other sages and disciples. Though Dadheechi had earlier condemned his action, when the messengers met him, Daksha thought he was attending the yâga, as he feared his anger. So, he welcomed him with due respect and gave them all seats.

Sage Dadeechi looked at those assembled there and then called Daksha near him.

"O Daksha Prajapati! You have invited me to come for a yâga, which you are to conduct. What is the purpose for which this is arranged? May I know about it?", he asked. Daksha narrated what all happened earlier. "Oh Sage! When Devi came as my daughter, I wanted to give her in marriage only to Lord Siva. He also willingly accepted her hand. When the marriage festivities were over, he alone disappeared from our midst, putting me to shame in the presence of my guests. Then he met my daughter when she was alone, meditating on Him and took her away without my permission. When I went to Mount Kailas to see my daughter, he prevented my entry by asking his demons to stop me and also the demons insulted me very badly. When he did not respect me as his father-in-law, I prevented my father giving him respect in the yâga conducted by him. That beggar's messenger Nandideva blabbered something there and my father Brahma gave up the yâga midway for fear of consequence due to Nandi's curses. From then on nobody does yâga out of sheer fear. So, I decided to conduct this yâga, without Lord Siva and hence invited you all".

When Sage Dadeechi heard this long background to the yâga, he laughed in ridicule.

"Daksha Prajapati! You condemn Lord Siva and keep Him out of your yâga for your personal reasons and anger. I feel sorry for your vain attempts. How can we conduct a yâga without the presiding deity Lord Siva! Who else can be Yagnapathi or the God for Yâgas? Brahma, Vishnu and Devas were all created by Him only. They are given various specific assignments. Lord Siva is God Supreme and keeping him out of this yâga will not be honourable for you. This shows your foolishness only. If you do not follow the vedic rituals and customary practices according to rules and regulations laid down traditionally and conduct anything according to your own whims and fancies it will not be proper or complete. Lord Siva will stop it. All those who particpate in it along with you will also incur His wrath. So I suggest you give up this evil thought and do things the right way."

Daksha said, "I shall give Lord Siva's place to Vishnu and conclude the yâga".

Dadeechi was quite aggrieved at his stupidity. "O fool! What you say is improper. How can you keep the Lord Supreme out of this yâga? If you try to substitute him with some one lesser than Him, you will face hell of a trouble", he said.

Daksha was not ready to accept the advice of the sage. As he refused to be guided by him, a long debate ensued between the two. The merits and demerits of the arguments on both sides were discussed at length.

## 84. Daksha raises a query

Daksha raised a query with sage Dadeechi. "Maharishi! You say that Rudra is the God of yâga. There are 11 other Rudras also. They are the Easanya Rudras, who guard the Northeastern direction. If Vishnu is not to be given the first offering, I will give it to these Rudras and complete the yâga".

"O Daksha! Lord Siva is the Rudra at the end of the ages – Pralayakâla Rudra – who destroys the entire universe for a recreation. The other Rudras that you mention are not equal to Him. They all are devotees at

His feet. They just carry His form and name. But Lord Siva and they are not one and the same. Just as devotees, who meditate on Him acquire His graceful form, these Rudras are mere replicas of the Lord. Unlike Indra and Devas, they cannot come here", replied the sage.

"Maharishi! Brahma and Vishnu do the creation and protection respectively. Lord Siva is only the destroyer. Why should He be known as Lord Supreme or God Almighty?", Daksha asked.

"Daksha Prajapati! Just because Vishnu and Brahma are also included along with Rudra and known as Trimurti or three Gods, you think all of them are equals. One who has no birth and death is known as Lord Supreme, who has no single name, form or work. In order to retrieve the souls, which are carried away by their pride and desires, he has given the name and forms and duties to different manifestations of his own self as Brahma, Vishnu or Indra. He has delegated them various responsibilities and has aksed them to execute them. As destruction is a specialized job, which cannot be assigned to others as any other job, He does it Himself.

When Devas wanted to acquire the necessary powers to execute the responsibilities assigned to them God told them, 'My dear Devas, you fulfill your duties throughout your lives. Chant the mantras and apply sacred ash on your bodies and meditate on my Panchakshara ie. Namasivaya. You will easily acquire the requisite powers to carry on with your jobs. Whatever you do not know, they will be clear to you.' Thus, except destruction, He has delegated all other powers to others for various jobs. Vedas still call him 'Panchakrithya Kartha', as He is the supreme master of all the five parts of the duties. Those who suffer in the big ocean of birth-death cycles get salvation by following the vedic guidance. So, God's children as well as those who have been blessed by Him are also known by his own name.

"Once upon a time there was a battle between Devas and Asuras. Before Devas started to go to the battle, they gave their wealth to Agnideva and asked him to keep them safe in custody. When they returned from the war, they went to Agni and asked him to return their wealth. But Agni did not do so, but ran away with their wealth. When Devas chased him and tortured him from all sides, he cried. So he was also called Rudra.

All these names, therefore do not mean Maharudra. If you analyse the places where He has been mentioned, you will know his greatness. Let me explain another incident also.

Once upon a time, the sages were debating as to who was God Almighty. Finally they went to Brahma and asked him to clarify. He was also very happy to tell them all about Him. With tears of joy in his eyes and a heart full of devotion, he raised his hands above his head in reverence to God and swore thrice that Lord Siva was God Almighty beyond doubt.

He also told them, "O Sages! God Siva created me and Vishnu. He taught us the Vedas. He is extremely kind to all the souls and so he does the five fold jobs. He is endless; He is the purpose for all purposes; He does not take birth; He is the Lord of everyone; He surpasses everything; He has no end for himself; Vedas say that He is supreme and ultimate. We are still unable to understand him fully'.

"The sages took leave of Brahma after getting convinced that Lord Siva is God Supreme. Daksha, please realise that He is the mastermind for all. I have only repeated what your father Brahma told us. You had been taught all Vedas by him and that is how you attained such a status after meditating on Siva as directed by your father. You seem to have forgotten all about the past. Is your end approaching? Pride goes before a fall. If you want to keep up your honour, Please do not nurse anger and enmity towards Lord Siva. Do not become a target for His anger. You offer him His due place and conduct the Yâga".

After listening to the long sermon from the sage, Daksha laughed aloud; "Maharishi! Will the Lord Supreme wear bones and garland of skulls? Will He wear ashes of Deva's burnt bodies? Will He go about with a begging bowl? Will He wear a hair as Upaveetam? Should elephant skin be his dress? Should he carry Agni, Deer, mazhu and Soolam? Why should he go begging? Why does he dance like a mad man? Should He be surrounded by demons? Should poisonous snakes be His ornaments? Should He wear the crescent moon? Why should He be half-naked? Why should He take various forms? Should He ride on an ox? Was He obliged to drink the poison? Is He to dance in the graveyard? Why should He have two women, one on His head and another by His side? Why did He beget children? Should He be so sluggish in action? By all these yardsticks, I can judge your Lord Siva only as a sub-standard person. He has absolutely no single good feature to talk about. Lord Supreme has to be immaculately pure.

"He has to be all kindness incarnate. He should be endowed with all excellent qualities. Then only we can accept Him as the source of all that is good. He is beyond any reasonable noble feature to adore. So, I won't propitiate Him in the yâga", Daksha firmly replied.

Sage Dadeechi was extremely angry at Daksha's casual mention of Lord's name and form. He felt that it was all futile to talk to him as he can never get to know God in His true colours. Even then, he wanted to give him a fitting reply for all the stupid statements he made about God. He expected that his mind may perhaps change after listening to his eloborate elucidation.

## 85. Sage Dadeechi explains the significance

Sage Dadeechi spoke to Daksha in detail. "O Daksha! You have talked so much ill of Lord Siva. You found fault with many of His activities and said that He was not virtuous. This shows that you do not know about Him fully well. I can give you explanations and reasons for all the queries you have raised. Listen to me carefully.

God Almighty first created Brahma and Vishnu and assigned them the work of creation and protection. He kept the work of destruction to Himself. At the end of the ages, there will be a deluge in which the whole universe will be wiped out and all the souls will attain salvation by uniting with the Lord Supreme. At that time God Almighty will absorb in Himself Brahma and Vishnu and all Devas and become the one great entity amalgamating everything in Him. He will then wear a garland of all their heads. He will spin their hairs into Upaveetam and wear it on his chest. He would pick them up using his Soolayudham. He will burn all the bodies with his third eye. This is all because of Devas' good fortune of their previous births. He does not do all these to be praised for anything. He wants all the souls to accept and understand Him as the great master. Please understand his limitless grace now.

Once upon a time, as asura named Hiranyakshan kidnapped the Earth, and put it in his stomach and hid himself in Paatalaloka.

The Devas were so afraid of him that they went to Vishnu and complained. He took the form of a pig, went to Pathalalokam, fought with the asura and redeemed the Earth. As he had successfully done it, he became so conceited that he thought that he was the all powerful God Almighty. In that ecstasy, he tore the ground with his sharp teeth, jumped into the sea and made it muddy. As he was exceeding limits, Lord Siva appeared there and pulled out one of his sharp teeth. Vishnu came back to his senses and worshipped Lord Siva. It is that tooth which Siva is still wearing on his chest.

When Devas and Asuras were churning the milk ocean to get the nectar, the Mandra mountain, which was used as the churning rod, was not steady and tilted into the ocean. Vishnu became a tortoise and took the mountain on his shell back so as to make it stand erect. Only after that Devas and Asuras could churn the ocean and get the nectar. There ensued a big fight between the Devas and Asuras as to who is to take the nectar. Vishnu who was responsible for making the churning possible did not intervene and settle the issue. Instead he went crazy and proud about his feat and revelled by enjoying himself in playing about in the sea.

If the sea water gets polluted, the people will suffer. So, Lord Siva appeared there, brought him to senses and curbed his revelry. Vishnu repented for his mistake and changed his form from the tortoise to his original self. Lord Siva took the shell back and wore it on his chest and also helped Devas to get the nectar.

Because of these two incidents, the sharp tooth of the pig and the shell cover of the tortoise are adorning Lord Siva's chest from then on.

At another point of time, the sages who lived in Daruka forest did not care for Lord Siva. They thought that their good deeds alone will pay rich dividends and so gave up worshipping God. They started doing very complicated yaagas and meditations. Lord Siva wanted to enlighten them on the right codes of conduct. He called Vishnu and told him about his intentions to go to Daruka forest in order to educate the sages.

"He also told him to do certain thing in this regard. Accordingly, Vishnu took the form of Mohini by which he had settled the nectar issue between the Devas and Asuras. Lord Siva took his Soolayudham and went with him.

As soon as they reached near Daruka forest, Lord Siva asked Vishnu to distract the sages so that they give up their routine activities. Vishnu went there in the most beautiful Mohini form. Enchanted by her immense beauty, all the sages abandoned their daily chores crowded around her and began to sing in praise of her exquisite charms.

After the sages were drawn to the place of Mohini, Lord Siva went to their ashrams. He sang the vedic hymns in a sweet voice and went along the streets. All the wives of the sages came out and were attracted by the handsome Lord. They forgot their status and surrounded the begging Siva, enticed by his majestic personality. In a state of mind full of lust, the wives of the sages forgot all their pure doctrines of chastity and were following the unknown handsome beggar, blabbering in extreme desire. They entirely forgot their true selves and fully enjoyed themselves in the company of Siva. Lord Siva blessed them with 48,000 sons. He ordained that all of them will meditate on Him from there. He came out of the Ashram with the wives of the sages and thought of Vishnu. When Vishnu in the form of Mohini reached Siva, all the sages who were mad after Mohini also followed.

"As soon as the sages reached the Asram, they came out of their spell bound attraction for Mohini. They saw their wives enjoying themselves in the company of a stranger. They got angry and also realised the truth behind what all happened. Lord Siva wanted to outrage the modesty of their wives and so had come as a naked handsome man. Vishnu had come in the guise of Mohini, in order to distract their minds from a life of principles to cheap desires. They told their wives, "You have all been cheated. You have lost your chastity. Please go away from the company of this beggar and go home. The women did not care for them. They continued to laugh and enjoy themselves in the company of Siva, without realizing the presence of their husbands. The sages went wild with anger and did treacherous yâga in order to destroy Lord Siva, who enticed and waylaid their women. Out came a wild tiger, which was directed to kill Siva. The Lord killed it and wore its skin as his dress.

A Soolayudham came out of the yâga. The sages threw it at him. Lord Siva grabbed it and made it his armour.

When these two tricks failed, the sages conducted a more terrific yâga. From the flames of the fire, a deer calf came out. The sages directed it on Siva. It pounced on the Lord. When He looked at it, it became subdued. He took it in his left hand and asked it to provide sweet music always.

Next came poisonous snakes from the yâga fire. They were also directed to kill Lord Siva. When they approached the Lord, they became quiet and became his ornaments. Then came out a lot of demons that were ordered to devour Siva. They could not stand the loud taunt from him and so became His slaves.

"The sages further intensified their yâga. An awful head alone emerged, which was too gruesome even for the sages to look at. The white fearful head was directed to Lord Siva who caught it by the hand and wore it in His head.

The sages were boiling with anger. They chanted evil mantras to annihilate Siva. They took the form of a Udukkai – a musical instrument, which sounded loudly to shake all directions. Lord Siva took it in his hand, so that it can produce melodious rhythm near his ears.

When Siva could not be cowed down by any evil tactic, the sages conducted a "homam" – a holy fire worship with an evil design. A great demon, Muyalakan came out. The sages asked the fire and the demon to destroy Siva. Lord Siva took the fire in his hand and stamped on Muyalakan by one of his feet and stood.

The sages gave Siva a series of curses, but nothing could affect the Lord. Muyalakan tried to lift his head from underneath the Lord's foot. Lord Siva started dancing on his back. The worlds trembled. The sages fell down unconscious. The Devas were very happy at the cosmic dance of Siva but they also fell down tired.

When Lord saw that all the souls were shivering, He stooped dancing. Indra and Devas worshipped Him. Lord Siva blessed the sages of Daruka forest also, though they had given him all problems. They were made to realise their folly. They came out of their mistaken notions and begged pardon from the Lord. When they repented for their sinful acts and behaviour, God pardoned them and asked them to adhere to the vedic rules and regulations".

Sage Dadeechi further explained to Dakshan some other aspects of Siva also.

## 86. Gajasamhara Moorthi

Once upon a time, there was an asuran with the elephant form called Gajaasuran. He meditated on Brahma and got boons, which gave him an unending, long life and undefeatable might. When Brahma gave him the boons, he also warned him that as and when he faces Lord Siva, the boons will not be functional.

Gajaasuran travelled all over the three worlds and with his excessive might, troubled everybody. Diggajas ran away; Indra went into hiding; Devas obeyed all his orders.

Gajaasuran made Bhoolokam his sole target. He wanted to do away with all brahmins and sages. All the sages went to Kasi city fearing his attacks. They went to Manikarnika temple, worshipped Lord Visweswara and pleaded with him to save them from the mighty asura.

Gajaasuran came to know that all the sages have run away to Vârânasi (Kasi city), fearing his onslaught. He chased them to Manikarnika temple and trumpeted loud outside the precincts of the temple. The sages got terribly afraid of him and hugged Lord Siva for succour.

**The asura laughed at them and came in. Lord Siva came out of the Lingam with the brightness of crore Suns. When he saw the Lord in great anger, he forgot Brahma's warning and tried to fight Him. The Lord kicked him with his leg and he fell down on the ground powerless. The Lord stamped on**

his head and back with his feet and skinned him with his nails. Umadevi got too terrified at the fierce sight. The Lord wore the elephant's skin on his shoulders and reduced his excessive brightness. Devas and sages got his superb darshan as Gajasamhara Moorti – the supreme power who destroyed the elephant asura and at last became free from the fear of the asura.

## 87. Brahma loses his head due to his pride

Once upon a time, Brahma and Vishnu were camping at one of the peaks of the Meru Mountains. The Devas and sages came to see them there. "O Sirs! We want to know who is the Lord Supreme amongst the Trimoortis – Brahma, Vishnu or Siva", they asked.

As both Brahma and Vishnu were part of the world of illusions, they forgot their exact status. Each one of the claimed that he was supreme. Brahma said he was Lord Supreme. Vishnu said that as Brahma was born only from his navel, he was greater than him. Both of them had serious arguments on the subject and it ended in a big fight. The sages and Devas felt that they were guilty of initiating the discussion and so left the place quietly. Then Pranava and Vedas came there in human forms. "Lord Siva is the Lord Supreme. He is the greatest among you. Why do both of you fight on the subject", they asked.

Their efforts to settle the issue failed, as both Brahma and Vishnu did not care for these words.

Lord Siva appeared as a huge column of fire before them in order to cry halt to the fight. On seeing a marvellous light before them, they shuddered and wanted to know who it was! Lord Siva revealed his form to them with his consort Pârvathi amidst the great fire.

"Vishnu came out of his trance, accepted Lord Siva as Supreme and praised him. Brahma had not come out of his mental distortions and so talked ill of Siva from his fifth head on top. Siva wanted to put down his pride and so asked Bhairava to come there. With a garland of skulls in the chest, Soolam, Mazhu, Paasam and Udukkai in his hands and with sparks of fire emitting from the three eyes, red locks of hair and sharp teeth, Bhairava appeared there with his blue – coloured image. Lord Siva asked him to pluck off the fifth head of Brahma, which spoke with contempt for him. Brahma was to be brought back to life afterwards with the blood donated by Devas and again giving them life. Then, Lord Siva asked Bhairava to stay in his own mansion – Bhairava Bhavanam. Whoever prayed to Lord was to be blessed by him and all their grievance removed. Then the light disappeared. Bhairava alone stood there. He plucked off Brahma's head on top with his finger nails. Brahma was bleeding profusely. He fell down dead. His blood was flowing all over the Earth. Bhairava opened his eye on his forehead, produced fire and made the blood streams evaporate. Brahma, by His grace, came back to life.

Thus, Brahma's conceit was put down. He realised the truth and understood clearly that Lord Siva was the Lord Supreme. With folded hands, he worshipped Bhairava. "Oh Lord! In my folly and ignorance, I failed to know the Supremacy of Lord Siva and talked very ill of him. So, I was punished for my pride. Just to make my fifth head get free from its guilt of having insulted Siva, let it adorn your hand, just as Soolayudham does".

Bhairava agreed and carried Brahma's skull in his hand. Brahma was thereafter known as Nânmukhan, as he was left with four heads only.

Bhairava then created Kâlavegan, Agnimukhan, Chomakan, Âlakâlan, Atibalan and such demons and visited the places of conceited sages and Devas at the heavens, with his demons' team accompanying him everywhere. He got their blood donated, cured them of imaginary illusion and finally gave them lives. Eventually he reached Vaikuntam, the abode of Vishnu.

Vishwaksena, the gatekeeper, did not allow Bhairava and his demons inside. The demons fought him and Bhairava picked up Vishwaksena by his Soolayudham and went inside.

Vishnu and his two wives welcomed Bhairava with due respect and asked him the purpose of his visit. "I have come to you as a beggar. I want the blood in your head to be donated to me", said Bhairava.

Madhava happily cut the vein in his forehead and made blood from his head flow into the skull in the hands of Bhairav. Even after all the blood from Vishnu's body had flown into the skull of Brahma, it was not even half-filled. Vishnu fainted and both his wives begged Bhairava for his life.

Bhairava resurrected Madhava and also released Vishwaksena from his Soolayudham. He also was revived to life and later Bhairava left with his demons. He went and stayed at Bhairava Bhavanam, earmarked for him by God. At the time of deluge, he will carry out Siva's orders and destroy all the creatures. In the graveyard of their ashes, he will happily go round on his dog mount of Vedas.

Lord Siva took the skull of Brahma as his begging bowl and went begging only to put down the conceit of others who deserved to be taught a lesson.

## 88. Indra fights with Lord Siva

Once, Indra came to Kailasa to meet Lord Siva. He was too proud of his leadership of Devas. Lord Siva knew this and so, appeared as a demon at the gate.

Indra did not recognize Lord Siva in the form of a demon. He thought that the gatekeeper was a stranger to Kailasa.

He asked him, "You seem to have recently come to Kailasa. Who are you? Is Lord Siva free now, for me to see him?"

Lord Siva did not answer him and just kept silent. Indra became angry thinking that the watchman was arrogant and indifferent in his attitude towards him. He attacked him with his Vajrayudha, which went to pieces on touching the body of the Lord. Siva took His original form and gave him darshan.

Indra was sorry that he did not know the Lord in disguise. He worshipped at His feet and begged to be excused, with tears in his eyes.

"Maheswara! I am even lower than a dog and I did not understand your omnipresence. Kindly excuse me, for having tried to hit you with Vajrayudham out of sheer foolishness on my part", he pleaded remorsefully.

God was kind enough to forgive him. His anger was thrown into the Western Sea. Indra was thrilled at his magnanimity, praised the Lord and returned with his blessings.

Thus, Lord Siva took a different form only to cure Indra of his conceit and thoughtless unkind treatment of the subordinate.

## 89. Asura takes birth from anger

Lord Siva's anger, which was thrown into the Western Sea took the shape of a child and grew with Varuna. Whenever the child cried all the worlds were trembling with its noise. Brahma was startled and wanted to know where it came from. So, he went to the sea to check the source of the noise.

On seeing Brahma, Varuna came with the child and put it on his lap. "Kindly bless this child of mine", he said. The child pulled all the four beards of Brahma which was painful and brought tears from his eyes. He slowly got out of the hold by the child and told Varuna. This child has been born out of Siva's anger. He will not obey anybody. All the Devas and Indra will fear him and run away. Vishnu also will not be able to control him. He will rule over all the three worlds for a long time and finally die at the hands of Lord Siva only. He alone who gave him birth, can bring about his death", he said.

Varuna wanted Brahma to name the child. As he was growing with the waters of Varuna, Brahma named him Jalandhara.

When Jalandhara grew up, he conquered all the three worlds and established his sway over every kingdom. Indra and Devas went to take shelter in Meru mountains. Jalandhara got the asura's architect to create a wonderful city called Jalandhara on Earth and ruled from there. Asuras accepted him as their leader. He married Brundai, daughter of an asura, Kâlanemi.

When Jalandhara was governing his kingdom with all prosperity and happiness, he came to know that Devas and Indra were hiding in Meru mountains. He went there with his army to fight him.

On hearing about asura's coming, Devas appealed to Vishnu for protection. Vishnu came to their help and fought with Jalandharan. The war continued for quite some years. As it was indecisive for both sides, Vishnu understood that the asura can never be defeated. So, he praised and made peace with him.

When Vishnu and the asura were fighting, the Devas had run away to Mount Kailas in fear. Jalandhara returned to his city without seeing Devas. When he knew that they were in Mount Kailas, he wanted to go there and fight them. Brundai, his wife, pleaded with him not to go to Mount Kailas or fight the Devas, as he will then incur the wrath of Siva. Jalandhara dismissed her fears lightly and started with his army.

When the Devas took refuge in Lord Siva, He went to the asura in the disguise of an elderly brahmin. "Who are you? Where do you live? Why have you come here?", the old man asked.

"O! Old man! I live in Bhoolokam. My name is Jalandhara. I am the King of Asuras. As Devas who ran away fearing my might are here, I have come to fight them and Lord Siva who gave them asylum", Jalandhara said.

"O! King of asuras! I live close to Siva. I know him very well. If you treat Siva as your enemy, you will certainly be destroyed. Please go back", Lord said, who was in disguise as the brahmin. "O Great Man! You are not aware of my strength! If you can stay here for sometime, you can see for yourself", Asura said.

"Let us see", said the Lord. He drew the figure of a wheel on the ground with his toes. It turned out to be a wheel in reality by His grace.

"Asurendra, just take this wheel on your head. Let us see if you can hold it there with your strength".

Jalandhara replied flippantly. "I have made the Devas retreat. This is after all nothing for me".

He took the wheel on his head. It cut him into two pieces and reached Lord back. The asura forces were also burnt down by Siva with fire emitting from his third eye. Devas praised Him for killing the asura and allaying their fears.

Jalandhara's wife Brundai was a great beauty. Vishnu wanted to marry her. He used to sit as an ascetic on the way through which she used to go to the temple in a garden near Jalandhara's palace. Brundai did not know that Jalandhara had been killed. She came to the garden worrying about her husband who waged a war with Lord Siva. Vishnu made a trick by which two lion headed men started teasing her. Brundai began to run with fear and reached the place where Vishnu was sitting as an ascetic. He told her, "O Beautiful girl! Do not be afraid. I can drive them away." The two men created by Vishnu Maya ran away in fear on seeing Vishnu.

Brundai now was impressed by his bright serene personality acquired by meditation and so asked him about her husband who went to Kailasa. She thought he can find out with his vision of yoga power.

**Vishnu closed his eyes for a moment as if he was deploying his inner vision. The next minute, two monkeys brought the two pieces of Jalandhara's dead body before Brundai by his magic. Brundai could not stand the grief of her husband's death and hence fainted. Vishnu helped her to wake up and consoled her saying that he will revive her husband Jalandhara using his powers. By his magical skills, he got into the dead body of Jalandhara.**

When Brundai saw her husband alive, her joy knew no bounds and she hugged him. Madhava, in the disguise of Jalandhara took her to the palace and both of them enjoyed life, day in and day out.

One day Vishnu was deep asleep leaving his illusory body. Brundai came to know the truth. She grew very wild and felt Vishnu had cheated and molested her. "The two lion headed people were also your accomplices in the crime. The two monkeys were also your men only. You cheated me badly and made me a fallen woman. I curse you to be born as a king on Earth. The two lion headed men will then be your enemies. You will also loiter here and there with monkeys. Your enemies will cheat you and kidnap your wife". Afterwards, she made a big fire and sacrificed her life.

Vishnu could not bear the separation from Brundai. He rolled on the ground in her ashes like a mad man. Brahma and Devas took pity on his plight and informed Siva. He gave a seed to Brahma and asked him to plant it in Brundai's ashes. He did so and poured nectar as the nonrishment for it. There came up a Tulasi plant and Vishnu was consoled. He forgot Brundai and started loving Tulasi. Brahma and Devas got her married to him. Vishnu

now wanted to get the Chakrayudham, with which Lord Siva killed Jalandhara. He worshipped at his feet with thousand lotus flowers every day.

One day, when there was one flower less for the worship, Vishnu took out one of his eyes and used it in the place of the missing lotus flower for the pujas. Lord Siva was pleased with his devotion. He appeared before him and gave him the Chakrayudham. From that day Vishnu was also known as "Nemiyaan", one who carries the Nemi or wheel.

## 90. The goddess of Dharma becomes the Rishabham

For Brahma, one day is equal to two thousand yugas. Such thirty days become a month. 12 such months make one year. Hundred such years is the total time of life for Brahma.

For Vishnu, the total period of Brahma's life makes one day. 100 such years will be his lifetime.

When Vishnu nears his end, that is the time of the great deluge. Then all creatures will perish, fire will break out everywhere in all the continents and everything will be burnt to ashes. Everywhere it will look like a graveyard. There, Lord Siva will dance in the presence of Devi.

Looking at the great deluge of fire, the goddess of rightenousness or Dharma feared that her end has come. She shuddered at this thought and surrendered to Lord Siva. She took the form of an ox or Rishabham and pleaded with the God for mercy.

God Almighty, who is the embodiment of utmost kindness gave refuge to the Goddess of virtues. He granted her the blessing of eternity and endless wisdom and the fortune to be his mount all the time. "You will be my vehicle throughout.

You will be the leader of all my forces. You will also take the form of human being and worship me". The Lord said.

From that day, Lord Siva appears before His devotees only on Rishabha mount. When the three forts were burnt down, Vishnu took the form of Rishabham and carried the Lord. So, God rides on Rishabham only to help others. It is nothing demeaning for him.

## 91. Poison in the throat

As Devas and Asuras were fighting among themselves every now and then, many of them died. Devas went to Brahma and asked him to get the nectar from the milk ocean, so that they get to live forever. He took them to Vishnu, who was residing in the Milk ocean.

Vishnu heard the Devas' desire and suggested that they take Mandra mountain as the churning rod, the moon as the supporting pillar and Vasuki, the snake, as the rope to churn the ocean. When the Asuras and Devas standing on either side were churning, Vishnu himself supported both the ends of the rod.

During the process, Vasuki could not stand the strain, and spit poison from all her thousand mouths. The poison from inside the ocean also came up as a ball, because of the churning. Both poisons together became the most poisonous Âlakâla poison and started spreading all over the place. Its intensity was so great that all the Devas and Asuras had to run away leaving the churning, as they were unable to withstand it. When Vishnu tried to control its ferociousness, he was also affected. His fair skin became blue. He was also on the run. From them on, he was called "Neelameghan" (Blue coloured)

Devas and Asuras went to Kailasa. Brahma and Vishnu accompanied them. Nandideva stopped all Devas including Indra and allowed Brahma and Vishnu alone to see the Lord. As Vishnu had turned blue skinned, the Lord asked for the reason. Vishnu detailed all that happened and said, "We started on this work without thinking of you. The venom is spreading all over the universe. You have to step in and save us. Who else is our saviour?" Lord Siva called Nandideva and asked him to permit those waiting outside. When they came in, he gave them refuge. He sent one of his devotees, Sundarar to bring the treacherous poison to him. Sundarar brought the venom, Âlakâlam, in his hands to Lord Siva. Taking it in his hand, Lord Siva asked, "Shall I drink it or shall I throw it somewhere?" The Devas were again shivering. "Mahadeva? Who else can destroy it if you throw it somewhere? It has no action now because you have it in your hand. You must kindly take it yourself and save us from all sufferings". Lord Siva swallowed it immediately.

When it reached his throat, Devas requested him to hold it there itself as there are many continents inside his holy body. So, God contained the poison at the throat itself without gulping it down. It stayed there as a blue ornament. The Devas thanked and praised Him again. If they churn the milk ocean again, God blessed them that they will get the nectar. The Devas and Asuras took his advice, churned the ocean and got the nectar and many other precious gifts.

## 92. Lord Shiva takes the Ganges

Once Lord Siva and Devi were in conversation with each other at a garden in Kailas. Devi closed the Lord's eyes from behind playfully. The whole world gets the light from His eyes and when they were closed, there was no light in the world. The sun and the moon lost their brightness. There was a total blackout everywhere. All the creatures in the world suffered in the dark.

Lord Siva opened his third eye to provide light for all suffering creatures. The darkness got dispelled and the Sun and the Moon got their light back from the third eye on his forehead.

When Lord Siva opened his third eye, Devi got a shock and took off her fingers form the Lord's eyes. Her fingers were sweating due to fear. She sprinkled her sweat on the ground. From those drops, ten Ganges rivers started flowing down. Devas saw the sudden flow of ten rivers and came to Siva running in great fear. "Maheswara! Please save us from the sudden gush of the Ganges!" They surrendered at His feet.

Lord Siva took the Ganges water in his hand and put it in the locks of His hair. Ganges, which was in a big spate as to drown all the worlds was controlled and that stayed in his head as small drops. Lord explained the origin of the river to Devas. They were thrilled to hear that. "O Lord! Ganges had been born due to your graceful power of Devi and now resides in your locks of hair. She becomes thus the holiest of all rivers. We too want to take her to our cities", they said.

Lord Siva gave drops of Ganges water to those devotees. They took it with them in all reverence to their cities.

In order to get the Sagaras, salvation from the cycle of births and deaths, their descendant Bhageerathan made great attempts to bring Ganges to the Earth. He brought it with His grace from Brahma. When she was flowing from Brahmalokam to the Earth, she was too proud of her great speed of flow and thought that none can control her. Bhageerathan prayed to Lord Siva who took her in His locks of hair so that her flow down the Earth was with a regulated speed and not in spate. When the Ganges water flowed on the ashes of Sagaras, they attained liberation.

Lord Siva taking Ganges in his head is not due to his love for a second woman. In order to prevent the Earth from being washed away by her floods, he had to carry her for checking her high speeds and suppress her undue pride.

## 93. God gives his left side to Devi

When Brahma started his job of creations, he got four sons and they were the four sages – Sanaka and others. They attained wisdom and led a life of meditations as ascetics. So, Brahma's task of creation did not progress and got stagnated. Brahma, became perturbed and took them to Vishnu and complained. Vishnu took them all to Lord Siva and said, "Maheswara! Brahma's work of creating progeny does not progress and has stagnated. You should kindly do something to remove the hurdle".

Lord Siva first made Brahma, Vishnu and the four sages get lost by a loud taunt. When he stood alone, He looked at His shoulder where Devi appeared. He retained her on His left side and got Vishnu, Brahma, Sanaka and others back to life. When the Lord and the Devi gave darshan together, all of them sang His praise. 'I am now in unison with my graceful power of Devi. So, hereafter, Brahma will be able to create without any problem", Lord said. All of them worshipped and took leave of him. Lord Siva has his consort Devi on his left side only to prolong and promote creations in the world.

## 94. The birth of Vinayaka

Once upon a time, when there was a war between Devas and Asuras, many of the Asuras got killed by Devas, who won the war. Asurendran was quite upset about it and hence consulted his Guru Sukracharaya to get the upper hand over Devas. The teacher of Asuras consoled him and said, "There is a sage called Maakadar in the family of Vasishta. He is well versed in all the sastras. You send an asura girl to him and ask her to get a son. He will have an elephant head. He will be devoted to Lord Siva, meditate on him and get enormous benefits. He will bring all credit to Asuras".

Asurendran followed his Guru's advice and sent the most beautiful asura girl called Vibudhai to sage Maakadar. He asked her to get a son by marrying the sage so that he will save the Asuras. When she saw the sage with an extraordinary brightness, sitting in meditation with closed eyes, she was hesitant. She prayed to Lord Siva to give her success in her mission and sat in meditation by his side.

**Maakadar woke up from his meditations and saw two elephants making love to each other. He was also desirous of having sensuous pleasures and when he looked around, he saw a beautiful maiden sitting in meditation. He approached her with great**

**love and asked her "O girl! Who are you? What
did you come here for?"**

Vibudhai saluted the sage and said, " Swami! I came in
search of a suitable husband for me. When I saw you I felt
you are the right person. As your were meditating, I was
waiting here."

The sage happily agreed to her proposal. He felt that
both of them should take the form of elephants and make
love. By their mating, they had a son called Gajamukhan.
From Vibudhai's body, many Asuras were born.
Gajamukhan with the elephant's head was very strong right
at his birth.

When the sage saw his son had the qualities of Asuras,
he got back to his original self. He asked Vibudhai with
anger. "Oh! You shall tell me the truth now. Who are you?
Why did you come in search of me?" Vibudhai shivered
with fear and answered, "In order to promote the Asuras
clan, the king of asura wanted me to get a son by marrying
you. I was sent to you by him". The sage felt sad that he
has been the root cause for great disasters, which will
overtake men and Devas. He dismissed Vibudhai from his
presence at once. She went and reported all that happened
to Asurendra, who was quite happy.

Gajamukhan and his friends roamed all over the place
and behaved in their own wicked ways. He caused
unlimited miseries to all saints ad seers. He entered their
ashrams and prevented them from doing their rituals.
Many gave up doing their daily routine rituals to Gods
fearing his intervention. The sages were suffering without
being able to meditate in peace.

When Asurendra heard about Gajamukhan's activities,
he was very happy and sent Sukracharya to his place.
Sukracharya met Gajamukhan and said, "My dear Child!

I am the teacher of your family. Your king has sent me to you, hearing all about your mighty deeds. Your activities have made Devas turn against you. They are tricky people and can cause a lot of problems for you. Let me suggest a way out to you, so that you can be safe from their botherations. Meditate on Lord Siva. If you get His blessings and boons, all Devas and Indra will obey you. Your glory will spread to all worlds and you will be the emperor of the Earth and heaven". Gajamukhan was happy to have his guidance and saluted him. "Swamy! I shall never forget you words, which mean all good things for me. You may kindly teach me the rules for meditation".

Sukracharya taught him the methods and sent him to Meru mountains. Gajamukhan reached Meru mountains and started on hectic meditation. He controlled his senses and chanted Panchakshara Mantra to propitiate Lord Siva. For thousand years he ate only grass and leaves. For the next hundred years, he lived on water. For another thousand years he sustained himself only on air. Lord Siva did not appear. He stood in the midst of Panchagni and meditated for ten thousand years. Agni himself was amazed at his strength of mind. Due to the most vigorous rules observed, Gajamukhan's body became as strong as diamond. His yoga gave him a terrific brightness. Devas were shuddering at his severe mediation.

At last, Lord Siva was pleased with him and appeared on his Rishabha mount. He asked him as to what he wanted of him. Gajamukhan saluted the Lord and requested the following:

"Oh My Lord! I should never be defeated by Brahma, Vishnu, Indra or Devas. I should not be killed by any weapon. Devas, Men, Asuras or beasts, none shall cause my death. All the worlds must come under my rule". God granted all his prayers.

Gajamukhan used his boons and won over all Devas and Indra. Brahma and Vishnu could not oppose him and so ran away. The entire world worshipped at his feet. Asurendran and Sukrachariar praised him immensely. Gajamukhan called the architect of the Asuras and founded a city for himself. Sukracharya named it as Mathangamaapuram. Gajamukhan married Vichitra Kaamati, the daughter of Asurendra and various other asura girls. He established his capital at the new city and started ruling from there. Kamadhenu, Kalpa Vruksham, Chintamani, etc., were in his control to give him whatever he desired. Asurendra and Sukracharya were his ministers, advising him on many issues. Indra and Devas were his slaves and carried out all his errands.

One day Gajamukhan called Indra and others and told them, "Whenever you come to see me, you should knock thrice on your head, hold your ears by crossing your hands and then prostrate before me". They did as he said being damn afraid to refute his orders.

Indra complained to Vishnu about the sufferings he and Devas suffered at Gajamukhan's hand. Vishnu took them all to Mount Kailas and apprised Lord Siva about their sad predicament. Lord Siva consoled them and said that he will get a son soon to annihilate Gajamukhan.

After Devas left, the Lord went to a garden nearby with his Devi. There was a beautiful hall with exquisite paintings. When both of them were going round there, seeing the paintings, there was a painting in which Pranava was in the form of two elephants making love. Devi wanted to know the significance of this painting.

"Devi, Pranava is the origin of all things and when you looked at them, it has taken the form of two elephants making love to each other", He said.

When the two elephant figures disappeared , the letter of Pranava alone remained there. A divine child of immaculate wisdom was born there with five hands, three eyes, hanging mouth, and locks of hair with the crescent moon and elephant face. It went round the parents and saluted them. Lord and Devi took the child in their arms and felt very happy.

"My dear child, whoever prays to you before starting any venture, you will bless them and see to it that they achieve their target without any hurdles. You create obstacles in all new ventures in case any one starts working on anything without thinking of you. You will be the master for all Devas and demons. You shall destroy Gajamukhan and remove Vishnu's fears."

They returned to Kailasa and made the child sit at the entrace as the leader of all his forces. Demons and Nandideva worhsipped their leader and all the Devas, on hearing the news, came to salute him.

One day, Vishnu went to Kailas to have a darshan of Lord Siva, who was then sitting down to play chess with Devi. When he saw Vishnu there, he wanted to have some fun. Whoever gets defeated in the chess game, He or She should give away the ornaments to the other. Vishnu was asked to be the referee there.

At the end of the game, Lord Siva was defeated. But he asserted that he had won and so wanted the ornaments from Devi.

Devi asked the referee Vishnu to give the verdict as to who won the game. If he utters the truth, Vishnu would incur the wrath of Siva. Vishnu was afraid to get into the trap and so declared Lord Siva as the winner. Devi got angry at Vishnu's resorting to falsehood. She looked at him angrily and cursed him.

"You witnessed the whole game as the referee. You ought to be impartial. But you took sides with Siva who was uttering a lie. Was it proper to drift from the path of rightenousness, even if the Lord adopts a falsehood? You are also a liar now and so I curse you to become a snake".

Vishnu was feeling sad and asked Siva as to when the curse would be lifted and how.

Lord Siva was kind to Vishnu. He said, "Madhava, you uttered a lie because of me. I will remove your sufferings. You go to Âlankâdu (a forest of banyan trees) in the south and meditate on me, living in the cavity of a banyan tree. My son, Vinayaka will come and relieve you from this curse". Vishnu went to.Âlankâdu accordingly and started meditating.

Indra worshipped Vinayaka and asked him to save him from the clutches of Gajamukhan. Vinayaka agreed to do the needful very soon.

Vinayaka got on the shoulder of Achalan, a demon, and started his journey to Mathangamaapuram. The rest of the demon army also followed him. Devas were showering flowers and walked along with them.

When Gajamukhan learnt about Vinayaka's coming, he came with 1000 vellam asura forces. The Demons and the asuras had a fierce fight. Because of the demon's fierce attack many Asuras were killed. Angry at this loss, Gajamukhan came to the front row. When he saw Vinayaka on the shoulder of Achalan, he asked his fellowmen as to who he was. They said that he was the son of Lord Siva and the demons have waged war under his leadership.

Gajamukhan laughed aloud and said, "My dear child! You perhaps do not know about the boons your father has given me. You cannot defeat me. No weapon can kill me. Even the Devas will not be able to win over me."

Vinayaka replied to Gajamukhan immediately. "Gajamukha! The same Lord Siva who gave you so many boons has created me to punish you for your atrocities on seers, sages and Devas. If you want to live, you better give up your hostility for Devas and do good to one and all. Otherwise your end is certain".

Gajamukhan was too proud of his powers and so sent several arrows at Vinayaka. They were all stopped and destroyed mid air by Vinayaka. He broke the asura's bow into two by his mazhu. Gajamukhan pounced upon Vinayaka with his Dandayudham. Vinayaka stunned him by hitting with his weapon on his chest. He threw his paasam to bind the asuran's army and killed all of them with his mazhu. Gajamukhan angrily deployed several other weapons at Vinayaka, but all of them bowed before him.

As per Lord Siva's boon, Gajamukhan was not to be killed by any weapon. So Vinayaka broke one of his tusks and threw it at Gajamukhan. It ripped his chest open, went to sea, cleansed itself in deep sea water and came back to Vinayaka. Asura's blood poured out like a river and spread all over a forest, which was known as Tiruchengadu from then on. (This place is now called Tiruchengattankudi in Nagapattinam district of Tamilnadu)

Gajamukhan had been blessed by Lord Siva for staying alive forever. So he took the form of a bandicoot and attacked Vinayaka. All his strength was shrunk by Vinayaka who rode on it and ordered that the bandicoot will carry him henceforth on his back. Asura who lost all his excessive powers became the vahana or vehicle for Vinayaka.

Devas were very happy as they are now rid of the fear for asura. They showered flowers and prayed to Vinayaka.

Asurendra and Sukracharya felt unhappy on hearing what happened. They were now afraid of Devas and left for Meru mountain in the form of birds. Asurendra hid himself there in a secret place. The demons went into Mathangamaapuram and killed the Asuras. Vinayaka went to Tiruchengattankudi, established a temple for Lord Siva and worshipped Him. This place where Vinayaka worshipped the Lord is called Ganapateeswaram. Then he left for Aalankadu to shower his grace on Vishnu. Vishnu came out of the cavity in the banyan tree as a snake and prayed to Vinayaka. The curse of Devi, which made him a snake, was nullified and he resumed his original form with his conch and wheel. "Oh Lord! Today is the sixth day (Shashti) of the first fortnight after newmoon in the month of Margazhi(Margasheersha). As I have been blessed by you, you should bless everyone who prays to you on this day".

Vinayaka granted his request and got back to Kailasa with his demon army. Indra and the Devas came to worship him there. "O Lord! We were knuckling on our foreheads and pulling our ears with crossed hands while worshipping at the feet of Asurendra so far. Hereafter we should be allowed to pray before you the same way", they said.

Vinayaka accepted their request and felt happy. Devas, from then on, worshipped Lord Vinayaka in the same method. The same form of worship continues for Vinayaka even today everywhere.

## 95. The curse of sage Dadeechi

Sage Dadeechi narrated several incidents in reply to set at rest all the queries raised by Daksha. "O Daksha! You find fault with Lord Siva on many counts. Of the three functions namely creation, protection and destruction, he has the responsibility for the third one. You need to have calmness to create and strength to protect. You need to be angry to destroy.

But God never gets angry so easily. When he was educating the sages like Sanaka and others under the Kallala tree do we see him angry? How can you understand him without any wisdom?

Vishnu has become blue and is resting on the milky ocean. As he was also proud, he had strength and anger. When he got back to his good senses and worshipped the Lord, he also acquired the calmness. Brahma is golden in colour and was also proud that he was the creator. When he worshiped the Lord , he also became calm. So, according to one's own circumstances and state of mind, the character changes. If we attribute anger to Lord Siva for his main function viz. Destruction, we cannot presume that he is always angry. You come out of your ignorance and accept him for his supremacy. You give him the due honour and start the yâga", he said.

Daksha did not budge an inch from his original standpoint. He refused to give the first offering to Lord Siva as required. The sage got mad with anger. When he got up from his seat, Devas dreaded the consequences of his unlimited anger.

Dadeechi addressed Dakshan. "You fool! I tried to do you good. You refuted all my advice. Let this yâga go incomplete as you are avoiding Lord Siva! Let all of you and Devas perish!"

After cursing him, he turned to the brahmins there. "Due to the greed for wealth, you have come to this yâga, conducted without observing the basic rules. So, you have lost your status. You will lead a treacherous life for many births decrying Lord Siva and his devotees wearing the sacred ash and Rudraksham and also disrespecting the Vedic rituals."

Thereafter he left the place with the sages and disciples, who had accompanied him.

## 96. The yâga gets disrupted

When sage Dadeechi left the yâgasâla in great anger and disagreement, Daksha's flag in the hall got cut and fell down. The crows and vultures sat on the staff. Whatever Daksha took in his hand slipped down. When he wanted to get up, he stumbled and fell on the nearby staff. Despite all these bad omens, Daksha did not worry. He stood firm. He worshipped Brahma and Vishnu and began the yâga.

The Devas and sages were given a lot of gifts. Women were given silk dresses and ornaments. Brahmins were given ornaments, costly dress, cows and other gifts. Everybody happily praised him.

The three types of Agni (Aagamaneeyam, Dakshinagni and Gâruhâpatyam) began to glow. Dakshan chose a centrally located place to sit and oversee the performance of yâga.

Narada who landed on the earth, came there when he came to know of Daksha yâga. All Devas except Lord Siva were seated there. Just to avoid giving the first offering to

Lord Siva, he was not invited, they said. He was worried that the yâga will not conclude properly as it was being done despising Lord Siva. So he went to Kailasa and called on Lord Siva.

"Mahadeva! Daksha Prajapati is doing a yâga on the banks of the river Ganges in Bhoolokam. All Devas are there. Your absence there is intriguing". Knowing what Narada had in his mind, Lord Siva smiled. Devi who was seated nearby had a desire to see the yaga performed by her father. She asked her husband's permission to go there.

"Devi! The very purpose for which the yâga is being conducted is different. Daksha has grown too arrogant of his status. He will not care for you. If you go there, you will get insulted by him", Lord said. Devi still wanted to go and see the yâga. She again worshipped and asked for permission.

"Oh! My Lord! My father has foolishly done a mistake. You must kindly bear with him. He has not invited us only because he is angry with us. When he sees me in person, his anger will subside. So, I want to go there. Please permit me", Devi said.

"If that is your desire, I do not want to stop you. You may go", he said.

Devi started in her air borne vehicle. Two girls, Sumali and Malini, carried her umbrella. Two other girls, Mangalai and Sumalai, carried her fans. Some others carried the festoons and showered the flowers. Nandideva's wife Sukesai carried her footwear. Malini and Aninditai brought garlands of flowers for her. Somanandi was playing on musical instruments. Twelve crore demons went in front of her as her guards.

Devi reached the yâgasâlâ with all this pomp and glamour. Dakshan became angry on seeing her. "I did not invite you here. Why did you come uninvited?", he shouted. "Father, you like my sisters and their husbands. Why do you hate me and my husband? Just as you have invited and honoured them, it was but proper that you extend equal courtesies to us also. Why did you not do that?" Devi asked.

"You loved and married that mad man dancing with the devils in the graveyard. I hate you. Look at your sisters' husbands. They respect me. Your husband does not. He insults me. So I do not love you. There is no place or offering for your husband in this yâga. I do not want you here. You may go back", he shouted.

Devi got wild at his words. She looked at Dakshan with red eyes. A friend, Vimalai, who was by her side, comforted her and asked her to calm down, saying the world would not be spared it she gets angry.

Devi addressed her father; "Father! I do not care very much for your insulting me in this assembly. But I will not tolerate your decrying my husband here.You called him a mad dancer in the graveyard. Because you are blind with your pride, you fail to realise the significance of his actions. In order to save the souls from birth and sufferings, he destroys them and saves them from miseries. You do not know his graceful deeds. Everything comes out of Him. All Vedas praise him. He is the Lord Supreme. Those who chant the two syllables Si Va get salvation. You refuse to give the first offering to God Almighty. None has escaped his anger, once someone wrongs him and condemns him. When you have asked me to go back I shall no longer remain here. Let me repeat. Your own misdeed will bring about your end."

Devi left the place at once and the demons also accompanied her back to Kailasa.

## 97. God who has no beginning or end

When Devi returned to Kailasa, she was full of mixed feelings of shame, remorse, insult and anger. She went to Lord Siva and saluted him; "I have returned because my father humiliated me by decrying you in an assembly of Devas and sages. The yaga that is being done, keeping you out of it, must be destroyed", she said.

Lord Siva was silent. He wanted to make sure whether she was talking out of anger or she really meant to destroy that yâga. Devi saluted Him again and said, "My lord! Even if you want to ignore what has happened, I want you to destroy it for my sake. From the moment he talked ill of you, the relationship between me and him as daughter and father has ceased to exist." Lord Siva now decided to thwart Daksha's yâgnaa. He produced a gruesome Veerabhadra, with a thousand heads, three eyes in each head. Sharply bent teeth, wearing a garland of skulls and bones. Devi also immediately produced Bhadrakaali with a thousand heads and two thousand hands.

Lord Siva looked at both of them and said, "On the banks of the river Ganges, Daksha is conducting a yâga, flouting all Vedic rules and keeping me out of it. You go there and ask him for my dues. If he gives you, take it and return. If Daksha refuses, you cut off his head, destroy all those present there and see that the yâga is stopped. I shall come there at that time."

Veerabhadra and Bhadrakaali took leave of the Lord. Veerbhadra produced countless demons from his breath and body. Bhadrakali also produced thousands of Kaalis similarly.

Accompanied by all of them, they reached Dakshan's yâgasâlâ. They kept the demon forces on all the four sides to keep a watch so that nobody escapes and then, both went inside.

Looking at their gruesome figures, all those present there were shocked. When Veerabhadra stood before Dakshan, he was also shaken."Who are you? Why did you come here?", he asked.

"I am the son of Lord Siva. I have come to take the offering due to him", replied Veerabhadra.

"Offering for Lord Siva! Not only here, but nowhere in the world He will be given any offering hereafter", Daksha said.

The four Vedas and the Pranavam who were present there, got up and said, "Daksha Prajapati, Lord Siva is the presiding deity of all yâgas. It is foolishness to deny him the offering. Please give it without delay".

Daksha did not care for their words. He affirmed that he will not change his decision. Pranavam and the four Vedas immediately walked out saying that they had no place where Lord Siva was not given due honour.

Veerabhadra asked Daksha again." Do you get me clear now? Please give the offering due to Lord Siva, the yagnapati".

"My decision is final. The mad dancer of the graveyard is not fit to own anything in this august assembly. I shall never give him a place here", he asserted.

Veerabhadra got angry. He looked at the Devas sitting on all sides. "One chooses to do a yâga denying the legitimate dues to God Almightly. You have not stopped him from doing this improper yâga and so are a party to his wrong decision".

What will they say? They were mortally afraid of Daksha and so kept silent. Veerbhadra grew wild at their incapacity and cowardice even to reply. He hit Vishnu with his Dandayudham. He fainted and fell on the ground. He dragged Brahma and hit him on his head. With his heads reeling, Brahma fainted in his seat. Bhadrakaali caught hold of Brahma's wives and cut their noses.

The Devas and sages started running out in fear. But the demons stopped them. There was utter confusion confounded everywhere.

Veerabhadra went round the place and punished whomever he saw. He pushed the Moon down and crushed him with his feet. He slapped Sun on his face and his teeth fell out.

He blinded Bhakan, who was one of the Adityas. Yama's head was cut off. Indra tried to escape taking the form of a cuckoo, but did not succeed. Veerabhadra cut him off with his sword. Agni's hands and seven tongues were chopped off. His wife Swaha's nose was pinched by his finger nails. Niruti was beaten up by his stick.

Rudras were shivering as they surrendered to Veerabhadra. He sent them out safely. He killed Varuna by mazhu. Vayu also fell a victim to mazhu. Kubera was killed with Soolayudham. Eesaanan saluted in fear and so was spared. Asurendran was chased and his head rolled. Yagnadeva wanted to escape like a deer amidst the melee, but he was killed by an arrow.

When Daksha saw the terrible commotion and punishments meted out to Devas and others, he realised that he was responsible for all the disaster. It was only because he spoke contemptuously of Lord Siva, all this suffering had followed. But it was too late. Who can help him if he comes to his senses after all the damage was done all around?

Veerabhadra caught hold of him and cut off his head. "You fool! You deserve this end richly for all that you spoke ill of my Lord, in your conceit", he said and threw his head into the fire where it was burnt down to ashes.

Bhadrakaali also moved among the women there and punished quite a few. Devas' wives and Dakshan's wife suffered most at her hands. The demons and kaalis who were guarding the yâgasâlâ outside broke the compound walls and entered. Yâgasâlâ became a battlefield. There were cries and wailing from those who lost their limbs.

The demons stamped on many; beat many to death; threw many into the fire; tore many with their sharp teeth; all materials there were destroyed. All men and women who were in the yâgasâlâ did get the due punishment for their being guilty of contempt of God Almighty.

Vishnu slowly opened his eyes after the attack by Veerabhadra. He saw the total destruction of yâgasâlâ and the painful suffering meted out to all invitees. He thought of Garuda, but he had been killed by the demons.

So, he converted his anger into Garuda and went to fight Veerabhadra getting on that mount.

By the grace of God, a beautiful chariot, drawn by Devas in the form of horses, reached there. At that time, Brahma who had fainted, regained his consciousness. He became the driver of the chariot and brought it before Veerabhadra.

"My Lord! This chariot has come to take you and your wife. Kindly oblige", he said. Veerabhadra excused Brahma, got into the chariot with Bhadrakaali and went to fight Vishnu.

Vishnu asked Veerabhadra, "You were right in punishing Daksha for his contempt of the Lord. Why did you punish others who were not guilty?"

Veerabhadra angrily replied, "Madhava! Daksha did a yâga, flouting all the prescribed rules and keeping the Lord out of it. Yourself and Devas partook in this improper yâga and took his offerings".

Madhava attacked Veerabhadra with his weapons. Veerabhadra destroyed all of them with his counter weapons. Both entered a stiff fight. Veerabhadra nullified all his arrows and also broke his bow called Sarangam. He cut off the wings of Garuda. Vishnu multiplied his image on all four sides with his magic and fought. Veerabhadra dispelled the magic and burnt down all the illusions with the fire from his third eye. When Vishnu angrily sent his Chakrayudham at him, Veerabhadra caught it by the hand and swallowed it. When Vishnu pounced upon him with his sword, Veerabhadra made a big noise which brought down all powers of Vishnu. He became fully exhausted.

There sounded a voice from heaven, "Cool down, Give up your anger", the Lord said. Veerabhadra changed his mind and abstained from tearing the chest of Vishnu. Brahma bowed before Veerabhadra and said, "O Lord! Kindly excuse me for my having attended Daksha's yâga and taken his offering". Veerbhadra forgave him.

Vishnu used this opportunity when Veerabhadra was a little cool. He bowed before him and said, "You are a great warrior by all means! I could not defeat you with all my weapons. Having been fully aware that there was no place for Lord Siva in Dakshayâga, we were guilty of partaking in it. You have given us the right punishment; I am not angry with you that you beat me. As I had also committed a blunder, I deserved the punishment as much as others. Lord Siva has four powers, Layasakti, Ghorasakti, Bhogasakti, and Purushasakti. Durgadevi is His Layasakti; Kaali is known as His Gorasakti; Umadevi is considered as His Bhogasakti; Purushasakti is myself. As I am part of the Lord, I am not against Him. I have worshipped at his feet and then only fought with you. So, kindly allow me to get back my original powers and the weapons forgiving my mistakes."

Veerabhadra accepted the request of Vishnu and gave up his anger against him.

Then, Lord Siva appeared there with Devi on His Rishabha mount. The demon forces accompanied him. Veerabhadra and Bhadrakaali bowed at His feet. Vishnu and Brahma also worshipped and praised him.

When Devi saw that the yâgasâlâ had been ruined totally and the Devas and sages had been killed, she addressed the Lord. "Oh Lord! I will be unduly criticised that I was responsible for all the sufferings borne by Devas and others. They will never realise that they earned it by their being accomplices in the crime of Daksha's contempt for you. Kindly take pity on them and get them back to life", she pleaded. Lord Siva looked at Veerabhadra with a smile.

Veerabhadra knew his mind and got all the dead back to life. They were all thrilled at the darshan of the Lord with Devi. They repented for the folly and worshipped at His feet. "Mahadeva! You are extremely kind to us though we had sinned against you by participating in an improper yâga. You did not make us suffer for long. How can we praise your kindness?", they said.

When all those who lost their lives at the hands of Veerabhadra came back to life, Brahma saw Daksha had not. He appealed to God, "Maheswara! Daksha foolishly condemned you and tried to conduct yâga in the most inappropriate manner. You have shown your mercy on us. Likewise you must forgive him also and show your mercy."

God granted his appeal. Veerbhadra asked Bhanukampan to bring Daksha's body. As his head had been burnt down to ashes, Veerabhadra cut off a goat's head from its dead body and put it on Daksha's body. Daksha came back to life with a goat's head. When he saw the Lord and Devi together, he realised his grievous mistake and was clear in his mind now.

He was moved to tears of repentance and worshipped at the Lord's feet. "My Lord! I was a great sinner. I had done unlimited blunders. Instead of singing your praise, I talked so ill of you always. I invited all the punishment given to me only by my obstinacy and foolishness. Now, after all the suffering, I am clear in my mind. You must kindly excuse me and show me your grace hereafter. I was so ungrateful, so wretched and worse even than a dog. You are my only saviour now", he prayed.

Lord Siva forgave him for all his mistakes, which he had profusely repented. Daksha got back his original status and was blessed to lead a life worthy of fame and name. Lord Siva left for Kailasa escorted by Veerabhadra and others.

## 98. God without a beginning or end

After the departure of Lord Siva, Brahma came to his son Dakshan and said, "My dear son! Think about the trouble that you had because of your improper conduct. Your high status and riches have been destroyed. Devas who supported you were also killed. In your pride over the superpowers that you had earned from Lord Siva, you grew head strong, got confused and forgot even your gratitude for the Lord. When He is the Lord Supreme, you took Him casually and insulted him. By God's grace, all your sufferings are over now. Do not think that I am finding fault with you. Power corrupts everybody. Myself and Madhavan were also no exceptions. At least from now on, you worship always at His feet and get His abundant grace".

Daksha bowed to his father and asked, "O Dad! You have shown the correct way to salvation. You said that, once, power corrupted your mind also. Kindly give me those details".

Brahma narrated his own experience.

When a thousand Chaturyugas pass by, it is a day for Brahma. When the day is over, Brahma goes to sleep. The night also covers the same period of thousand Chathuryugas. During the night, all the creatures in the world would perish. Even the Devas will be dead. The Sun, the Moon and the stars will not be there. All the sages in the heaven will go to Janalokam. The seas will raise and drown all the continents in the flood. Very few places like Kanchi alone will remain status quo.

Madhava will sleep on a banyan leaf thinking of Lord Siva. All the sages in Janalokam will sing his praise.

Once upon a time, during one such night, Brahma went to sleep. The night was about to be over. Vishnu woke up, hearing the songs of the sages from Janalokam. Immediately he looked around for the earth. As it had been drowned by the great deluge and pushed into Paatalalokam (underground), Vishnu took the form of a pig, went to Paathala and brought back the earth with the help of his teeth. Brahma also woke up by then as his day was dawning and resumed the duties of the creator.

As Vishnu had successfully brought out the Earth from paathala, he grew very proud. He rested in the milk ocean with a feeling that he was supreme. As Brahma had recreated all the worlds and the creatures, as soon as he got up from his sleep, he was also under the impression that he was the greatest. In his pride he asked Madhava, "Who are you?", without recognising him.

Madhava smiled and said, "O son! I am your father! Don't you know me?"

Brahma laughed aloud; "What are you blabbering? Are you still sleepy? I create the whole world and you call me your son! When my son Brughu had cursed you, you had taken ten incarnations on earth and I was responsible to give you those ten births. I am Supreme", he said in his heavy headedness.

Madhava got angry. "You are talking rubbish. Just because you create the world, would you become supreme? When you talked ill of Lord Siva, he plucked off your fifth head on top. Could you get it back? You came out from my navel and so, naturally you become my son. Because your mind is confused due to illusions, your have failed to see the truth. I am all in all and you better understand it", he said.

Brahma refuted this argument and there was a serious exchange of words between the two. This wordy dual led to a war when they fought each other with weapons. All the worlds and the creatures there suffered heavily due to this hectic fight. At that time, Narada appeared there by the grace of God, from Brahma's face. He started advising them.

"Why are you fighting with one another? None of you is supreme. Lord Siva who created both of you and also gave you the portfolios of creation and protection is the Lord Supreme. Please realise the truth and stop fighting".

Without heeding to Narada's advice, both of them fought for 100 years. All the worlds were in great distress. Lord Siva decided to save the situation and so appeared as a huge column of light between them. It was Chaturdasi day of Amarapaksham in Maasi month. It was exactly the mid night.

When Brahma and Vishnu saw a big column of fire emitting excessive heat all around, they came round and round that. "Lord Siva will decide who is the most powerful between you two. You may find out the head and feet of this form of glowing light", a voice from heaven said.

They accepted the word from the air. Whoever wins in this task will be taken as the mightiest of the two. Brahma wanted to see the head at the top most level and so flew into the air in the form of a swan. Vishnu took the form of a boat and went down the Earth to look for His feet.

Both carried on their search for several years. Vishnu's strength gradually got diminished and he became very tired. He could not reach and see the feet of the Lord at the bottom most point under the ground. His pride disappeared. He gave up the false idea of his supremacy.

He had no strength even to come back to the Earth's surface. He prayed to Lord Siva. "O Lord! I have come to senses now. I am clear that you are the super power. You should kindly excuse me for my stupid mistake."

God gave him the strength. He came out of Paatal and worshipped the luminous form of Lord Siva.

Even after hundred years of flying, Brahma could not reach the head of Lord Siva. He was feeling dizzy and tired. If he continued further, he was bound to fall. Some Siddha appeared there and ridiculed his vain attempt. When Madhava has accepted his defeat and surrendered, they wondered if the swan would win at all, even after many more thousand years of flight.

Hearing them, Brahma got back to his true senses. He came to Madhava and said, "Due to sheer ignorance we have fought with each other. Now we are clear that Lord Siva is God Supreme and stands above us. Let us be friends and pray to Him".

When Madhava agreed with Brahma, they installed a Sivalingam there and worshipped with devotion and Lord Siva gave them the darshan. "Lord of the universe! We were fighting amongst us due to absolute foolishness. You were kind enough to enlighten us and graced us with your presence. You should forgive us for our sins committed due to our vanity and pride", they prayed.

God blessed them and disappeared. Brahma and Vishnu worshipped the great bright light. It shrank in size and stood as a mountain. They went round the hill, which was in the shape of Sivalingam and worshipped Him.

Brahma gave the full account of his experience to Daksha. "Daksha! The great mountain where both of us went to see the head or toe of the Lord is known as 'Arunachalam', the red mountain". The day on which we worshipped is called 'Sivaratri'. Anyone who prays to him on this day gets rid of all his sins committed in the past and present. He is our mother, father, teacher, God and treasure all rolled into one. If you show absolute devotion to him always, without swerving from the path of virtues, you will never suffer from any wants", he said.

On getting the advice of his father, Daksha took leave of him and proceeded to Benaras. On the banks of the river Ganges, he built a temple for Lord Siva near Manikarnikai and worshipped him. God was pleased with him and granted him all his prayers. He was also made the leader of all his demon forces. Daksha returned to his capital with a clear mind.

Bruhaspati, the teacher of Devas, told Indra's son Jayanta about the life of Dakshaprajapati. Jayanta prayed to Lord thanking him for his love and grace for Devas.

## 99. Vratas dear to Lord Muruga

Emperor Musukundan went to sage Vasishta one day and requested him to explain about the vrathas that please Lord Muruga.

Sage Vasishta said, Fridays are ideal days for worshipping Lord Muruga. Those who worship him on Fridays will achieve whatever they desire for.

When Bhageeratha was ruling over this country, an asura called Goran usurped his kingdom from him. Bhageeratha was unable to oppose him and therefore he left his country. When he met Sukracharyar and asked for his advice, he consoled him.

"Bhageeratha, you do penance on Fridays which will please Lord Muruga. If you continue to do it for three years in full devotion, Lord Muruga will help you to get back your kingdom", he said. Bhageeratha took his suggestion and started meditating on Muruga on Fridays. He used to take one meal only on the previous day i.e Thursday and pray to Lord Muruga on Fridays without food or sleep. Next day i.e. Saturday also, he took only one meal. For three years, he followed his schedule strictly. Lord Muruga was pleased with his worship. When he sent his Velayudham aiming it at Goran, it returned with the asura's life. Bhageeratha got back his kingdom.

Narada wanted to become one among the seven leading sages. He prayed to Vinayaka with devotion and asked him to fulfill his desire. Vinayaka gave darshan to Narada and asked him to worship Lord Muruga on Karthigai days for twelve years.

Narada came to Bhoolokam and started on Karthigai Vratham for Lord Muruga. Every month on Bharani day, he will take only one meal in the day.

Next day, i.e. on Karthigai day, he will take his bath early in the morning wear a white dress and do the daily rituals as per rule. He will worship Lord Muruga during the day, taking a little water only and read his puranas, sitting in front of his idol. He will sleep on Darbha grass for the night and get up thinking only of Muruga. Next day i.e. on Rohini day, he will take bath early in the morning and eat with the other sages to conclude the vrata. He will keep awake throughout the day. If he goes to sleep in the day, he will be guilty of the sin of killing hundred Brahmins without any reason. In this manner, Narada observed the vrata for twelve years and secured the first place among the Saptarishis.

A brahmin who was steadfast in observing the Krittigai vrata became the first Manu. Another brahmin, by observing the vrata, obtained all the riches that he desired. He became Raja Trisanku in the next birth.

Once a king and a hunter observed Kritigai vrata and became the greatest philanthropists, Andiman and Sandhiman. Later they also ruled over kingdoms on Earth.

Shashti is another favourite vrata for Lord Muruga. During Aippasi (Thula) month, the vrata should be started from the first day after the full moon (Suklapaksha prathamai) and followed upto shashti, the sixth day. On all the six days, one should take bath early in the morning and worship Lord Muruga as prescribed. Puja has to be done in three forms namely image, kalasam and agni. Modakam has to be offered as holy food to him. On seventh day, i.e. saptami, special pujas are to be done and vrata concludes with feeding Brahmins. Those who can observe shashti vrata like this get high status as well as all that is good in the world.

## 100. Veerabhahu gets a curse

Emperor Musukundan observed all the vratas, as advised by sage Vasishta for quite a long time. Lord Muruga was immensely pleased with him and so, he appeared before him and asked as to what he wanted.

"Oh Lord! I want the help of soldiers like Veerabhahu Thevar for me to rule over the world", he asked.

Lord Muruga granted the boon to him and called Veerabhahu and other soldiers to go to Bhoolokam and be helpful to emperor Musukundan.

Veerabhahu raised a query with the Lord. "O My Lord! We had destroyed the dynasty of Soorapadman. How can we go and help the man of the Sun's dynasty?"

Lord Muruga was not happy at his query. "Muchukundan has great regard for me than all of you. When he asks me for something, I shall not deny it. As you chose to question the validity of my orders, you will be born as a man in Bhoolokam", he cursed him thus.

**Veerbhahu and others got a shock. They fell at His feet and asked for pardon for their mistake.**

"You will obey my orders first. After helping emperor Musukundan in his kingdom, you can meditate and get back to me". Accordingly, Veerabhahu and his men came to Earth to help the emperor ruling from a city called Karuvur. Musukundan gave them large four fold armies, riches, countries and all honours. By the grace of God, women of the celestial kingdom were born as maidens on Earth and Musukundan got them married to Veerabhahu and others.

Veerabhahu married Pushpagandhi and got a daughter Chitravalli. He got her married to the emperor. He got two other sons, Anakan and Sanakan. The other soldiers also

had a number of children.

Musukundan's wife Chitravalli had a pet parrot. Yama's wife wanted to have the parrot. She sent her messengers to bring it somehow. They stealthily abducted it and gave it to Yama's wife.

Chitravalli complained to her husband when she did not see her pet parrot. When Musukundan knew that it was in the palace of Yama, he sent Veerabhahu to fetch it back. Veerabhahu and his soldiers went to Yamapuri, fought with Yama, defeated him and brought the parrot back.

Later, when Chitravalli was pregnant, she wanted a particular fruit for which Musukundan sent the soldiers to the hilly region. When the tribes there refused to give them the fruits and also talked ill of them, Veerabhahu had to fight them and get the fruits. Veerabhahu went all over the world, won over all kings and made them pay allegiance to emperor Musukundan. Chitravalli got a son called Agnivarman.

# 101. Musukundan brings Tyagesa

An asura named Valan wanted to conquer Devalokam and so laid a siege on Amaravati with his forces. Indra and the Devas opposed him. As the asura was more powerful, Indra could not win. He sent his messenger to Bhoolokam and asked emperor Musukundan for help. Understanding the sad plight of Indra, Musukundan went with his army and Veerabhahu to Amravati and fought the asura and his forces besieging the city. Most of the asuras were killed by Musukundan in the war. Indra, when placed in a comfortable position, fought with the asura, Vala and killed him. In view of this victory, Indra was known as Valâri.

After the war, Indra took Musukundan to his court and honoured him suitably. Afterwards, Indra took his bath wore new clothes and worshipped Tyagesa, an idol which was earlier brought by Vishnu.

Musukundan was very much attracted towards the idol of Tyagesa worshipped by Indra. Once upon a time when Lord Siva gave him darshan in Kailasa, he was with Umadevi and Arumukhan. The idol reminded him of that scene and made him very happy. He was so thrilled at Indra's worship and praised the Lord for his graceful darshan. Lord Siva who liked Musukundan very much, whispered in his ears without Indra knowing about it, thus: "Musukunda! Vishnu worshipped me at Vaikuntam for a long time with great devotion. He then gave the idol to Indra who is now worshipping me with equal devotion. Now I want you to take me to Bhoolokam and worship me there". Musukundan was delighted to take the Lord's command and decided to carry it out.

After the prayers. Indra gave a good feast to the emperor and gave him lots of gifts like silk robes and ornaments.

He also gave him many weapons and offered to give him anything that he wanted. Musukundan was moved to tears and said, "King of Devas, I want to worship the Lord whom you were praying to so far. Kindly give me that idol with all your love."

Indra got a shock to hear the emperor's desire. How can he part with the idol, which he is worshipping with all devotion?

"O King! I have to know the opinion of Vishnu before I part with the idol of the Lord. Once upon a time, Vishnu prayed to Lord Siva for ages, to be blessed with a son. Umadevi got angry with Vishnu that he prayed to the Lord only ignoring her and so cursed him by saying that the son to be born to him with Lord's grace will die as a victim of Lord's anger".

Madhava was quite upset about Devi's curse. So he worshipped Lord Siva with Umadevi and Kumaran in Somaskanda form and meditated on Lord Siva again. When God appeared before him in response to his prayers, Madhava worshipped Devi first and wanted her blessings. Devi was kind to him now and said that her curse will go through as already given but the son who dies will be revived back to life by God's grace.

As per God's blessings, beautiful Manmatha was born from the mind of Madhava. He was the God of love who sent his amorous arrows at Lord Siva and got burnt for waking him up from his yoganishta. As per Devi's blessings, he got back to life with God's grace at the time of their wedding.

Once an asura named Vaarkali attacked me and I was so weak that I ran to Vishnu at the milk ocean. He was then asleep hugging the Somaskanda idol to his chest. I woke him up and told him my problem. He gave me this idol and asked me to worship him with devotion in order to overcome my crisis. From that day, I am worshippig this idol everyday with utmost devotion as directed. Madhava defeated the asura and killed him in the war. Our suffering ended by his graceful help. So, without consulting Vishnu, how can I part with it?," Indra asked. Musukundan went to Vishnu at the milk ocean and got his permission to take the idol of Somaskanda from Indra. Indra was reluctant even then. So, he got a smiliar idol made exactly the same way without any difference and gave it to Musukundan.

Musukundan took it in his hands and then to his eyes. When the Lord did not speak to him as before, he came to know that Indra had duped him. He gave it back to Indra and said, "King of Devas! I did not want this. I want the same idol worshipped by you." Indra brought another one, which was also returned. Six times, Indra tried to give him six similar duplicate idols, but Musukundan refused to accept them.

At last, Indra had no other go except to part with the original idol of Tyagesa worshipped hitherto by him. As soon as he got it, The Lord said, "I have come to you". Muchukundan praised Indra for his kindness and took leave of him. Musukundan returned to his capital with Tyagesa and also the six idols made by Indra to resemble the original. Within one day, he installed all the seven idols in seven different places.

At Tiruvarur where Vanmeekinatha has his temple, the idol worshipped by Indra has been installed. As these idols were not chistled by any sharp tool, they were swayambhus i.e. they take the form on their own. So they are also called Vitankar. There is Veedhi Vitankar in Tiruvarur; Azhagu Vitankar in Tirunagaikkâronam; Nagura Vitankar in

Tirunallar; Adivitankar in Tirukanayal; Avanida Vitankar in Tirukolili; Neela Vitankar in Tiruvanmiyur; Bhuvani Vitankar in Vedaranyam alias Tirumaraikkâdu. Musukundan installed all the seven idols at the above places and conducted a festival at Tirvarur where he installed the idol himself. On the same day, festivals were conducted at the other six centres also.

As Indra had to give away the idol worshipped by him to Musukundan, he was born as a pulaya (Drummer) in bhoolokam, to cleanse himself of the sin. He sat on an elephant and beat the drum in the streets of Tiruvarur announcing to people to come and see the Lord during the festival. He had to do this to get back to his position in Amaravati).

After enjoying the darshan of the Lord at Tiruvarur during the festivals conducted by Muchukundan for very many years, Indra could come out of the form of the drummer and reach heaven. Musukundan ruled his country for a long time in the most appropriate manner and made his son Agnivarman the king. He then meditated on Lord Siva and went to Kailas. Veerabhahu and others also appointed their sons to their posts, meditated on God and returned to Lord Muruga's abode.

As Musukundan observed all the vratas dear to lord Muruga, he got the exalted status and finally reached Lord's feet. Whoever follows his footsteps to worship Lord Muruga with devotion will be certainly blessed with all that they want to achieve in this world and thereafter.

## 102. Velavan marries Valli

There is a mountain called Vallimalai near the town Melpadi in Tondaimandalam in Tamil Nadu. In this mountain valley, there were hunters with their chief called Nambi. He was an ardent devotee of Lord Siva and he was unhappy that he had no children for a long time.

In the Vallimalai valley, there was a sage called Sivamunivar. While he was meditating on Lord Siva, there came a deer by the grace of Lord Muruga. When he saw the deer, the sage expressed his great love for it. The deer got pregnant by his amorous glances. Sundaravalli, daughter of Vishnu, was meditating in that forest to get married to Lord Muruga. She began to grow as a child in the deer's womb. At the proper time, the deer gave birth to a girl bady inside a pit dug by the hunter women for taking out sweet potatoes. When the deer saw the beautiful girl child, it was afraid and so ran away.

Sundaravalli was wearing ornaments to indicate that she was a divine child, right from the time she was born to the deer. Soon after the deer ran away, the child started cyring for milk. At that time, Nambirajan was passing through that side with his wife and soldiers. When he heard the child cry, he looked around only to find a pretty girl child in a pit nearby. His joy knew no bounds. He thought God has blessed him with a child and ran to take it. His wife Kodikki took the child in her hands and put it to her breast. Soon after, they returned to their palace where everyone greeted Nambirajan and blessed the child. As she was taken out from a pit dug for sweet potatoes or valli roots, she was named Valli and brought up with due care and concern.

Valli became 12 years old when Nambirajan as per his family customs, asked her to guard his millet fields. She

stayed there in the field with her friends and drove away birds like parrots and animal like pigs from spoiling the crops.

Lord Muruga who was in Kandhapuri with Veerabhahu and others decided to shower his grace on Valli. So he came to Tiruttani hillock which is near Vallimalai. Narada knew the Lord's mind and so visited Valli first. He felt that she will be an ideal match for Muruga and so went to Tiruttani to see Lord Muruga.

"Swami! Valli who was born to sage Sivamuni and the deer is guarding the fields of Nambirajan with her friends. She is extremely beautiful and she is none else than Vishnu's daughter, Sundaravalli. You had already promised that you will marry her at the right time", Narada said.

**Lord Shanmukhan went to Vallimalai fields in the guise of a hunter. He went near Valli and asked, "O dear girl! What is your name? Who are your parents? Where do you live? How did your parents leave you in the forest, all alone, without any male escort, especially when you are so young?"**

Valli was hesitant when a stranger suddenly appeared and questioned her. Still she gave a suitable reply. At that time, Nambirajan came there with his forces. Shanmukhan did not want to be seen by him and so, stood there like a neem tree.

Nambirajan enquired after his daughter's welfare and gave her all that she needed, as usual. He incidentally looked at the neem tree. Someone nearby commented that the tree was not there earlier. Someone else wanted to pull down the new tree. Nambirajan looked at his daughter who could not definitely say whether the tree was there earlier without proper maintainance or it is a new one!

Though Nambi was doubtful, he left it without pulling it down, as it may be useful for a good shadow.

After the hunters went, Muruga took the original form and told Valli. "My dear girl! You are very beautiful. I have fallen in love with you. You come along with me. I will give you a wonderful life making people envious of you."

Valli did not realize that the hunter there was none else than Muruga, whom she was worshipping daily. She replied, "Sir, though I am a hunter's daughter, my father is the chief of hunters. I shall not do anything unbecoming of my lineage. My parents will decide on my marriage. You may please go."

She heard some birds chirping at a distance. She thought that her father Nambirajan was coming back there, perhaps for something he has forgotten. So she told Muruga, "Sir, my father is quick-tempered. His soldiers are quite brave and strong. If he sees a stranger like you talking to me, when I am alone, he may harm you or even kill you. It is better that you leave this place at once."

Muruga moved from there and took the form of on old saivite saint. He went to Nambirajan and blessed him. He fell at his feet and said, "O Sage! I feel honoured by your darshan. You have come to this forest at this old age, without realising that there are wild beasts here. Tell me, if I can do something for you."

"O king of hunters! I have come for achieving peace of mind here by taking bath in Kumari teertham and meditating on Lord Siva".

Nambirajan happily said, "Swami! You can stay with my daughter here. Kumari teertham is quite close by". He took the old man to Valli, introduced him to her and made all arrangements for his stay there.

After Nambirajan left, Muruga in the guise of the old man told Valli that he was hungry. She gave him honey and millet powder to eat. He said at once that he was thirsty. "Swami! if you go seven mountains beyond this mountain here, you have a clear stream there, you can drink water there as much as you please", Valli said. "My dear girl! I am new to this region. If I go alone, I may lose my way. You can come with me and show me that place", he said.

Valli took him to the stream. He drank water there and told her. "Thank you for quenching my thirst. I want you to fulfill my desire for you also likewise."

Valli was startled. "Swami! What did you say? These words do not become of a devotee of Lord Siva who meditates on him. You are a great sage. I am born in a hunters' family. You are as old as my father and so I came along with you and that was my mistake. After having known your mind now, I cannot allow you to stay with me. You may go now". So saying she started speeding away to her fields.

Muruga thought for a while as to how to call her back as she was moving away from him in anger. He thought of Vinayaka in his mind and asked for his help. Vinayaka appeared before Valli as an elephant.

Valli was afraid of elephants. She was shocked to see an elephant in front of her, all of a sudden. So she ran back to the stream and hugged the old man, saying, "Swami! Please save me! An elephant is chasing me".

Muruga was happy to hug her. He then told Vinayaka, "Brother, because of your help Valli has come back to me. My desire is fulfilled. You may go now.'

The elephant disappeared. In fact, Vina yaka who had come there as an elephant. withdrew. Muruga showed his true self to Valli. With six faces and twelve hands, Muruga gave her darshan on his peacock mount. Valli was immensely happy and worshipped at his feet.

"Swami, you could have told me earlier about yourself. I had no idea about who you were and so said many harsh words. You must pardon me for my folly", she said. "Valli, you were the daughter of Vishnu in your previous birth. You meditated on me, with a desire to marry me. I asked you to go to Bhoolokam and wait for me in meditation. In this birth, you are born as the daughter of Nambirajan. I came to see you only. Very soon, I shall marry you in the presence of one and all", he said.

Later Muruga left her in the fields and disappeared. Valli told her friends confidentially about what all happened and waited for the Lord, meditating happily all the time for him.

The fields got ready for the harvest. Valli had to return home when the harvest began. She was quite sad now.

Valli was becoming quite moody. She did not speak to anyone. She did not eat properly. She was always thinking of Lord Muruga and growing thinner and thinner. Her parents got worried and called the soothsayers for consultation. They performed a puja in which Lord Muruga appeared on the soothasayer. He said that he had seen Valli in the field and wanted pujas to be done worshipping him.

Muruga came in search of Valli to the field. As he could not find her there, he was quite depressed. After searching here and there, he reached the house of Nambirajan at midnight. When he reached the backyard of the house, Valli's bosom friend knew about his arrival. She told him about her condition. "If she has to be alive, you have to accept her now. She is unable to stand the separation from you and is becoming weak". She went inside the house, informed Valli about Muruga's presence and brought her out. She fell at his feet and said, "If my kith and kin see you now, there will be a big fight. Please take me to your place right away".

Lord Muruga returned with her to Tanigai mountains. Nambirajan woke up next morning only to find his daughter Valli missing from his house. His wife was shocked not to see her early in the morning. They were worried that some thief had kindnapped her. He started on a search for her with his soldiers.

The hunters saw Muruga and Valli enjoying themselves in a garden on Tanigai mountains. Nambirajan came near them in great anger. When Valli saw her father and his men approaching them in great anger, she expressed her fears to Muruga.

"Valli! Do not worry! I shall see to it that they do not harm us", said Muruga.

Nambirajan and his men attacked them with many weapons. Due to Muruga's grace, all of them fell at their feet. When the Lord looked at the cock in his flag, it jumped and gave a long crowing. Nambirajan and his men were shocked and fell down dead. Muruga left the place with Valli.

Narada appeared there and worshipped Muruga. "O Lord! Is it proper for you to kill Nambirajan and his soldiers and take Valli away like this? You must bring them back to life", he said.

Muruga asked Valli to do it. She thought of His grace and prayed that her father and his soldiers should get back to life. All of them woke up as if they were asleep till then!

Nambirajan was bestowed with wisdom to realise the truth by Lord's grace. He praised him and pleaded, "Swami! If you kidnap my daughter like this, it does not befit the honour of our family. So, you should come back to our place and marry Valli in the presence of my whole community and people".

Muruga agreed and came to his small town. Nambirajan invited all the people and gave Valli in marriage to Him in a grand scale. Narada was present to conduct the wedding. Devas gathered in heaven to see Murugan's wedding with Valli. They showered flowers and rejoiced partaking in all the festivities of the function.

Muruga returned to Tanigai mountain with Valli. She asked him to tell her about the greatness of the mountain.

Though Muruga resides in several hillocks and mountains, Tanigai is his favourite abode. After destroying Soorapadman and others, Muruga landed on this hill, where he calmed down from the hectic anger he had against the asuras.

Cheru means anger and Tani means cool down. As Muruga was quite calm and cool with kindness after he reached this place, quitting his anger, this place was first called – Cheruttani – Give up anger and become cool. Indra saw to it that three blue flowers blossom in a stream on this mountain – one in the morning, one in the mid-day and another in the evening and worshipped Muruga thrice a day with these flowers. Those who see this mountain and worship it get rid of all their sins.

If people stay on this hill for five days and pray to the Lord they will get anything that they desire. Your meditations on this mountain will become ten-fold in their strength and gains. The good deeds done here, charitable acts and donations will yield great results. Devas come and worship the Lord here, on the mountain.

Muruga installed his father Lord Siva's idol here and worshipped him. He stayed here with Valli for sometime and left for Kandhapuri.

Deivayanai welcomed both of them at the entrance to Kandagiri. Muruga took both of them on either side and entered. He introduced Valli to Deivayanai.

"Both of you were Vishnu's daughters in your previous birth. Both of you wanted to marry me and meditated on me. I had asked you two to wait and I promised to come at the right time and marry you. Amirtavalli was born as Deivayanai, daughter of Indra and married me. Sundaravalli was born to sage Sivamuni and grew as Valli, in the palace of Nambirajan and fell in love with me. I have just married her at her place in Vallimalai", he explained.

Deivayanai hugged her sister in great happiness. They lived in great unity as flower and fragance and stayed with Muruga to shower grace on all the devotees.

## 103. Shower of gold

The august assembly was in rapt attention, observing absolute silence. Kachiappa Sivachariar concluded his exposition of Sri Kandha Puranam with tears of joy filling his eyes.

**Long live the twelve broad shoulders;**
**Long live the six faces;**

**Long live the unique vel, which ripped**
**open the mountain;**
**Long live the cock;**

**Long live the peacock mount of the**
**beautiful Lord;**
**Long live Deivayanai, daughter of the**
**divine elephant.**

**Long live Valli, the steadfast lover;**
**Long live all His great devotees.**

The inaugural presentation of Sri Kanda Puranam was completed to the great joy and ecstasy of all devotees.

Kachiappa Sivachariar arranged the palm leaves on which he had written the great work and got up to bow before the assembly of scholars.

But the audience did not see him as mere mortal – a simple man called Kachiappa Sivachariar. They saw Lord Muruga himself in him as he had made them all sing His praise in that literary work. All of them worshipped at his feet. They brought gold and gems and showered on him.

They were still not satisfied. They thought they had expressed their gratitude only a wee bit. So they gifted silks and made him seated on an elephant. They took him in procession through all the four streets of the town to the accompaniment of pleasing musical renderings on auspicious instruments.

People thronged the streets to see him and take his blessings. They welcomed him with 'Poorna Kumbham' (Pots of holy water kept in Puja) and honoured him to their hearts' content. The women performed 'Ârati' in order to dispel the effect of evil eyes on him.

Kachiappa Sivachariar was immersed in their waves of affection and love. He did not speak a word; his eyes were filled with tears of joy.

After the procession along the four streets reached the temple, the devotees carried him on their shoulders and placed him before the Lord in the sanctum sanctorum. He raised his folded hands above his head, prostrated on the ground and worshipped the Lord.

There was an excessive stretch of devotion and dedication all over the place. The temple bell was ringing for a long time continuously. Its sweet sound filled the air as well as the devotees' minds with exquisite ecstasy and eternal bliss.

### Subham

# GLOSSARY

| | | |
|---|---|---|
| Âdisesha | : | The primordial serpent, which is Lord Vishnu's bed. |
| Âgneayâstra | : | The missile charged with an invocation to the God of fire – Agni. |
| Airavatha | : | Indra's elephant |
| Âsram | : | Hermitage |
| Âsuric Yâga | : | Sacrifice pertaining to Asuras. Demonical sacrifice and necro mancy for gaining power |
| Abhisheka | : | Religious rite of pouring or sprink ling sacred waters on the head of one, who is installed as a King. |
| Adharma | : | Sin; Unrighteous action; Opposite of Dharma. |
| Agni | : | The God of fire. |
| Alakapuri | : | The Capital of Kubera, the God of Wealth. |
| Amaravati | : | The city in heaven where Indra has his abode. |
| Amrit | : | Ambrosia, the food of the God, which make the partakers immortal. |
| Astras | : | Miraculous weapons, whose power lay in the invocations with which they are charged. |
| Asuras | : | Enemies of the Gods / Devas. |
| Avatar | : | Incarnation. |

| | | |
|---|---|---|
| Brahmin | : | The first of the four castes devoting their lives to study, teaching and the performance of religious ceremonies. |
| Brahma | : | The creator of the universe; one of the Trinity. |
| Brahmâstra | : | The most powerful among Astras. A divine weapon, given by Lord Brahma himself. |
| Brahmacharya | : | Celibacy, chastity. |
| Bruhaspati | : | The preceptor of the Devas. |
| Darbha | : | A species of sacred grass used for religious rites. |
| Dharma | : | Righteous code of conduct |
| Gandharvas | : | A class of semi-divine beings. Celestial musicians. |
| Garuda | : | The bird kite, who is Vishnu's vehicle. |
| Guru | : | Acharya; Preceptor, Teacher. |
| Gnâna | : | Spiritual knowledge; Realisation. |
| Himavân | : | The king of the Himalayan range of mountains |
| Indra | : | The chief and the king of Devas. |
| Kailâs | : | Abode of Siva. |
| Pâtâlalokam | : | The nether regions. |
| Prajâpati | : | The creator. |
| Purânas | : | Sacred legends. |
| Sâstras | : | Sacred lore. |

| Siddha | : One who has attained special powers through penance. A class of heavenly beings. |
| Slóka | : Couplet in Sanskrit |
| Siva | : The Lord Supreme, destroyer, one of the Trinity. |
| Varuna | : The Lord of the ocean. |
| Védas | : Basic Hindu scriptures. There are four Vedas namely Rig, Yajur, Sâma and Atharvana. |
| Vellam | : A count of numbers. |
| Viswakarma | : The celestial architect. |
| Yâga | : Sacrifice; a religious ceremony accompanied by oblations. |
| Yakshas | : A class of celestial beings. |
| Yojana | : A measure of distance equal probably to nine miles. |

\* \* \* \* \* \*